FARM JOURNAL
Christmas Idea Book

BY THE EDITORS OF FARM JOURNAL

Edited by Kathryn Larson
Design: Al J. Reagan

COUNTRYSIDE PRESS
a division of Farm Journal, Inc.
Philadelphia

Distributed to the trade by
DOUBLEDAY & COMPANY, INC.
Garden City, New York

Contents

Library of Congress Catalog Card Number 72-80795

Make Christmas Meaningful

Christmas comes just four days after the shortest—and often gloomiest—day of the year. Small wonder that this exceedingly bright and hope-filled day is so eagerly anticipated and so long planned for. In the deepening dark of winter, we need to look forward to, and get involved in, a celebration of this magnitude. We need the joy and promise—and the thoughtfulness of others—that only Christmas seems to motivate.

A rich source of inspiration for thoughtful ways to observe this Holiday has been the farm families of America. For in their homes and communities it has been traditional to "put yourself into Christmas." There, celebrating Christmas means getting involved in it, with flour on your nose and paint in your hair, scarcely finishing one project before launching the next. Being "too busy" is half the fun. And busy farm homemakers know the value of planning ahead to make the season less hectic. By October they are happily stitching away at odd moments on handmade gifts, for fund-raising bazaars as well as family and friends. In November they start filling the freezer with make-ahead goodies and food gifts. The catch-all drawer yields odds and ends the children turn into fabulous decorations for the house.

For many years, FARM JOURNAL magazine has been featuring the ingenious gifts, decorations—and superb holiday foods from country kitchens. During the past five years, these ideas have been shared in the Farm Journal Christmas Book, to the delight of both city and farm people. The current yearning to return to the values of simplicity and sincerity—and the joys of the handmade—prompts this all-new Three-in-One Christmas Idea Book, collected by the editors of FARM JOURNAL.

This book is packed with ideas that will help you give of yourself this Christmas. You'll find irresistible the old-fashioned crafts like patchwork, adapted to the most contemporary materials and fashions. While doing for others, you can also give yourself a creative adventure. Try one of the new crafts, like needleweaving, casting candles in sand, making gifts from plastic. If you prefer to cook your treats, you'll find pages of tested recipes for country feasting and food gifts. The recipes, ideas and patterns have been collected from good cooks and craftsmen all over the country . . . warm-hearted people who, like you, know that the best way to keep Christmas is to share it.

Gather together for a festive feast

Sugar Plum Loaf

Serve for holiday brunch or tea

1 c. milk, scalded
¼ c. sugar
¼ c. shortening
1½ tsp. salt
2 pkg. active dry yeast
2 eggs, beaten
4 c. sifted flour
1 c. chopped walnuts
¾ c. seedless raisins
¼ c. chopped candied cherries
¼ c. chopped candied pineapple
1 tsp. chopped candied lemon peel
1 tsp. ground cardamon

• Combine milk, sugar, shortening and salt; cool to lukewarm. Stir in yeast. Add eggs; beat well. Add enough flour to make a soft dough.

• Turn onto a floured surface. Knead in walnuts, fruit and cardamon; continue kneading dough until smooth. Place in a greased bowl and let rise until double. Punch down and let rest 15 minutes. Divide dough in half.

• Shape into 2 round loaves. Place on greased baking sheet. Let rise until double. Bake in moderate oven (350°) for 25 minutes or until golden brown. Cool slightly; frost with your favorite confectioners sugar icing. Decorate with bits of candied fruit and walnuts. Makes 2 loaves.

IN THE PICTURE: Foods that bring back memories for Countryside families. Fruit-filled stollen called Sugar Plum Loaf that one family has cut and served with coffee for over 50 years. A light, crisp Norwegian cookie called Fattigmann. A mushroom-studded bread stuffing that's light and fluffy, and a cabbage salad that sparkles with color and flavor.

Christmas is family reunion day. We all remember it from childhood: the flurried, foot-stomping arrival of aunts, uncles and cousins. The high-pitched hellos and kisses of the grownups and the shy or wary greetings of youngsters who will soon be reacquainted. The careful carrying of tea towel-covered baskets and baking pans to the kitchen, as each one of the family's good cooks brings her specialty to the feast.

Remembering such a Christmas, we indulge our own little ones today with sweets forbidden on ordinary days. We empathize with the 10-year-old, squirming as the inevitable aunt beams, "My, *my,* haven't we grown!" We finally (but tactfully) rescue the baby from too many loving "strangers".
In the snowy stillness, we imagine we hear jingle bells and the clop-clop of a horse-and-sleigh. But no, it's the Seventies sound of a snowmobile, the squeal of excited passengers.
Still, when Aunt Maggie puts on the *Christmas Sing with Bing* record and Uncle Chris puffs the fireplace embers back to life, we can imagine we're the ones sitting on the floor, as we did years ago when the feast was over and the dishes done, when everyone collected in the living room to visit. This was the best time.

How many memories are triggered by food: the smell of it, the talk about it. Grandma *always* explained how thrilled she was to find an orange in the toe of her stocking Christmas morning. This was said to remind us of our blessings and it did—it does. Mother *always* apologized that her potato filling wasn't quite up to Grandma's, but over the years she'd learned the lesson well—and now we have the precious recipe written down.

While we tried to remember which Christmas it was that we had all mince pies and no pudding (because the aunts bringing dessert both got the same message), Grandpa cracked a mountain of nuts, passing them out to each child in turn. Jim's dad does that now, and we hope our sleepy kids are storing up the remembrance of what they've heard and seen and eaten today.

Fattigmann

Delicate, crisp Norwegian cookies that are perfect for gift-giving

6 egg yolks
½ tsp. salt
⅓ c. light cream
⅓ c. sugar
1 tblsp. melted butter
2¼ c. sifted flour
¼ tsp. ground nutmeg
1 tblsp. grated lemon rind
Confectioners sugar

• Beat together egg yolks and salt until thick and light. Beat in light cream, sugar and butter.
• Sift together flour and nutmeg. Add to egg yolk mixture with lemon rind, mixing well. Chill 1 hour.
• Roll out ¼ of dough at a time, keeping remaining dough chilled. Roll 1/16" thick and cut in strips about 1½" wide with sharp knife. Cut diagonally at 4" intervals. Make 1" slits lengthwise in center of each piece. Slip one end through slit. Fry a few at a time in deep hot fat at 350° for 1 to 2 minutes or until golden. Remove from fat with slotted spoon. Drain on paper towels and sprinkle with sifted confectioners sugar. Store in an airtight container. Makes 6 dozen.

Mushroom Bread Stuffing

Surprise your guests with this delicious mushroom-studded stuffing

1 c. chopped onion
1 (4 oz.) can sliced mushrooms, drained
½ c. melted butter
12 c. soft bread cubes
¼ c. minced parsley
1 tsp. sage
¼ tsp. pepper
1 (10½ oz.) can condensed cream of mushroom soup
1 tblsp. milk

• Sauté onion and mushrooms in ¼ c. melted butter. Toss together bread cubes, parsley, sage, pepper, ¼ c. butter and sautéed vegetables. Stir soup and add to mixture.
• Place in a greased 2 qt. casserole and sprinkle with milk. Bake in moderate oven (350°) for 35 minutes or until brown. Makes 6 to 8 servings.

Christmas Cabbage Salad

This festive salad will add color to your holiday buffet table

½ c. sugar
1 tblsp. flour
1 tblsp. cornstarch
½ tsp. salt
⅛ tsp. pepper
⅛ tsp. dry mustard
1 (8½ oz.) can pineapple tidbits
Water
¾ c. white vinegar
2 eggs, beaten
6 c. shredded cabbage
1 c. miniature marshmallows
1 unpared red apple, cored and cut in wedges
Pecan halves

• Combine first 6 ingredients in a saucepan. Drain pineapple; add enough water to make 1½ c. juice. Stir juice and vinegar into dry ingredients. Beat in eggs. Cook over medium heat, stirring constantly, until mixture thickens. Cool well. Toss with cabbage, marshmallows, apple and pineapple. Garnish with pecans. Serve immediately. Makes about 8 servings.

Sweet Potato Bonbons

Look and taste very special

3 lbs. sweet potatoes, peeled and cooked
¼ c. butter
½ c. brown sugar, firmly packed
1 tsp. salt
½ tsp. grated orange rind
6 marshmallows, halved
4 c. cornflakes, crushed
⅓ c. melted butter
12 pecan halves

• Mash sweet potatoes until light and fluffy. Beat in butter, sugar, salt and orange rind. Let cool. Divide into 12 portions. Press potatoes around each marshmallow half, being careful to keep marshmallow in center. Shape into ovals.
• Coat each with melted butter. Roll in crushed cornflakes, top with pecan half and place on lightly greased baking sheet. Bake in very hot oven (450°) for 7 to 8 minutes. Serves 6 to 8.

Cranberry/Orange Glazed Ham

This is a real holiday beauty

1 (10 to 12 lb.) fully cooked bone-in ham
2 large oranges, sliced
3 maraschino cherries, halved
Whole cloves
1 tblsp. flour
⅓ c. brown sugar, firmly packed
2 tblsp. prepared mustard
1 c. cranberry cocktail
¼ c. cider vinegar
¼ c. honey
2 tblsp. butter

• Trim and score ham. Place fat side up on rack in shallow pan. Insert meat thermometer into center; do not let it touch bone. Bake in moderate oven (350°) for 1 to 1½ hours. Remove from oven. Cover top and sides with orange slices. Place a cherry half in center of each orange slice. Insert cloves around edge of each cherry.
• In 1½ qt. saucepan, combine flour, sugar, and mustard; stir in remaining ingredients. Bring to a full boil; cook 1 minute. Pour over hot ham. Return to oven. Continue baking ½ hour or until thermometer registers 160°, basting often with glaze. Makes 20 servings.

TRY SOME NEW TREATS for your Christmas Feast—you may launch a tradition this year. Cranberry-Orange Glazed Ham looks spectacular and it's easy to tote if you're bringing part of the family dinner. Cranberry Chutney is a delightful elaboration on cranberry sauce. Sweet Potato Bonbons have a surprise center—a sweet, melting marshmallow. Holiday Cauliflower is cloaked in a superb Swiss cheese sauce; Olive Wreath Mold is named for its decorative red and green crown.

Holiday Cauliflower

You'll love the delicate sauce

1 large head cauliflower
1 (4 oz.) can sliced mushrooms
¼ c. diced green pepper
¼ c. butter
⅓ c. flour
2 c. milk
1 tsp. salt
1 c. shredded Swiss cheese
2 tblsp. chopped pimiento

• Break cauliflower into medium-size flowerettes; cook in boiling water until crisp-tender, about 10 minutes. Drain well; set aside.
• In a 2 qt. saucepan, sauté mushrooms and green pepper in butter until tender. Blend in flour. Gradually stir in milk. Cook, stirring constantly, over medium heat until mixture is thick. Stir in salt, cheese and pimiento.
• Place half of the cauliflower in a buttered 2 qt. casserole. Cover with half of the sauce; add remaining cauliflower. Top with sauce. Bake in slow oven (325°) for 15 minutes. Makes 8 servings.

Olive Wreath Mold

So festive—good eating, too!

1 (3 oz.) pkg. lime gelatin
1 c. boiling water
⅔ c. cold water
2 tblsp. lemon juice
1 c. heavy cream, whipped
⅓ c. sliced stuffed olives
1 (8 oz.) can crushed pineapple, drained
½ c. shredded American cheese
½ pimiento, chopped
½ c. finely chopped celery
½ c. chopped walnuts
½ tsp. salt
24 slices of stuffed olives

• Dissolve gelatin in boiling water. Add cold water and lemon juice. Chill until syrupy. Stir in whipped cream; fold in the ⅓ c. sliced olives, pineapple, cheese, pimiento, celery, walnuts, salt.
• Arrange the 24 olive slices in a circle around the bottom of an oiled 9″ ring mold. Pour mixture into mold. Chill until firm. Makes 8 servings.

French-Style Turnips

The seasonings do something special to turnips—taste-testers approved

2½ lbs. medium turnips (about 9)
¼ lb. bacon in one piece
⅔ c. minced onion
1 tblsp. flour
¾ c. canned beef bouillon, or 1 bouillon cube dissolved in ¾ c. water
½ to 1 tsp. salt
1 tsp. sugar
¼ tsp. rubbed sage
¼ tsp. pepper

• Peel, quarter and cook turnips in 1″ boiling salted water 5 minutes. Drain.
• Cut bacon in ¼″ cubes; you should have ¾ c. Cook bacon 4 minutes in skillet, stirring constantly. Add onion and cook 5 minutes (do not let brown). Blend in flour; add bouillon, salt (the exact amount depending on saltiness of bacon), sugar, sage and pepper. Cook 2 minutes, stirring constantly.
• Add turnips; cover and simmer 15 to 20 minutes, or until turnips are tender. Makes 6 to 7 servings.

Potato Filling

Hearty potato filling made in the traditional Pennsylvania Dutch way

10 c. seasoned mashed potatoes
2 eggs
3 c. chopped onion
3 c. chopped celery
⅔ c. butter
6 c. soft bread cubes (½″)
½ c. minced parsley
2 tsp. sage
½ tsp. salt
¼ tsp. pepper
2 tblsp. butter
2 tblsp. milk
Paprika

• Mix eggs with mashed potatoes; set aside.
• Sauté onion and celery in ⅔ c. butter. Add bread cubes, parsley, sage, salt and pepper; toss until golden.
• Combine with mashed potato mixture. Turn into a buttered 3 qt. casserole. Dot with 2 tblsp. butter and sprinkle with milk and paprika. Bake in moderate oven (375°) for 40 minutes or until golden brown. Makes 10 servings. Traditionally served as a substitute for bread stuffing.

Brussels Sprouts with Lemon

Lemon brings out a garden-fresh taste

1½ qts. Brussels sprouts
¾ c. butter
Salt
Pepper
Lemon slices

• Trim sprouts, removing any imperfect leaves. Pour boiling salted water (1 tsp. salt to 1 qt. water) over them to cover; let stand 5 minutes; drain.
• Melt butter in heavy skillet; add sprouts. Cover tightly and cook over very low heat just until they are tender, 10 to 20 minutes. Test for tenderness with a kitchen fork.
• Add salt and pepper to taste. Serve garnished with thin lemon slices. Makes 4 to 5 servings.

French Onions and Rice

Absolutely delicious with poultry

¼ c. long grain rice
2 qts. boiling water
1 tsp. salt
¼ c. butter or margarine
4 c. thinly sliced large white or yellow onions (about 3)
½ tsp. salt
⅛ tsp. paprika
2 tblsp. grated Parmesan cheese

• Drop rice into rapidly boiling water with 1 tsp. salt added; boil uncovered 5 minutes; drain at once.
• Melt butter in 2-qt. casserole in oven; stir in onions. Add ½ tsp. salt and stir onions in butter until nicely yellowed and coated. Then add rice and stir to distribute evenly. Cover and bake in slow oven (325°) 1 hour. Sprinkle with paprika and cheese. Makes 8 servings.

Note: Large onions are easier to slice if first cut in halves lengthwise and placed, cut side down, on a chopping board. Cut a thick slice from top and bottom, enough to remove top and root growth, and slice lengthwise.

Red and Green Christmas Salad

Tomato aspic in green pepper frames

5 whole green peppers
2 envelopes unflavored gelatin
½ c. chicken broth
2 c. tomato juice
¼ c. finely chopped onion
⅓ c. finely chopped celery
2 tblsp. lemon juice
2 drops Tabasco sauce
2 tsp. worcestershire sauce
½ tsp. celery salt
1 tsp. sugar
1 c. crushed ice

• Wash green peppers, slice off tops and seed them. Set aside.
• Sprinkle gelatin over chicken broth; let stand 5 minutes to soften; then dissolve over hot water.
• Stir gelatin mixture into tomato juice; add onion, celery, lemon juice, Tabasco sauce, worcestershire sauce, celery salt and sugar. (For a satin-smooth aspic, whirl ingredients in blender—the ice, too.)
• Stir in crushed ice. When mixture starts to thicken, fill pepper shells. Chill until set.
• To serve, slice peppers across and place on lettuce leaf. Makes 8 to 10 servings.

Caraway Cabbage and Oranges

Good with pork chops, barbecued spareribs, baked ham or sausage

1 small head cabbage, shredded
4 oranges, peeled, thinly sliced, then slices cut in halves
Caraway Dressing (recipe follows)
1 c. dairy sour cream (about)
Grated peel of 1 orange

• Layer cabbage, orange slices and Caraway Dressing in a shallow serving bowl, ending with orange slices. Pour on remaining dressing.
• Cover and chill for 2 hours or more. At serving time drop sour cream in big spoonfuls over top of salad (or pass), sprinkle with orange peel. Makes 6 servings.

Caraway Dressing: Beat together with rotary beater until thickened: ¼ c. sugar, 2 tsp. whole caraway seeds, 1 tsp. salt, 1 tsp. dry mustard, 1 tsp. onion juice (scraped from onion), ¾ c. salad oil and ¼ c. vinegar.

The marinating dressing is sharply sweet and sour. The sour cream topping mellows it.

Fruited Cucumbers with Black Pepper-lemon Dressing

Serve with chicken or turkey

1 cucumber, peeled and thinly sliced
3 c. thin slices of fresh melon and/or pears
Black Pepper-lemon Dressing (recipe follows)
Crisp lettuce
Finely chopped fresh parsley

• Toss cucumber and fruit gently with dressing. Cover and chill for 2 hours or more.
• At serving time, arrange on lettuce-lined, chilled serving platter or individual plates; spoon dressing over salad. Sprinkle with chopped parsley. Makes 6 servings.

Black Pepper-Lemon Dressing: Beat or shake together: ½ c. salad oil, 3 tblsp. fresh lemon juice, ¾ tsp. prepared Dijon-type mustard (or dry mustard), ½ tsp. salt, ½ tsp. freshly ground black pepper, ¼ tsp. crushed dried rosemary (or about ¾ tsp. finely minced fresh rosemary).

The rosemary in Black Pepper-lemon Dressing must be only a whiff . . . it shouldn't overpower the salad. When it isn't fresh-melon season, use only sliced fresh pears (or well-drained, firm, canned pears).

Cucumber-Walnut Salad Bowl

Good with ham or smoked tongue

2 large cucumbers, peeled and thinly sliced
6 c. torn crisp lettuce (loosely pack to measure)
1 c. finely chopped walnuts, toasted
Onion Dressing (recipe follows)

• Toss cucumbers thoroughly with half the dressing; cover and chill for 2 hours or more.
• Drain cucumbers well. In a chilled salad bowl, toss drained cucumbers, lettuce and walnuts with remaining dressing. Serve immediately. Makes 6 servings.

Onion Dressing: Shake or beat together: ⅔ c. salad oil, ¼ c. vinegar (preferably wine vinegar), 1 tblsp. finely grated onion, 2 tsp. dry mustard and 1½ tsp. salt.

Toasting brings out the nutty flavor of walnuts. To toast: Sprinkle chopped walnuts on baking sheet; place in a moderate oven (350°) until lightly browned, about 4 minutes; shake and stir occasionally.

Sunshine Citrus Salad

Serve with either turkey or ham

1½ c. shredded iceberg lettuce
1 c. coarsely chopped chicory
2 c. coarsely chopped romaine
1 white grapefruit
2 pink grapefruit
3 oranges
1 avocado, sliced
½ c. macadamia nuts or almonds

Dressing:

½ tsp. grated lime rind
2 tblsp. lime juice
1 tsp. salt
¼ tsp. ground pepper
½ tsp. crushed basil leaves
½ c. oil
6 tblsp. heavy cream

• Combine greens and keep chilled.
• Peel citrus fruit, carefully removing all the white skin. Cut out fruit sections by cutting as close to the membrane as possible, on both sides of each section. Chill.
• Combine dressing ingredients in blender; blend well. Dressing can also be mixed with rotary beater or shaken in a bottle. Chill at least 2 hours before serving.
• Aternate layers of greens and citrus fruit in salad bowl. Top with avocado. Sprinkle with nuts. Pour on dressing. Toss and serve immediately. Makes 6 servings.

Danish Pork Roast

Garnish platter with whole red crab-apples and watercress or parsley

½ tsp. salt
½ tsp. ground cinnamon
½ tsp. ground allspice
½ tsp. ground pepper
¼ tsp. ground cloves
¼ tsp. ground mace
3 to 3½ lb. boned pork loin
12 pitted prunes
2 medium apples, pared, cored and cut into sixths
2 tblsp. raisins
¼ tsp. ground cinnamon
¼ c. brandy or apple juice
1½ tblsp. currant jelly, melted
1 c. fresh bread crumbs
¼ c. melted butter

• Mix salt, spices; rub in surface of roast. Refrigerate overnight.
• Combine the fruits, cinnamon and brandy. Refrigerate overnight.
• Cut a long, deep pocket the length of the roast. Stuff with fruit. Sew closed with large needle; tie with kitchen twine. Brush roast with liquid left from fruit.
• Roast on rack in slow oven (325°) 1 hour. Remove from oven; brush with jelly. Roll in bread crumbs. Baste with butter; roast 1½ hours more. Let stand 15 minutes before carving. Makes 6 servings.

CHRISTMAS is a time for embroidered linen and candle shine . . . and food that's frankly fancy. The Danish Pork Roast wrapped in buttery crumbs and filled with delectable apple-prune stuffing is a beauty. The Viennese Raisin Rolls (a kind of brioche) will melt in your mouth.

Viennese Raisin Rolls

Also perfect for brunch or breakfast

½ c. white raisins
½ c. dark raisins
¼ c. brandy or water
3½ c. sifted flour
1 pkg. active dry yeast
2 tblsp. sugar
⅓ c. lukewarm water
1 tsp. salt
4 eggs, slightly beaten
1 c. soft butter
¼ tsp. ground cinnamon
½ tsp. grated lemon peel

• Steep raisins in brandy or water overnight, stirring once.
• *To make yeast sponge:* Combine 1½ c. flour, yeast, sugar, water. Moisten hands to form dough into a ball. Immerse ball in a bowl of water at 110°F. Let ball rise to the surface; this takes about 15 minutes.
• Meanwhile, place 2 c. flour into large bowl. Make a well in center; add salt, eggs, ¼ c. butter and flavorings. Mix to form a soft dough. Remove yeast sponge from water (let excess water drip off) and blend with dough. (Dough is *very* soft, sticky and shapeless.)
• Turn dough onto *unfloured* board. Lift it (about 18" high) with one hand and throw it back, hard, onto the board. With other hand, use a spatula to scrape dough together. Continue lifting and throwing dough until smooth and satiny. It will pull together when lifted and no longer stick to board (takes about 10 minutes). Blend in remaining butter, 2 tblsp. at a time with fingers. DO NOT KNEAD. Add raisins.
• Put into a buttered bowl; cover with damp cloth. Let rise until doubled (2 to 3 hours); punch down. Let rise again until doubled (about 2 hours). Punch down.
• Fill buttered, floured muffin tins about two-thirds full. (Dough is too soft to shape.) Let rise until doubled. Combine 1 egg yolk and 3 tblsp. milk. Brush on rolls.
• Bake in hot oven (425°) for 10 minutes. Remove from the pan immediately; serve rolls while they are lukewarm. Makes 18 2½" rolls.

Pears Cardinale

Delightful! This light fruit dessert won bouquets from taste-testers

1 (10 oz.) pkg. frozen red raspberries
8 poached pear halves (recipe follows) *or* 1 (1 lb. 13 oz.) can large pear halves, chilled
¼ c. sugar
2 tblsp. cornstarch
2 tblsp. toasted slivered almonds

• Defrost raspberries. Drain well, reserving liquid. Drain pear halves, reserving liquid.
• Pour liquid from drained raspberries into a 1-cup measure. Add enough pear liquid to make 1 c.
• Mix cornstarch and sugar in a small saucepan. Gradually stir in the 1 c. fruit liquid. Cook over moderate heat, stirring constantly, until clear and thickened. Simmer gently for 3 minutes. Cool to room temperature.
• Fill cavities of pear halves with well-drained raspberries and invert in individual glass serving dishes. Allow 1 pear half per serving.
• Spoon raspberry glaze over pear halves. Sprinkle toasted almonds over glazed pears. Refrigerate until serving time (up to 2 hours). Makes about 7 servings, depending on number of pear halves in can.

Poached Pears

Nice to keep on hand in the refrigerator for desserts and salads

4 firm pears
1½ c. sugar
1½ c. water
½ lemon, sliced

• Cut pears in halves lengthwise. Peel and core.
• Combine sugar and water in saucepan. Bring to boil. Add lemon and pears. Simmer until pears are tender (about 10 minutes). Remove from heat. Chill to serve.

white Christmas desserts

You can finish all these desserts the day before. Cherries on snow and the White Christmas Pie must be thoroughly chilled before serving—overnight is best

Cherries on Snow

Serve at Christmas Dessert Buffet

1½ c. graham cracker crumbs
1 tblsp. sugar
¼ c. melted butter
1 pkg. unflavored gelatin
¼ c. cold water
¼ c. milk
1 (8 oz.) pkg. cream cheese
½ c. sifted confectioners sugar
2 tsp. grated lemon peel
2 pkg. whipped topping mix
1 (1 lb. 5 oz.) can cherry pie filling

• Mix cracker crumbs, sugar and melted butter. Press into bottom of 8" spring-form pan. Line sides with waxed paper.

• Soften gelatin in cold water. Heat milk, stir in gelatin and heat until gelatin melts. Set aside.

• Beat cream cheese with confectioners sugar until smooth. Add gelatin mixture, lemon peel and beat until well blended. Reconstitute prepared whipped topping mix according to package directions. Fold into the cream cheese mixture.

• Pour filling into spring-form pan. Refrigerate until firm. Gently spread cherry pie filling on top and refrigerate until serving time, overnight if possible. Makes 9 servings.

Snowdrift Mardi Gras Cake

Freeze ahead for unexpected guests

½ lb. butter
1 (8 oz.) pkg. cream cheese, softened
1½ c. sugar
1½ tsp. vanilla
4 eggs
2¼ c. sifted cake flour
2 tsp. baking powder
2 c. mixed candied fruit (1 lb.)
¼ c. sifted cake flour
½ c. coarsely chopped pecans
½ c. finely chopped pecans

• Thoroughly blend butter, softened cream cheese, sugar and vanilla. Add eggs, one at a time, beating well after each addition.

• Sift together 2¼ c. sifted cake flour and baking powder. Add to batter and blend well.

• Combine remaining ¼ c. sifted cake flour with candied fruit and ½ c. chopped pecans. Fold into batter. Spoon batter into a 10" bundt or angel cake pan that has been greased and sprinkled with ½ c. finely chopped pecans.

• Bake in a slow oven (325°) 70 to 80 minutes, or until cake tests done. Cool in pan 5 minutes. Remove from pan; cool on rack.

• Sprinkle with sifted confectioners sugar. Garnish with candied cherries and candied pineapple if you wish. Makes 16 servings.

White Christmas Pie

Top each wedge with a sprig of holly

1 envelope plus 1 tsp. unflavored gelatin
¼ c. cold water
¼ c. sugar
¼ c. sifted flour
½ tsp. salt
1½ c. milk
½ c. mixed candied fruit, chopped fine and rolled in confectioners sugar
1½ c. heavy cream
¼ c. sugar
1 tsp. vanilla
¼ tsp. almond extract
1 (3½ oz.) can flaked coconut
Baked 9" pie shell

• Soften gelatin in the cold water.

• Combine ¼ c. sugar, flour, and salt in saucepan. Add milk gradually and cook, stirring, until mixture is thickened and smooth. Remove from heat; stir in gelatin until melted. Chill until it starts to set.

• Beat cream with ¼ c. sugar.

• Beat gelatin mixture until smooth. Stir in vanilla, almond extract and candied fruit. Fold in whipped cream and 1 c. flaked coconut. Garnish with remainder of coconut. Chill until firmly set—overnight is best. Makes 6 to 8 servings.

Garnishes add the festive touch

Vegetable Garnishes

Tomato Roses: Select large, bright red tomatoes. Start at the stem end and cut a crosswise slice only *two-thirds* of the way through (this slice serves as the base of rose). From this cut, start paring the tomato round and round in a continuous spiral—the strip should be about ¾" wide and ⅛" thick. To form rose, place stem end on plate, skin side down. Starting at free end, roll up spiral toward stem; secure with toothpick.

Radish Roses: Trim root from red radish. With small paring knife, make several petal cuts from root end to stem end, leaving petals attached at stem end. Crisp in ice water.

Radish Accordions: Cut slightly elongated red radishes in thin slices, but not quite through. Chill in ice water. The radish slices will spread apart.

Carrot Curls: Peel large carrots. Hold the large end of a carrot on cutting board and shave off long slices with vegetable peeler. Roll each strip around your fingertip; place in bowl of ice cubes for at least 1 hour.

Lemon or Lime Twists: Cut lengthwise grooves in lemon or lime with citrus stripper. Cut slices across. Cut from one side to just beyond center of slice; grasp the resulting two ends and pull apart, twisting.

TO SIMPLIFY SERVING a crowd, bring the soup course to the living room in mugs. They'll look festive when you add a quick garnish. Here we show a crust of French bread in consommé, slivered radishes on tomato soup and sour cream on borsch. Other attractive dress-ups appropriate for most soups are: shoestring potatoes, snipped celery leaves and crumbled sharp cheese (see photos). Nuts, corn chips or bacon pieces add welcome crunch. Eat the garnish first with a spoon.

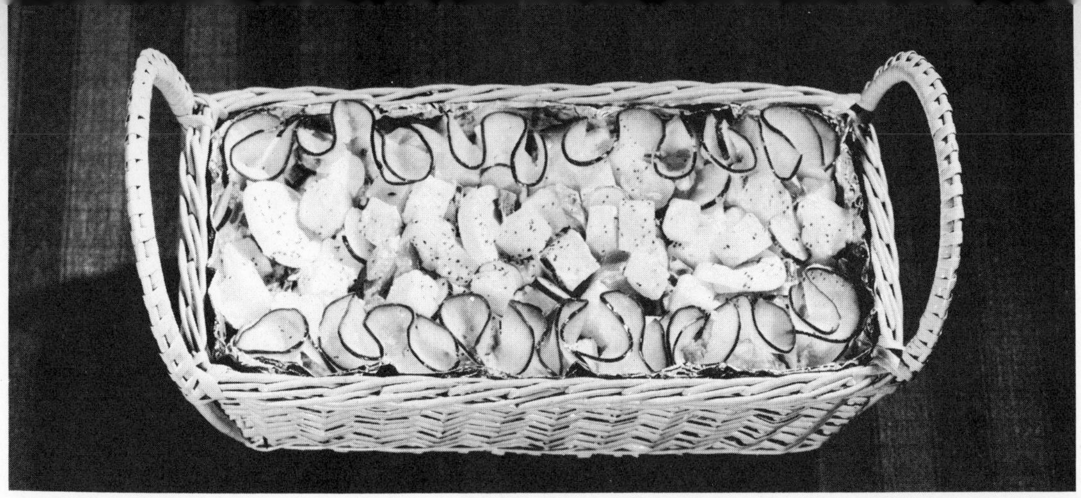

A SALAD SHOWS OFF to advantage in a basket spray-painted jonquil yellow and lined with a double layer of heavy-duty foil. Brighten it with radishes, green pepper and a cucumber ruffle (see photo)—our eye-catching border. To make cucumber ruffle: Slice off one end of the cucumber; hold cuke upright. With vegetable peeler at a right angle to it, pare around on top of cut end, turning cucumber carefully to keep strip in one thin spiral. Your salad will taste extra good if you keep pieces sizable and coat them lightly with creamy dressing.

MEAT IS A MEAL'S attraction so the platter deserves attention. Add color with broiled cheese-topped tomatoes or fruit kabobs—one for each person. We garnished the Holiday bird (see photo) with onion lilies in green pepper cut-outs. To make onion lilies: Cut a small, peeled onion into 16 pie-shaped wedges to within ½" of the bottom. Crisp lilies for at least 1 hour in ice water tinted with food color; drain. Cut a green pepper in half, saw-tooth fashion, to hold lily. Keep in ice water until serving time.

A SIMPLE DESSERT turns elegant if you bring it to the table in an impressive dish. Our English Trifle is layers of cubed angel food cake, prepared fruit pie filling and instant pudding, but it's an eye-catcher in a large glass bowl. Serve into delicate glass sherbet dishes for added drama.

Between-holidays eating

Something different to serve

With most of us, the Christmas menu must be the traditional one, so it's easy enough to plan. But what about the potlucks you'll be going to, or the "stay for supper" invitations you'll extend? Or just feeding the family on the everydays?

Look over the recipes on these pages and see if they aren't just what you're looking for: food that's tasty and economical, that you can start early in the day and finish later, or freeze . . . and just a little bit "different."

Stuffed Meat Loaf

This freezes—make several ahead

1 lb. lean ground beef
1 lb. ground pork
1 c. dry bread crumbs
½ c. grated carrot
¼ c. finely chopped onion
2 eggs, beaten
½ c. milk
2 tsp. salt
1 tsp. Worcestershire sauce
⅛ tsp. pepper
1 (4 oz.) can mushrooms, drained and chopped
1 tblsp. finely chopped onion
2 tblsp. butter
2 c. soft bread crumbs
1 tblsp. chopped parsley
½ tsp. poultry seasoning
¼ tsp. salt

• Mix together ground meat, bread crumbs, carrot, onion and eggs. Add milk, salt, Worcestershire sauce and pepper. Mix lightly, but well.
• Place on a double-thick square of greased aluminum foil. Shape into a 14x 8" rectangle.
• Sauté mushrooms and onion in butter over medium heat. Combine with bread crumbs, parsley, poultry seasoning and salt.
• Spread stuffing over meat; roll up, starting with long side. Press overlapping edge into roll to seal. Bring foil edges together in a tight double fold on the top. Fold ends up, using tight double folds.
• Place wrapped meat loaf on rack in shallow pan. Bake in moderate oven (375°) for 1 hour. Open foil; continue baking for 15 minutes or until loaf browns.
Note: If you freeze meat loaf, bake it wrapped in very hot oven (450°) for 1½ hours, then brown as directed. Makes 4 to 5 servings.

Pineapple Chicken

Delightful with a crisp green salad

2 (2½ to 3 lb.) broiler-fryers, cut up
2 tsp. salt
1 tsp. rosemary
½ tsp. pepper
10 small white onions, peeled and parboiled for 15 minutes
2 c. unsweetened pineapple juice
1 tsp. ground ginger
1 tblsp. cornstarch
1 tblsp. water

• Rub chicken with a mixture of salt, rosemary and pepper. Place skin side up in a 13x9x2" baking dish. Arrange onions around chicken. Combine pineapple juice and ginger; pour over chicken.
• Bake in moderate oven (350°), uncovered, for 1 hour or until chicken is tender. Remove chicken and onions from pan and arrange on platter. Combine cornstarch and water. Slowly stir into pan juices. Bring to a boil; boil for 1 minute. Pour ⅓ cup sauce over chicken; pour remaining sauce into serving bowl. Serve with hot boiled rice. Garnish with parsley. Makes 6 to 8 servings.

Chicken-Rice Pyramids

Lovely addition to a buffet supper

3 c. cooked rice
3 c. diced, cooked chicken
½ c. chopped celery
½ c. chopped onion
½ c. chopped walnuts
3 eggs, beaten
1 tsp. poultry seasoning
1 c. shredded Cheddar cheese
1 tsp. chili powder
½ tsp. oregano
½ c. melted butter
1 c. corn flake crumbs

• Mix together rice, chicken, celery, onion, walnuts, eggs, poultry seasoning, cheese, chili powder and oregano. Chill. Form into 12 cone-shaped mounds. Dip each cone into butter and then into crumbs.
• Place on greased baking sheet. Bake in moderate oven (350°) for 30 minutes or until golden brown. Serve with homemade or prepared chicken gravy. Makes 6 servings.

Ham and Broccoli Royale

A nourishing meal in one dish

3 c. cooked rice
2 (10 oz.) pkg. frozen broccoli spears, cooked and drained
6 tblsp. butter
2 c. fresh bread crumbs
2 c. chopped onion
3 tblsp. flour
½ tsp. salt
¼ tsp. pepper
3 c. milk
4 c. cubed ham (about 1½ lb.)
1 (8 oz.) pkg. sliced process American cheese

• Spoon cooked rice into a greased 3-qt. casserole. Layer broccoli over rice. Melt butter; remove 2 tblsp. and sprinkle over bread crumbs in a bowl; set aside.
• Sauté onion in remaining butter. Blend in flour, salt and pepper. Slowly stir in milk. Cook, stirring, until thickened. Add ham; heat until bubbly. Pour into casserole. Layer cheese over ham mixture.
• Sprinkle on buttered crumbs. Bake in moderate oven (350°) for 45 minutes or until top is golden brown. Makes 8 to 10 servings.

Meatball Stew

Hearty dish for skaters and skiers

1½ lbs. ground beef
1 c. soft bread crumbs
¼ c. finely chopped onions
1 egg, beaten
1 tsp. salt
½ tsp. marjoram
¼ tsp. thyme
2 tblsp. cooking oil
1 (10½ oz.) can condensed tomato soup
1 (10½ oz.) can condensed beef broth
4 med. potatoes, pared and quartered
4 carrots, scraped and cut in 1" chunks
8 small white onions, peeled
2 tblsp. chopped parsley

• Combine ground beef, bread crumbs, onions, egg, salt, marjoram and thyme. Shape into 24 meatballs.
• Brown meatballs in oil in a 4 qt. dutch oven. Remove as they brown. Combine soup and broth in dutch oven. Add meatballs and potatoes, carrots and onions. Bring to a boil; cover and simmer for 30 minutes or until vegetables are tender. Add parsley. Makes 6 to 8 servings.

Neapolitan Lasagna

Spinach is a great addition

Sauce:
⅓ c. oil
2 tblsp. finely chopped onion
½ tsp. minced garlic
1 (2 lb. 3 oz.) can plum tomatoes, sieved
2 beef bouillon cubes
1 c. water
1 (6 oz.) can tomato paste
½ bay leaf
2 whole cloves
½ tsp. basil
½ tsp. oregano
½ tsp. salt
¼ tsp. pepper
¼ tsp. sugar

Filling:
1 lb. cream-style cottage cheese
1 (9 oz.) pkg. frozen spinach, cooked, drained and chopped
2 eggs, slightly beaten
½ c. grated Parmesan cheese
¼ tsp. salt
¼ tsp. ground nutmeg
⅛ tsp. pepper
1 (1 lb.) pkg. lasagna noodles, cooked and drained
¼ lb. Mozzarella cheese, shredded
Grated Parmesan cheese

• Sauté onion and garlic in oil. Stir in remaining sauce ingredients. Bring to boil; simmer 1 hour. Stir occasionally. Remove bay leaf and cloves.
• Blend together cottage cheese, spinach, eggs, Parmesan cheese, salt, nutmeg and pepper. Set aside.
• Spread 1 c. sauce in 9x13x2" baking dish. Lay ⅓ of noodles in single layer on top. Spread with sauce; spoon on ½ spinach mixture; sprinkle with ⅓ of Mozzarella cheese. Repeat layers, topping with sauce. Add remaining noodles; cover with remaining sauce. Sprinkle with Mozzarella and Parmesan cheeses. Cover loosely with foil. Bake in moderate oven (350°) 40 minutes. Makes 12 servings.

Double Cheese Bake

Take this to your next potluck

1 c. elbow macaroni
¼ c. butter
1 c. soft bread crumbs
1 c. shredded Cheddar cheese
½ c. shredded Swiss cheese
½ c. slivered ham
3 eggs, well beaten
1 tblsp. minced onion
1 tblsp. chopped parsely
¼ tsp. salt
⅛ tsp. pepper
1½ c. milk, scalded
Paprika

• Cook macaroni according to package directions; drain. Add butter; toss until coated.
• Add bread crumbs, Cheddar and Swiss cheese, ham, eggs, onion, parsley, salt, pepper and milk. Mix well. Turn into greased 2 qt. casserole. Sprinkle with paprika. Bake in slow oven (325°) 40 to 45 minutes. Makes 6 servings.

Timballo with Cheese Sauce

Beautiful enough for a banquet

1 lb. spaghetti (break strands in half)
⅓ c. butter
1 lb. pork sausage
1 (4 oz.) can sliced mushrooms, drained
3 tblsp. finely chopped onion
⅓ c. sliced stuffed olives
½ c. grated Parmesan cheese
2 tblsp. chopped parsley
½ tsp. salt
¼ tsp. pepper
¼ c. dry bread crumbs
2 eggs, well beaten
¼ lb. Mozzarella cheese shredded
Cheese Sauce (recipe follows)

• Cook spaghetti for 10 minutes in boiling salted water. Drain, toss with butter; coat well.
• Sauté sausage until almost done. Pour off all fat except 2 tablespoons. Add mushrooms and onion. Sauté in fat until tender.
• Toss together spaghetti, sausage mixture, olives, Parmesan cheese, parsley, salt and pepper.
• Coat a buttered 9" spring-form pan with bread crumbs; reserve some for top. Place half the spaghetti mixture in pan; pour eggs evenly over all. Sprinkle with Mozzarella cheese; put remaining mixture on top. Sprinkle with remaining crumbs. Cover with foil; bake in moderate oven (375°) 40 minutes. Let stand 5 minutes. Serve with Cheese Sauce.

Cheese Sauce: Stir ¼ c. of Parmesan cheese and 1 tblsp. chopped parsley into 2 c. of medium white sauce. Makes 6 to 8 servings.

Pressure-cooker Baked Beans

We give "oven" method, too

1 lb. navy beans
⅓ lb. bacon, cut in pieces
3 tblsp. brown sugar
3 tblsp. molasses
3 tblsp. ketchup
½ c. chopped onion
1½ tsp. salt
½ tsp. prepared mustard
2 c. water

• Wash beans. Soak overnight in water to cover. Rinse and drain.
• Sauté bacon in 4-qt. pressure cooker. Add brown sugar, molasses, ketchup, onion, salt, mustard, water and drained beans. Close cover securely. Cook beans at 15 lbs. pressure (following manufacturer's directions for your pressure cooker) for 50 minutes. Let pressure drop of own accord. Makes about 6 servings.

Oven Method: Soak beans (as above) overnight. Rinse and drain. Add enough water to cover beans. Bring to a boil; reduce heat. Cook for 20 minutes.
• Put beans and liquid in a 2-qt. bean pot or casserole. Add remaining ingredients. Cover. Bake in slow oven (300°) for 6 to 8 hours, adding more water as needed to keep beans moist. Uncover for last 30 minutes of baking. Beans should be tender and not mushy. Makes 6 servings.

It'll keep them happy the busiest night of the year

Christmas Eve soup supper

Be sure to make enough for second helpings when you serve a soup supper. Our recipe for Cream of Potato Soup (pictured) or any of these other satisfying hot soups may be doubled—or tripled.

To go with the soup, cut crusty squares of corn bread, hot from the oven. Add a crisp tossed green salad and call the family to come serve themselves.

Desert is easy, too: a big plateful of bar cookies. We recommend tart, tangy Apricot Snowdrifts.

Cream of Potato Soup

Prepare ahead. . . then heat and serve

6 c. sliced potatoes (5 large)
½ c. sliced carrots
6 slices bacon
1 c. chopped onion
1 c. sliced celery
1½ tsp. salt
¼ tsp. pepper
2 c. milk
2 c. light cream
Finely shredded Cheddar cheese
Parsley sprigs

• Cook potatoes and carrots in boiling water until tender. Drain.

• Sauté bacon until crisp; drain and crumble. Sauté onion and celery in 2 tblsp. of the bacon fat.

• Combine potatoes, carrots, sautéed vegetables, bacon, salt, pepper, milk and cream. Simmer for 30 minutes. (Do not boil.) Garnish with shredded Cheddar cheese and parsley. Makes about 2 qts.

Virginia Cream of Peanut Soup

As served at King's Arms Tavern in Colonial Williamsburg

2 tblsp. butter or margarine
¼ c. minced onion
⅔ c. chopped celery (include some tender leaves)
3 tblsp. flour
4 c. chicken broth (skim fat)
½ c. peanut butter
1 c. light cream, half and half or evaporated milk
Salt and pepper to taste—season after cooking
Salted peanuts

• Melt butter in saucepan. Add onion and celery; cook until tender but not brown. Blend in flour; remove from heat. Gradually add chicken broth and bring to boil over medium heat, stirring constantly. Add peanut butter; blend smooth. Stir in cream and seasonings. Heat, but *do not boil.* Garnish each serving with salted peanuts. Makes about 5½ cups.

Savory Split Pea Soup

Delicately flavored special of the Commonwealth Club in Richmond

1 lb. (2¼ c.) dried split green peas
4 qts. water
Large smoked Smithfield ham bone or 1 lb. hocks
1 large onion, sliced
¼ c. bacon fat
2½ c. milk
Salt and pepper to taste—season after cooking

• Wash peas, add water and bring to a boil in heavy kettle. Cover and let stand 1 hour. Do not drain.
• Add ham bone and onion. Simmer, uncovered, down one third (3 to 4 hours); stir occasionally.
• Remove bone and strain soup through sieve. Add bacon fat.
• Remove portions to be frozen. Cool, package, label and freeze.
• To portion not frozen (or when ready to serve frozen soup), add milk and seasonings and heat, but *do not boil.* Soup will be thin and creamy. Makes about 3 quarts.

Herbed Potato Soup

Garnish soup with minced parsley

8 medium potatoes
2 onions or 2 tblsp. minced dry onion
4 tblsp. butter
2 tblsp. chopped parsley
½ tsp. crushed basil
4 tblsp. flour
2 tsp. salt
½ tsp. pepper
2 c. cold milk
4 c. scalded milk
2 c. hot potato water

• Cook potatoes and onion together until potatoes are tender. Drain; *save the potato water.* Put the potatoes through ricer or coarse strainer.
• While potatoes are cooking, melt butter in heavy 6-qt. saucepan. Add chopped parsley and basil.
• Blend in flour, seasoning; gradually stir in cold milk. Add scalded milk and potato water. Cook over medium heat; stir constantly, until mixture thickens slightly. Stir in potatoes and onions; heat. Makes 12 cups. (Soup freezes well.)

Corn-Oyster Soup

Call this Christmas Eve soup—it's a real special-occasion treat

1 tblsp. butter
1 tblsp. flour
1 qt. milk
1 (1 lb. 1 oz.) can whole kernel corn
1 lb. oysters (about 2 c.)
1½ tsp. salt
¼ tsp. pepper
Paprika (optional)
Chopped parsley (optional)

• Melt butter in large saucepan. Blend in flour, then milk. Cook, stirring constantly, until mixture comes to a boil. Add corn, oysters (with their liquid), salt and pepper. Simmer 10 minutes. Serve sprinkled with paprika and parsley, if desired. Makes 6 servings.

Boula Boula Soup

A fashionable combination of mock turtle and split green pea soups

Mock Turtle Soup: Dilute 1 (10½ oz.) can of condensed onion soup with ½ can water. Heat; strain out solids. To remaining soup add 1 c. cooked diced veal, which resembles turtle meat.

Jig-time Split Green Pea Soup: Dilute 1 (10½ oz.) can condensed split green pea soup with 1 can water. Heat; mash through strainer. Reheat, stirring well.

• Combine mock turtle and pea soups; ladle into serving bowls. Garnish with mounds of unsweetened whipped cream or sour cream. Sprinkle with Parmesan cheese. If desired, broil 1 minute, 4 inches from flame (use ovenproof bowls). Makes about 4½ cups. You may substitute 2½ c. Savory Split Pea Soup, recipe follows, for canned split green pea soup.

Apricot Snowdrifts

Perfect meal ending for a soup supper

⅔ c. dried apricots
1⅓ c. sifted flour
¼ c. sugar
½ c. butter
½ tsp. baking powder
¼ tsp. salt
2 eggs
1 c. brown sugar, firmly packed
½ c. chopped walnuts
½ tsp. vanilla

• Cook apricots in boiling water for 10 minutes; drain. Cool and cut up. Set aside.
• Combine 1 c. flour, sugar and butter, mix until crumbly. Press into a greased 9" square pan. Bake in moderate oven (350°) for 18 minutes.
• Sift together ⅓ c. flour, baking powder and salt. Beat eggs slightly. At medium speed, slowly beat in brown sugar. Add flour mixture; stir well. Add apricots, nuts and vanilla. Spread over baked layer. Bake in moderate oven (350°) 25 minutes or until golden brown. Cool and cut into bars with a wet knife. Roll in confectioners sugar. Decorate each bar with candied cherry half. Makes 32 (2x1") bars.

PICTURED (top to bottom) are zippy Cider Mold Salad, quick and easy Paper Cup Frozen Salad and glistening frozen Cranberry Chunk Salad.

Make ahead fruited salads

It's no trick to add eye appeal to Christmas salads that are ready and waiting in the refrigerator or freezer. The mold you choose gives you a head start (see photo). All you do at serving time is turn the salad out on a pretty plate and decorate with your favorite green garnish.

Cider Mold Salad

A delightfully different molded salad from a New Jersey grower's wife

3 (3 oz.) pkgs. orange gelatin
5¾ c. apple cider or apple juice
½ c. seedless white raisins
½ c. apple cider or apple juice
2 large apples, cut in cubes (peeled or unpeeled)
½ c. chopped walnuts

• Dissolve gelatin in 2 c. boiling cider. Add 3¾ c. cold cider. Chill until slightly jelled.

• In the meantime, soak white raisins in ½ c. cider for about ½ hour. Drain raisins (discard this cider) and add them with the apples and walnuts to the gelatin mixture. Pour into 2½ qt. mold and chill until firm.

• To serve, run a knife around edge of salad. Dip mold into warm water for a few seconds. Unmold on platter. Garnish with frosted grapes or greens. Makes 9 to 12 servings.

To frost grapes: Dip small bunches of seedless green grapes in slightly beaten egg white. Roll in superfine granulated sugar and dry on cake racks.

Cranberry Chunk Salad

Chunks of jellied cranberry sauce make this frozen salad different

2 (3 oz.) pkg. cream cheese, softened
¼ c. salad dressing
¼ c. lemon juice
⅛ tsp. salt
1 c. drained crushed pineapple
1 c. diced walnuts
1 c. diced bananas
1½ c. heavy cream
1 (1 lb.) can jellied cranberry sauce, chilled and cut into chunks
Decorations (optional, see directions that follow)

• Beat cream cheese with salad dressing and lemon juice and salt until smooth. Stir in pineapple, walnuts and bananas. Whip cream and fold into mixture. Lightly fold in cranberry chunks.

• Turn into a 9x5x3" bread pan that has been lined on all sides with a double thickness of waxed paper. Freeze.

• To unmold, place pan in warm water for a count of 15. Turn out on a chilled platter. Place in refrigerator for about 30 minutes before serving. Slice to serve. Makes 12 servings.

Decorations shown in picture: Prepare 1 pkg. whipped topping mix according to package directions. Reserve ½ c. of prepared mix. Spread remainder over sides and top of frozen salad. Make an edging from whipped topping using a cake decorator, #30 tip. Decorate top with bells cut from jellied cranberry sauce. Freeze to set decorations.

Paper Cup Frozen Salad

Easy way to mold a frozen salad. Delicious flavor; smooth texture

2 c. dairy sour cream
2 tblsp. lemon juice
½ c. sugar
⅛ tsp. salt
1 (8½ oz.) can crushed pineapple, well drained
1 banana, diced
4 drops red food color
¼ c. chopped pecans
1 (1 lb.) can pitted Bing cherries, well drained

• Combine sour cream, lemon juice, sugar, salt, crushed pineapple, banana pieces and enough red food color to give a pink tint.

• Lightly fold in nuts and Bing cherries. Spoon into fluted paper muffin cups (large size) which have been placed in 3" muffin cup pans. Freeze. Cover with plastic wrap and store in freezer.

• Remove from freezer about 15 minutes before serving to loosen paper cups from pan. Peel off paper cup and place salad on greens. Fills 12 large paper muffin cups.

The yule log cake

A cake roll not only makes a perfectly delicious Christmas dessert but it also has a symbolic history. It's traditional for French confectioners to bake their *Bûche de Noël* for the holidays, which is a cake roll frosted and decorated to look like a Christmas log. They use a decorating tube to pipe chocolate or mocha frosting over the cake to resemble bark. Elaborate cake rolls may have "branches" or be decorated with meringue "mushrooms" and spun sugar "moss" or have Christmas messages written on in tinted frosting.

If you want to decorate a Yule log, use the recipe for Basic Cake Roll (see next page)—the chocolate version if you prefer. Fill it with whipped cream, sweetened and flavored with vanilla. Spread the rolled-up cake with creamy canned chocolate frosting; then rough up the "bark" with a table knife or wide-toothed comb.

A wonderful way to serve cake roll at a large party is to bake and fill three or four of them, offering your guests a choice of flavors, fillings and sauces. We give you a marvelously spiced Coffee and Cream Ginger Roll as well as the versatile basic recipe to fill and glaze as you choose: strawberry, butterscotch, pineapple or chocolate. You can easily manage such a display; the recipe includes directions for filling and freezing the rolls ahead of time.

Coffee and Cream Ginger Roll

Spiced with authority, soothed with whipped cream

5 eggs, separated
½ tsp. cream of tartar
1 c. sifted confectioners sugar
3 tblsp. sifted flour
¼ tsp. salt
1/16 tsp. ground black pepper
1½ tblsp. instant coffee powder
1½ tsp. ground ginger
1 tsp. ground allspice
1 tsp. ground cinnamon
1 tsp. ground nutmeg
1 tsp. ground cardamom (optional)
½ tsp. ground cloves
Sifted confectioners sugar
1½ c. heavy cream
½ c. sifted confectioners sugar
1½ tsp. vanilla
Amber Candy Shatters (recipe follows) or fruit to garnish

• Beat egg whites (at room temperature) with cream of tartar until soft peaks form. Gradually add ½ c. of sifted confectioners sugar, beating until stiff peaks form. In a separate bowl, beat egg yolks until thick and light colored.

• Sift together 3 times the remaining ½ c. confectioners sugar, the flour, salt, pepper, coffee and spices. Fold into yolk mixture until just blended.

CONTINUED

USE A SMALL SIEVE to sprinkle a light dusting of confectioners sugar over Coffee and Cream Ginger Roll. Serve with Amber Candy Shatters or with fruit.

Gently fold yolk mixture into egg whites. Spread gently and evenly in a 15½x10½x1" jelly roll pan which has been greased, lined with waxed paper and the waxed paper greased.

• Bake in moderate oven (350°) 15 minutes or until cake springs back when touched lightly. Turn out on a towel sprinkled with confectioners sugar. Quickly and gently peel off paper. Starting at narrow end, roll cake and towel together; cool thoroughly on rack.

• Whip heavy cream, gradually adding the ½ c. confectioners sugar and vanilla. Unroll cake and spread with cream. Roll up again and roll onto serving platter. Chill thoroughly, at least 3 hours.

• Sprinkle lightly with confectioners sugar. Slice to serve and accompany each slice with fruits or top with Amber Candy Shatters. Makes 10 servings.

Amber Candy Shatters: In a heavy frypan, cook ½ c. sugar over medium heat, stirring, until sugar melts and turns deep brown. Pour into buttered shallow pan to cool and harden. Break into pieces, then crush with rolling pin.

Frozen Cake Roll, Four Ways

Basic cake roll with variations

- 4 eggs, separated
- ¾ c. sugar
- 1 tsp. vanilla
- ¾ c. sifted cake flour
- ¾ tsp. baking powder
- ¼ tsp. salt

• Beat egg yolks until light and lemon-colored. Slowly add sugar, beating until creamy. Add vanilla; beat.

• Sift together flour and baking powder; gradually add to sugar mixture. Beat only until smooth.

• Beat egg whites with salt until stiff, but not dry. Fold into batter.

• Spread batter evenly in greased 15½x10½x1" jelly roll pan lined with heavily greased brown paper.

• Bake in moderate oven (375°) 15 minutes, or until top springs back when lightly touched. Loosen cake edges at once; invert onto clean towel sprinkled with confectioners sugar. Cut off hard edges. Roll up, leaving towel in; cool. Unroll; fill (recipes follow); reroll.

• Wrap, seal, label, date and freeze seam side down.

Recommended storage time: unfilled cake rolls, 6 months; filled rolls, up to 1 month.

• To serve, take cake roll from freezer. See recipes following for glazes and sauces to go with each flavor filling. Spread top of cake roll with glaze; slice to serve; pass sauce. Makes 1 roll or 10 (1") slices.

Chocolate Cake Roll: Follow above recipe, sifting ¼ c. cocoa with flour.

Cake Roll Fillings, Glazes and Sauces

Basic Filling: Whip 1 c. heavy cream until it begins to thicken. Gradually add 3 tblsp. sugar and ¼ tsp. vanilla (use almond extract instead of vanilla for Pineapple Roll); beat stiff.

Strawberry Roll: Fold 1 (10 oz.) pkg. frozen strawberry slices, drained, into whipped cream. Spread on cake; roll. Bring to boil ¼ c. strawberry jam and ¼ c. light corn syrup; brush on top of roll. Serve with Strawberry Sauce.

Strawberry Sauce: Mix 1 c. strawberry jam and 1 c. light corn syrup; bring to boil. Cool. Makes 1 pint.

Pineapple Roll: Fold 1 (8¼ oz.) can crushed pineapple, drained, into whipped cream. Spread over cake; roll. For glaze, bring to boil ¼ c. apricot jam and ¼ c. light corn syrup, brush on top of roll. Serve with Pineapple Sauce.

Pineapple Sauce: Mix 1 (8¼ oz.) can crushed pineapple, drained, with 1 c. light corn syrup. Bring to boil and cook until mixture thickens. Makes 1 pint.

Butterscotch Roll: Fold 1 (3 oz.) can chopped pecans into whipped cream. Spread over cake; roll. For glaze, heat ¼ c. light corn syrup and 1 tblsp. melted butter or margarine. Brush on top of roll. Sprinkle with ¼ c. chopped pecans. Serve with Butterscotch Sauce.

Butterscotch Sauce: Combine ⅔ c. light corn syrup, 1¼ c. brown sugar, firmly packed, ¼ c. butter and ¼ tsp. salt; boil to heavy syrup; cool. Add 1 (6 oz.) can evaporated milk. Makes about 1 pint.

Chocolate Roll: Spread whipped cream over cake; roll. Sift ¼ c. confectioners sugar over roll. Serve with Chocolate Sauce.

Chocolate Sauce: Put 4 squares unsweetened chocolate, ½ c. butter and 2¼ c. evaporated milk in top of double boiler; heat until butter and chocolate melt. Slowly add 3 c. sugar; heat until sugar dissolves. Cool; refrigerate. (Sauce will thicken. If too thick, thin with corn syrup.) Makes 1 quart.

Note: Cake rolls may be filled with different kinds of ice cream, softened just enough to spread and returned to the freezer. Serve sliced with a sundae sauce.

Party pies...

sized just right

When your regular 9″ pie isn't enough to serve company and two pies would leave you with leftovers, try our compromise pie: a big 10″ pie that cuts into eight generous wedges.

Delicious combinations of fruits make these pies standouts for flavor and originality: pear-pineapple, pumpkin-apple and cranberry-apple-mince.

If you use packaged pie crust mix, use 1¾ c. mix and about 4 tblsp. cold water for a one-crust 10″ pie. Use 2½ to 2¾ c. mix with 4 to 6 tblsp. cold water for a two-crust 10″ pie.

Pumpkin-Apple Pie

Combination of two pie favorites

10″ Pie	9″ Pie
⅓ c.	⅓ c. firmly packed brown sugar
1 tblsp.	1 tblsp. cornstarch
½ tsp.	½ tsp. ground cinnamon
¼ tsp.	¼ tsp. salt
⅓ c.	⅓ c. water
2 tblsp.	2 tblsp. butter
3 c.	3 c. sliced tart apples
2 eggs	1 egg
½ c.	⅓ c. sugar
1 c.	¾ c. canned or cooked, mashed pumpkin
¼ tsp.	¼ tsp. salt
½ tsp.	¼ tsp. ground ginger
¾ tsp.	½ tsp. ground cinnamon
¼ tsp.	⅛ tsp. ground cloves
1 c.	¾ c. evaporated milk
10″	9″ pie shell, unbaked

• Combine the brown sugar, cornstarch, ½ tsp. cinnamon and ¼ tsp. salt in a large saucepan. Stir in water, butter. Bring to a boil; add apples and cook 4 minutes over medium heat. Set aside.

• Beat eggs in separate bowl. Add sugar, pumpkin, ¼ tsp. salt, ginger, ¾ tsp. cinnamon, (½ tsp. for 9″ pie), ground cloves, and evaporated milk. Blend well.

• Spoon apple mixture into pie shell. Carefully spoon pumpkin layer over apples. Bake in moderate oven (375°) 50 to 55 minutes. Larger pie makes 8 servings, smaller pie makes 6 servings.

Pear-Pineapple Pie

Use pears that hold their shape. We used Anjou pears

10″ Pie	9″ Pie
Pastry for 2-crust pie	
3 tblsp.	2 tblsp. flour
½ c.	⅓ c. sugar
¾ tsp.	½ tsp. salt
¾ tsp.	½ tsp. ground nutmeg
7 c.	5 c. thinly sliced pears
½ c.	⅓ c. crushed pineapple, well-drained
2 tblsp.	2 tblsp. raisins
3 tblsp.	2 tblsp. lemon juice

• Roll out a little more than half of the pastry and fit into pie pan.

• Combine flour, sugar, salt, nutmeg. Toss with pears and remaining ingredients. Spoon into pie shell. Roll out top crust; make cutout in center. Place on filling; seal and crimp edges.

• Bake in moderate oven (375°) 50 to 60 minutes. Larger pie, 8 servings; smaller pie, 6 servings.

Apple-Cranberry-Mince Pie

Tasty, attractive, open-faced pie

10″ Pie	9″ Pie
1 (1 lb.) can	1⅓ c. whole cranberry sauce
1 c.	¾ c. prepared mincemeat
4 c.	2½ c. coarsely chopped tart apples
3 tblsp.	2 tblsp. melted butter
⅓ c.	¼ c. sugar
¼ c.	3 tblsp. cornstarch
½ tsp.	¼ tsp. salt
10″	9″ pie shell, unbaked

• Combine cranberry sauce, mincemeat, apples and butter. Combine dry ingredients; stir into fruit mixture. Spoon into pastry shell.

• Top with pastry cut-outs in leaf shapes. Bake in hot oven (400°) 40 to 50 minutes. Larger pie, 8 servings; smaller pie, 6 servings.

Slick Trick:
Machine-stitch circles on your pastry cloth to indicate crust sizes you need most often. This is a quick guide and saves guesswork.

Pie Crust Recipe

Ingredients	9″ one-crust	9″ two-crust 10″ one-crust	10″ two-crust
Flour	1 c.	2 c.	3 c.
Salt	½ tsp.	1 tsp.	1½ tsp.
Shortening	½ c. + 1 tblsp.	¾ c.	1 c. + 2 tblsp.
Cold water	2-2½ tblsp.	4-5 tblsp.	6 tblsp.

• Combine flour and salt in mixing bowl. Cut in shortening with pastry blender until mixture is the consistency of coarse cornmeal or tiny peas.

• Sprinkle on cold water, 1 tblsp. at a time, tossing mixture lightly and stirring with a fork. Add water each time to the driest part of mixture. Dough should be just moist enough to hold together when pressed gently with a fork. It should not be sticky.

• Shape dough in smooth ball with hands and roll out; or wrap in waxed paper and refrigerate until ready to roll and fill pie.

Desserts *ready and waiting in the freezer*

Frozen desserts are just great for a big do, when you want to breeze in and out of the kitchen, with a minimum of fussing. If you have a helper, you can cut and serve these frosty squares in no time. And aren't they festive looking?

Each one of the dessert trio has its own distinct flavor. The crimson and white Raspberry Swirl has creamy undertones of cheesecake. Gelatin based, the Velvety Lime Squares taste equally as good when you allow them to thaw for several hours. Vanilla Almond Crunch has a smooth ice cream base with a crunchy coconut/almond crust. Vary the ice cream flavor to taste–chocolate or peach would be delicious, too.

All three can be held in the freezer compartment of your refrigerator, too. However, if you plan to store them for a long period of time only the regular freezer with its 0° temperature assures that these desserts will keep properly.

Be sure to wrap these frozen pretties snugly with foil to seal in their delicate flavor and to prevent freezer burn. They will be easier to cut if you allow them to stand at room temperature for about 20 minutes before serving,

Velvety Lime Squares

Garnish with a perfect pecan half

1 (3 oz.) can flaked coconut
½ c. vanilla wafer crumbs
2 tblsp. melted butter
2 tblsp. sugar
2 (3 oz.) pkgs. lime gelatin
2 c. boiling water
1 (6 oz.) can frozen limeade concentrate
1 qt. plus 1 pt. vanilla ice cream, softened
⅛ tsp. salt
Few drops green food coloring

• Carefully toast ½ c. coconut in moderate oven (375°) until lightly browned, about 5 minutes. Set aside.

• Combine remaining coconut, crumbs, butter, sugar. Lightly press into 7x11x1½" pan and bake in moderate oven (375°) 6 to 7 minutes. Cool.

• Dissolve gelatin in boiling water. Add limeade, ice cream and salt; stir until dissolved. Pour into crust. Top with reserved toasted coconut and garnish with pecans, if you wish. Freeze until firm. Cover tightly. Return to freezer.

• Remove dessert from freezer 20 minutes before cutting. Makes 6 to 8 servings.

Vanilla Almond Crunch

Try a splash of chocolate sauce on it for a special sundae

1 (4 oz.) pkg. slivered almonds
¼ c. melted butter
1 c. crushed rice cereal squares
½ c. light brown sugar, firmly packed
½ c. flaked coconut
⅛ tsp. salt
½ gal. vanilla ice cream, softened

• Toast almonds in the melted butter. Remove half of almonds from butter and set aside.

• Combine crushed cereal, brown sugar, coconut and salt with remaining almonds and butter. Pat mixture gently into 13x9x2" pan. Bake in moderate oven (375°) 5 minutes. Cool.

• Spread ice cream over cooled crust. Decorate top with reserved almonds. Freeze until firm. Makes 10 servings.

Raspberry Swirl

Cool and tangy finale to a meal

¾ c. graham cracker crumbs
3 tblsp. melted butter
2 tblsp. sugar
3 eggs, separated
1 (8 oz.) pkg. cream cheese
1 c. sugar
⅛ tsp. salt
1 c. heavy cream
1 (10 oz.) pkg. frozen raspberries, partially thawed

• Combine thoroughly crumbs, melted butter and 2 tblsp. sugar. Lightly press mixture into well-greased 7x11x1½" pan. Bake in moderate oven (375°) about 8 minutes. Cool thoroughly.

• Beat egg yolks until thick. Add cream cheese, sugar and salt; beat until smooth and light.

• Beat egg whites until stiff peaks form. Whip cream until stiff and fold with egg whites into cheese mixture.

• In a mixer or blender, crush raspberries to a pulp. Gently swirl half of fruit pulp through cheese filling and spread mixture into crust. Spoon remaining purée over top; swirl with a knife. Freeze, then cover and return to freezer. Makes 6 to 8 servings.

Desserts *ready and waiting in the refrigerator*

After indulging in too much turkey and trimmings, most folks appreciate a light dessert. If you chill one of these luscious whipped desserts in a tall mold, you can serve it forth most festively. Turn it out on a pretty glass plate and wreathe it with a circlet of whipped cream and a sprinkling of chopped nuts or a grating of fresh orange or lemon rind.

Do you have trouble unmolding desserts and salads? Lightly brush the mold with salad oil before filling—then your dessert will slide out easily.

Whipped Strawberry Delight

Wonderful mix of flavors

1 (9 oz.) can crushed pineapple
1 (3 oz.) pkg. strawberry gelatin
1 c. boiling water
1 env. whipped topping mix
½ c. milk
⅔ c. chopped nuts

• Drain pineapple, reserving juice. Add enough water to juice to make 1 c. of liquid.
• Dissolve gelatin in boiling water. Stir in juice and water. Chill until thick and syrupy.
• Whip topping mix with milk until soft peaks form.
• Whip gelatin until fluffy. Beat in whipped topping. Add pineapple and nuts. Turn into a lightly oiled 5 c. mold. Chill until set.

Blueberry Lime Imperial

Cloud-light and luscious

1½ c. reconstituted frozen lime-ade
1 (3 oz.) pkg. lime gelatin
1 c. heavy cream, whipped
1 c. frozen blueberries, thawed and drained

• Bring 1 c. limeade to a boil. Dissolve gelatin in hot limeade. Stir in remaining ½ c. limeade. Chill until thick and syrupy.
• Beat with electric mixer until light and fluffy. Fold in cream and blueberries.
• Turn into a lightly oiled 5 c. mold. Chill until set.

Mint Mist

A towering beauty

1 (20 oz.) can crushed pineapple
1 pkg. unflavored gelatin
⅓ c. mint-flavored apple jelly
1 c. heavy cream, whipped

• Drain pineapple, reserve juice.
• Soften gelatin in ½ c. pineapple juice. Place over low heat, stirring constantly until gelatin dissolves. Remove from heat; add jelly; stir until melted. Add pineapple and remainer of juice.
• Chill until thick and syrupy. Fold cream into gelatin mixture. Turn into a lightly oiled 4 c. mold. Chill until set.

Russian Cream Mold

Double for company

1 (3 oz.) pkg. lemon gelatin
1 c. boiling water
1 c. sour cream
1 (1 lb.) can sliced peaches, drained and diced
⅓ c. flaked coconut
1 c. sliced strawberries

• Dissolve gelatin in boiling water. Chill until thick and syrupy.
• Add sour cream; beat until blended. Fold in peaches, coconut and strawberries. Turn into lightly oiled 4 c. mold. Chill until set.

Fruit Tree

• Follow the Christmas Tree shape to stack up a dazzling display of fruit and cheese. It's a splendid way to serve everyone's favorite meal ending. Bring the tree out before dinner, to decorate buffet or coffee table. Then, after the feast, invite guests to pluck their favorite fruits from your tree.
• To build the tree, assemble trays, cake stands and footed dishes, graduated in size; place the heaviest pieces on the bottom. Roll florist's clay (available from a florist; about 60¢ per half lb.) into long thin strips. Use clay to anchor each dish firmly to the one below it. If your trays and dishes don't match in color and material, cover glass or metal pieces with contact paper and spray with copper or gold paint.
• Begin at the bottom to stack fruits and work up (we've used five layers). Intersperse fruits with green leaves from your yard—ivy, holly, laurel, or whatever you have.
• Supplement your own home-grown fruits with an assortment from the food store. Add color with a few out-of-season strawberries or cherry tomatoes. Quarter fresh pineapple by cutting right through the crown (leaves). Remove the core with a sharp knife, loosen fruit from rind, then cut in bite-size pieces to spear with toothpicks.
• Try cheeses for dessert that you've not tasted before. We recommend Pineapple Cheese, Blue or Roquefort, Neufchâtel, Liederkranz and a good Cheddar.
• Keep your tree to replenish throughout the holiday season. Refrigerate perishable fruits and most cheeses until guests arrive.

FRUIT TREE. For dessert and decoration in one, arrange a spectacular serving of fruit on trays and serving dishes stacked up to make a tree shape. Let guests help themselves.

Cranberries

Cranberry Chutney

Serve with poultry or cold meat—extra jars make nice gifts

1 (1 lb. 14 oz.) can fruit cocktail
½ c. orange juice
½ c. sugar
¼ c. light brown sugar, firmly packed
¼ c. cider vinegar
½ tsp. ground cloves
¼ tsp. red pepper
½ tsp. salt
2 c. cranberries
1 c. chopped, unpeeled apples
1 tblsp. finely chopped candied ginger
1 small clove garlic, minced
¾ c. seedless raisins

• Drain fruit cocktail. Measure 1¼ c. syrup; reserve fruit. Combine syrup, orange juice, sugar, brown sugar, vinegar, cloves, pepper and salt in a heavy 3 qt. saucepan. Bring to a full boil, stirring often. Add cranberries, apples, ginger, garlic, raisins and fruit cocktail. Cook until berries pop, about 5 minutes. Stir in fruit cocktail. Simmer, stirring often, until mixture thickens slightly, about 15 minutes.

• Pour into hot, sterilized jars. Seal immediately or store in refrigerator. Chutney will thicken as it cools. Makes about 2½ pints.

Holiday Cranberry Cake

Run berries through food chopper while still frozen—saves mess

1 (1 lb. 3 oz.) pkg. lemon cake mix
1 (3 oz.) pkg. cream cheese, softened
¾ c. milk
4 eggs
1¼ c. ground cranberries
½ c. ground walnuts
¼ c. sugar
1 tsp. mace (optional)

• Blend cake mix, cream cheese and milk; beat with mixer 2 minutes at medium speed. Add eggs; blend and beat for two additional minutes.
• Thoroughly combine cranberries, walnuts, sugar and mace; fold into cake batter. Pour into a well-greased and floured 10" tube or bundt pan. Bake in moderate oven (350°) for 1 hour or until done. Cool 5 minutes. Remove from pan. Cool on wire rack. Dust with confectioners sugar if you wish. Makes 12 servings.

Chewy Cranberry Squares

Excellent for lunch boxes

¾ c. sugar
6 tblsp. butter
2 eggs
1½ tblsp. lemon juice
1½ c. sifted flour
1½ tsp. baking powder
½ tsp. salt
1 c. chopped nuts
¾ c. jellied cranberry sauce, cut in ¼" cubes.

• Cream sugar and butter until light. Add eggs and lemon juice; beat until smooth and creamy.
• Sift together flour, baking powder and salt. Stir into creamed mixture. Gently fold in nuts and cranberry cubes. Pour batter into a greased 9x13x 2" pan. Bake in moderate oven (350°) for 25 to 30 minutes. Cut into squares while still warm. Makes 24 bars.

Cranberry Trenton Dessert

It's great either warm or cold

3 c. choppd cranberries
3 c. chopped tart apples
1 tblsp. cornstarch
⅓ c. light brown sugar
¾ c. sugar
1 tsp. salt
1 tsp. vanilla
1 c. oatmeal
½ c. light brown sugar
⅓ c. sifted flour
2 tblsp. crushed cornflakes
¼ c. butter
½ c. chopped nuts

• Combine cranberries, apples, cornstarch, ⅓ c. brown sugar, granulated sugar, ½ tsp. of the salt and vanilla. Pour into a buttered 7x11x2" baking dish.
• Mix together oatmeal, the ½ c. brown sugar, flour, cornflakes and the remaining ½ tsp. salt. Cut in butter until mixture is crumbly; stir in nuts. Sprinkle evenly over top of cranberry mixture. Bake in moderate oven (350°) for 35 to 40 minutes. Top with whipped cream if you wish. Makes 10 servings.

Yiftus

Doubles as a cranberry dessert

2 c. crushed saltines or soda crackers
2 (1 lb.) cans whole cranberry sauce
1½ c. heavy cream
1 tblsp. sugar

• Spread 1 cup saltines in a 7x11" oblong baking dish. Cover with 1 can of cranberry sauce.
• Whip the cream, sweetening it slightly with the sugar and spread half of it on the cranberry layer. Repeat layers.
• Refrigerate at least 1 hour. Serve as a relish with turkey or other poultry. Makes 6 to 8 servings.

Mincemeat

Everybody likes to come into the farm kitchen when you're cooking mincemeat. That wonderful spicy-sweet fragrance from a big kettle of gently simmering mincemeat promises lots of good eating to come.

You may use a commercial, prepared mincemeat in any of these recipes. But if you've never made mincemeat, try this Old-Fashioned Mincemeat recipe and see how good a homemade version can be. One of Farm Journal's Family Test Group homemakers has made this family recipe for years; it is a flavorful, chopped meat-fruit combination that has no vinegar tang.

Our taste testers rated the mincemeat excellent; we think you'll enjoy it in plump, golden-crusted pies or in the new dessert recipes that follow.

Old-Fashioned Mincemeat

For flavor variation, substitute other fruit juices for apple juice

1½ lbs, beef, trimmed of fat and cut in chunks
1½ lbs, pork, trimmed of fat and cut in chunks
½ lb. suet
2 oranges, quartered
2 lemons, quartered
½ lb. citron
8 c. peeled, chopped, tart cooking apples
2 (15 oz.) pkgs. seedless raisins
3 (11 oz.) pkgs. currants
4 c. sugar
1 (1 lb.) pkg. brown sugar
1 c. molasses
2 tsp. ground cloves
1 tblsp. ground cinnamon
1 tblsp. ground ginger
1 tsp. ground nutmeg
3 c. apple juice
2 c. meat broth

• Cook beef and pork in gently simmering water until tender, about 1½ hours. Drain, reserving 2 c. broth. Put meat, suet, oranges, lemons and citron through food chopper using coarse blade. (Chop apples by hand.)

• Combine all ingredients in a large kettle. Bring to a gentle simmer over low to medium heat; stir occasionally. Cover; simmer for 1 hour. Stir mixture occasionally.

• Remove from heat, cool immediately. Package in airtight containers; refrigerate or freeze. If you can mincemeat, reduce cooking time to 30 minutes; follow canning instructions in instruction book which came with your pressure canner. Makes 7 quarts.

Note: If mincemeat seems dry when you use it, add apple juice.

Mincemeat Refrigerator Dessert

Creamy, light filling in gingersnap crust; an easy-to-make, big dessert

Crust:
2 c. gingersnap crumbs
⅓ c. melted butter

Filling:
1½ tblsp. unflavored gelatin
5 tblsp. cold water
2 c. mincemeat
4 eggs, separated
¼ c. butter
½ c. lemon juice
½ c. sugar
1 c. heavy cream or 1 (2 oz.) pkg. dessert topping mix, whipped

• Combine crumbs and melted butter; mix thoroughly. Reserve ½ c. for topping; pat remaining crumbs in 13x9x2" pan and refrigerate while you make filling.

• Soften gelatin in cold water. Combine mincemeat, slightly beaten egg yolks, butter and lemon juice in heavy saucepan. Cook, over low heat, until slightly thickened, about 15 minutes. Stir constantly. Remove from heat; add gelatin, stir until dissolved. Refrigerate.

• When mincemeat mixture chills and begins to thicken, prepare a soft meringue of the egg whites and sugar. Fold meringue and whipped cream or topping mix into mincemeat mixture. Gently pour into crumb-lined pan. Sprinkle with remaining crumbs. Chill several hours. Makes 12 to 15 servings.

Mincemeat-Lemon Stacks

A frozen dessert to have on hand for last-minute company

1 (1 lb. 3 oz.) pkg. lemon cake mix
Confectioners sugar
1 c. mincemeat
1 qt. vanilla ice cream, softened

• Prepare cake as directed on package. Bake in paper-lined 15½x10½x1" jelly roll pan. Chill or let stand several hours so tender cake may be easily handled. Invert onto a piece of heavy aluminum foil, dusted with confectioners sugar; carefully remove paper from cake. Cut cake crosswise in half.

• Blend mincemeat into softened ice cream. Quickly spread on one cake half. Invert other cake half onto ice cream; use foil to assist in turning one half over the other.

• Quickly cut cake into 12 servings. Freeze; wrap well. Move dessert from freezer to refrigerator one half hour before serving. Serve with a tart lemon sauce, warmed. Makes 12 servings.

Mincemeat-Pumpkin Pie

A combination of two favorite fall flavors in one extra-good pie

1 (9") unbaked pie shell
1 c. cooked pumpkin
½ c. brown sugar, firmly packed
½ tsp. salt
¾ tsp. ground cinnamon
¾ tsp. ground nutmeg
3 eggs
½ c. heavy cream
1 c. mincemeat

• Combine pumpkin, sugar, salt, spices, eggs and cream and beat only until blended. Stir in mincemeat. Pour into unbaked pie shell. Bake in hot oven (425°) until filling is set, about 35 minutes. Serve warm. Makes 6 servings.

Ginger!

Ginger mingles wonderfully with lemon, molasses, and other spices in these unusual gingerbreads and gingercakes.

Serve sturdy Whole Wheat Gingerbread warm as an after-school snack. Cut it in inch-thick slices and spread with salted butter. Or cut cooled slices slightly thinner and spread with soft butter.

Moist, nutted Pecan Ginger Loaf has the tender texture of a cake. Carve thick slices and broil-toast it on one side. Turn slices, spread with butter and broil-toast them on the other side . . . a breakfast treat for frosty mornings when you want to be extra nice to your family.

These Pumpkin-Ginger Squares are rich and spicy!

Pecan Ginger Loaf

Served with a brick of cream cheese (soft, for spreading) and fruit

½ c. soft butter or margarine
1½ c. sugar
2 eggs
1⅔ c. unsifted flour
¾ tsp. salt
1 tsp. baking soda
¼ tsp. baking powder
2 tsp. ground ginger
½ tsp. ground cinnamon
½ tsp. ground nutmeg
¼ tsp. ground cloves
⅓ c. water
1 c. cooked, mashed pumpkin
½ c. finely chopped pecans

• Cream butter and sugar together with electric mixer. Add eggs, one at a time, and beat until mixture is light and fluffy.
• Sift together flour, salt, baking powder and spices, add to creamed mixture alternately with water. Beat well after each addition. Add pumpkin and beat until well blended. Stir in chopped pecans. Turn into greased 9x5x3" loaf pan and spread smooth.
• Bake in moderate oven (350°) for 60 to 70 minutes, or until tooth-pick inserted in center comes out clean. Cool in pan for 10 minutes, then turn out on wire rack to cool thoroughly. Makes 1 loaf.

Ginger Lemon Pudding-Cake

Molasses enriches the taste. Serve warm, topped with whipped cream

3 eggs, separated
2 tblsp. light molasses
6 tblsp. sugar
2 tblsp. flour
1 tblsp. melted butter or margarine
1 tsp. ground ginger
1/16 tsp. salt
1 c. milk
2 tsp. grated lemon peel
¼ c. lemon juice

• Beat egg yolks in a mixing bowl. Beat in molasses and sugar, then the flour, butter, ginger, salt, milk, lemon peel and lemon juice to make a smooth mixture.
• Beat egg whites until stiff but not dry. Fold into batter.
• Pour mixture into greased 1½ qt. baking dish. Set into pan of hot water about 1-inch deep. Bake in slow oven (325°) for 55 minutes or until top is browned and knife inserted halfway deep into center comes out clean.
• Spoon into serving dishes. Makes 5 to 6 servings.

Whole Wheat Gingerbread

Not too sweet and quite spicy

½ c. butter margarine
2 tblsp. sugar
¾ c. light molasses
1 c. sifted flour
1 c. stirred whole wheat flour
½ tsp. salt
¾ tsp. baking soda
1 tsp. ground ginger
½ tsp. ground cinnamon
½ tsp. ground mace or nutmeg
½ c. chopped walnuts
½ c. raisins
3 tblsp. minced candied lemon peel
2 eggs
½ c. milk

• Melt butter in a saucepan. Add sugar and molasses; stir to blend.
• Sift together flour, whole wheat flour, salt, baking soda, and spices into a large mixing bowl (include chaff from whole wheat flour. Stir in nuts, raisins and lemon peel.
• Beat eggs and milk together and add to dry ingredients along with molasses mixture. Stir to moisten. Then beat mixture with a wooden spoon for about 70 strokes. Turn into a greased 8x8x2" baking pan.
• Bake in moderate oven (350°) for 40 minutes or until cake tests done. Serve warm or cool on rack. Makes 10 servings.

Spicy Gingerbread Squares

A long-keeper. Serve warm as is or serve cold with a hot lemon sauce

2 c. sifted flour
½ c. sugar
½ tsp. salt
1 tsp. baking soda
2 tsp. ground ginger
1½ tsp. ground cardamom
1 tsp. ground allspice
1 tblsp. grated orange peel
3 eggs
½ c. light molasses
1 c. buttermilk
½ c. melted butter

• Sift together flour, sugar, salt, baking soda and spices into a large mixing bowl. Stir in orange peel.
• In a separate bowl, beat eggs until thick, light and foamy. Add molasses in a stream, beating constantly. Gradually beat in buttermilk.
• Add half of buttermilk-molasses mixture to dry ingredients. Beat with a spoon until well blended. Add remaining buttermilk-molasses mixture in two additions, beating well after each addition until well blended.
• Gradually add butter and beat with spoon until batter is blended and smooth. Pour into greased 8x8x2" baking pan.
• Bake in moderate oven (350°) 45 to 50 minutes or until toothpick inserted in center comes out clean. Makes 9 servings.

Pumpkin-Ginger Squares

Top with a puff of whipped cream

1 c. sifted flour
½ c. quick-cooking rolled oats
½ c. brown sugar, firmly packed
½ c. butter
1 (1 lb.) can pumpkin (2 c.)
1 (13½ oz.) can evaporated milk
2 eggs
¾ c. sugar
½ tsp. salt
1 tsp. ground cinnamon
½ tsp. ground ginger
¼ tsp. ground cloves
½ c. chopped pecans
½ c. brown sugar, firmly packed
2 tblsp. butter

• Combine flour, rolled oats, ½ c. brown sugar and ½ c. butter in mixing bowl. Mix until crumbly, using electric mixer on low speed. Press into ungreased 13x9x2" pan. Bake in moderate oven (350°) for 15 minutes.
• Combine pumpkin, evaporated milk, eggs, sugar, salt and spices in mixing bowl; beat well. Pour into crust. Bake in moderate oven (350°) 20 minutes.
• Combine pecans, ½ c. brown sugar and 2 tblsp. butter; sprinkle over pumpkin filling. Return to oven and bake 15 to 20 minutes or until filling is set. Cool in pan and cut in 2" squares. Makes 2 dozen.

ALWAYS READY FOR GUESTS WITH

Snack packs in the freezer

Tasty nibbles give a lift to any gathering, and our FARM·JOURNAL Countryside Test Kitchens' freezable Party Snack Packs will give the busy hostess a lift, too. If you prepare several packs with a variety of festive treats before the holiday rush, you'll be all set when guests drop in.

Snacks with tomato juice or hot consommé can start off your holiday buffet or open house, provide a light supper for TV watchers, or a snack-treat for hungry teens after caroling. They're handy to take to card parties or club meetings.

Your guests and family will appreciate this tasty change from the usual sweet holiday fare, and you'll know that snackers are getting needed protein. Try dressing a Party Pack with a holiday ribbon to extend Christmastide good wishes to a busy neighbor.

For Hot Snack Packs, select 2 to 4 of the following snacks per tray: Bean Tarts, Pizza Franks, Chicken Turnovers and the Deviled Ham Twists. Prepare according to recipe directions which follow.

• Place assorted unbaked snacks close together in a 7¼ x 11¼" disposable aluminum foil pan or pizza pan. Freeze until firm; next cover closely with a plastic wrap, then with aluminum foil. Seal foil to edges of each tray securely with freezer tape. Then tape all the snack trays in a neat stack for convenient storage in your freezer.

• To serve hot snack assortments, remove foil and plastic coverings and bake unthawed in a pre-heated hot oven (400°) for 13 to 15 minutes, until the snacks are nicely browned and puffed.

Deviled Ham Twists

Biscuit "butterflies," ham-filled

3 (4½ oz.) cans deviled ham
3 tblsp. chopped walnuts
3 tblsp. minced onion
¼ c. minced, stuffed green olives
½ tsp. cayenne pepper
6 finely crushed saltines
¾ c. milk
2¾ c. biscuit mix

EASY HOT SNACKS (ROUND TRAY): Bean Tarts, Pizza Franks, Chicken Turnovers and Deviled Ham Twists—from the freezer. In the cold assortment: Savory Ham, Tuna Toppers, Cheese and Beef Potpourri.

• Combine ham, walnuts, onions, olives, cayenne, and saltines, stirring until well-blended and smooth.
• Stir milk into biscuit mix to make soft dough; beat 20 strokes until stiff. Divide biscuit dough in half. Roll each portion to a 12x12″ square, and spread 1 cup of ham mixture on half of square. Fold uncovered half over the ham mixture to form a 6x12″ rectangle. With a sharp knife or pastry wheel cut into 36 rectangles, 1x2″. Twist each gently to form a bow and sprinkle with paprika.
• Repeat procedure with remaining dough and ham mixture. Makes 6 dozen twists.

Pizza Franks

Pizza-flavored biscuit dough

2¼ c. sifted flour
4 tsp. baking powder
½ tsp. cream of tartar
¼ tsp. garlic salt
¼ tsp. onion salt
1 tblsp. sugar
¼ c. Parmesan cheese
¼ tsp. dried basil leaves
½ tsp. dried oregano leaves
⅓ c. shortening
⅓ c. milk
⅓ c. tomato paste
1 egg, unbeaten
1 lb. wieners, cut in ½″ pieces

• Sift together flour, baking powder, cream of tartar, garlic and onion salt and sugar. Stir in cheese, basil, and oregano; cut shortening into flour mixture to make coarse crumbs. Add milk, tomato paste and egg; stir with fork until dough follows fork around the bowl.
• Knead on floured board five or six times. Roll dough ½″ thick. Cut into 1″ rounds (we used a doughnut hole cutter). Press dough around franks to form cups. Makes 8 dozen.

Chicken Turnovers

These have a delicate hint of curry

1 tblsp. chopped onion
¼ c. diced green olives
1 (3 oz.) can mushroom pieces (reserve liquid)
1 tblsp. butter
1 tsp. flour
1 tsp. curry powder
¼ tsp. salt
1½ c. cooked, ground chicken
1 (9½ oz.) pkg. pie crust mix, prepared according to package

• Sauté onions, olives, and mushroom pieces in butter. Stir in flour, curry powder and salt, then mushroom broth. Simmer one minute; add chicken. Place a teaspoonful of mixture in center of 3″ pastry circle. Fold pastry over, dampen edges and seal with a fork or handle-end of a table knife. Makes 2½ dozen.

Cornmeal/Bean Tarts

South-of-the-Border flavor excitement in a bite-sized tart

Filling:
1 (15½ oz.) can refried beans
¾ c. grated Provolone cheese (or other sharp cheese)
2 tsp. garlic salt
2 tblsp. red chili sauce
1½ tsp. crushed dried red pepper
¼ tsp. chili powder
2 tblsp. butter

• Combine ingredients in top of double boiler; heat until cheese melts. Spoon into cornmeal tarts.

Pastry:
2 c. sifted flour
1 tsp. salt
1 c. cormeal
⅔ c. shortening
⅔ c. grated Cheddar cheese
⅔ c. water

• Sift flour and salt; stir in cornmeal. Cut in shortening until mixture resembles fine crumbs. Stir in grated cheese. Sprinkle water over mixture, tossing lightly with a fork until pastry is uniformly dampened. Roll to about ⅛″ thickness on lightly floured surface. Cut with 2″ biscuit cutter. Press pastry circles into tiny tart cups, ruffling edges. For larger bean tarts, use small muffin-cup pans. Bake unfilled in hot oven (400°) for 13 minutes. Makes 30.

For Cold Snack Packs, cream butter and spread it to the edges of frozen bread slices. Stack several slices and trim off all crusts with a sharp knife.
• Spread filling on sandwiches and cut into triangles, squares or bars. Garnish and freeze according to directions given above.
• At serving time, uncover snack trays and thaw for 30 minutes at room temperature.

Savory Ham

Two-layer treat of ham and cheese

1 (3 oz.) pkg. cream cheese, softened
1 tblsp. chili sauce
1 tsp. chili powder
1 tsp. Worcestershire sauce
4 to 5 drops Tabasco sauce
1 tsp. capers and juice (optional)
1 clove garlic, crushed
1 tblsp. pickle relish
⅛ tsp. salt
4 oz. sliced, fully cooked ham

• Combine all ingredients except ham. Spread mixture on 6 slices white bread and top with a ham slice. Cut each slice into 4 triangles. To garnish, pipe ribbons of cream cheese on top in a decorative design. Makes 24.

Tuna Toppers

Mustard adds a special zing

1 (7 oz.) can tuna, drained and flaked
¼ c. diced stuffed olives
1 tblsp. prepared mustard
2 tblsp. sour cream
⅛ tsp. black pepper

• Combine ingredients. Flake finely with a fork. Spread mixture evenly on 4 slices buttered white bread. Cut each slice into quarters. If desired, garnish with sliced stuffed olives. Makes 16 snacks.

Cheese and Beef Potpourri

Its vivid colors add eye appeal

1 (8 oz.) pkg. cream cheese, softened
2 tblsp. blue cheese, crumbled
⅓ c. chopped walnuts
¼ c. crumbled dried beef
2 tsp. minced green onion tops
4 to 5 drops Tabasco sauce
⅛ tsp. cayenne pepper

• Whip cream cheese. Add remaining ingredients and spread on 6 slices buttered whole wheat bread. Cut each slice into 3 fingers. Garnish with additional chopped dried beef. Makes 18.

Party punches hot and cold

Hot Fruit Punch

Spicy, aromatic, refreshing

3 pts. canned apple juice
3" stick cinnamon
1 tsp. nutmeg
½ c. sugar
2 (1 pt. 2 oz.) cans pineapple juice
1 (46 oz.) can orange juice
2 medium oranges
30 whole cloves

• Simmer apple juice and spices 20 minutes. Add sugar and remaining juices. Stud oranges with cloves and add to punch. Heat, but do not boil. Fill heated punch bowl. Makes about 25 servings.

Cherry-Apple Drink

Unusual taste. The tanginess seems to soothe a dry throat

2 envelopes *unsweetened* cherry flavor instant soft drink mix
½ c. sugar
1 (6 oz.) can frozen lemonade concentrate, thawed
1½ qts. apple juice or apple cider
2¼ qts. ice water

• Combine ingredients: stir until sugar dissolves. Makes 1 gallon.

Christmas Punch

Festive red two-fruit holiday drink. Add ginger ale if you like the bubbles

1 qt. apple juice
1 (1 qt.) bottle cranberry juice cocktail
½ c. lemon juice

• Mix juices. Chill. Garnish with canned pineapple chunks, drained. Makes 12 servings.

Cardinal Punch

Tea and fruit juices join in this—float a thin lemon slice in each glass

2½ c. boiling water
2 tblsp. black tea
¼ tsp. ground allspice
¼ tsp. ground cinnamon
⅛ tsp. ground nutmeg
¾ c. sugar
1 (1 pt.) bottle cranberry juice cocktail
½ c. orange juice
⅓ c. lemon juice
1½ c. water

• Pour the rapidly boiling water over tea; add spices. Cover and let steep 5 minutes. Strain and stir in sugar.
• Add the cranberry, orange and lemon juices and cold water. Cover and chill thoroughly. Makes 8 servings.

Fruited Ice Ring Add decorative ice floats to punch bowl. Pour ½ to 1" water (distilled or boiled and cooled water makes clearer ice) into a ring or fancy shaped mold. Arrange maraschino cherries (rinsed in cold water to remove excess color and prevent "bleeding"), orange or lemon slices, mint sprigs, strawberries, green seedless grapes or raspberries in mold; freeze. Add water almost to top of mold and freeze. Unmold by dipping in hot water just until ice will drop out. Invert float in bowl of punch. Use a star-shaped mold for Yuletide punch. Decorate the float, if you wish, with a few tiny flowers, or use orange or lemon slices on the float instead of flowers.

Golden Punch

This punch is on the tart side. It's refreshing, colorful, easy to fix

1 (6 oz.) can frozen orange juice concentrate
1 (6 oz.) can frozen lemonade concentrate
1 (12 oz.) can apricot nectar
2 c. pineapple juice
½ c. lemon juice
1 qt. lemon-lime carbonated beverage, or 1 qt. ginger ale
Sherbet

• Reconstitute orange juice and lemonade as directed on cans. Combine in punch bowl with apricot nectar, pineapple juice and lemon juice.
• Pour bottled carbonated beverage or ginger ale slowly down side of bowl. Drop scoops of pineapple, orange, lime or raspberry sherbet into punch. (Sherbet is not necessary, but it is decorative and delicious.) Makes about 3½ quarts without sherbet.

Hot Spiced Punch

Float a clove-studded orange slice in each cup of this refreshing drink

1 tblsp. whole cloves
½ tblsp. whole allspice
3 sticks cinnamon
½ c. brown sugar, firmly packed
2 c. water
¼ tsp. salt
2½ c. pineapple juice
2 c. cranberry juice

• Combine spices with brown sugar and water in saucepan. Simmer 15 minutes. Strain through several layers of cheesecloth.
• Combine salt and fruit juices. Add strained spice mixture. Heat and serve from warmed punch bowl or electric coffee maker. Makes about 6½ cups, or 8 servings.

ALWAYS APPRECIATED:

Gifts from your kitchen

What will it be this year? Will you bake an assortment of cookies for your friends? Pastries? Miniature fruitcakes? Will you fill jelly jars? Cook candy? Or can relishes? Fry doughnuts? Don't decide until you've looked through the next 24 pages. We've collected the Christmas specialties of country cooks for you to sample.

Some of our cookie recipes make giant batches, enough for several gift boxes. Candy recipes include some do's and don'ts from a woman who teaches candymaking; with this good help you'll achieve perfection every time.

If you were provident, you've already stored summer garden relishes for December gift-giving. But if you weren't, it's not too late to put up a few jars—cabbages, cucumbers and peppers are still plentiful in the markets. And we have a new jelly idea for you to try—a combination of fruit and honey, using winter fruits.

Close-up pictures show you how to shape our buttery yeast dough to make butterflies, braids, knots, crescents and swirls. Try filling some of them with sparkling jelly—they'll look like jewels. We also include our best, man-pleasing recipes for raised doughnuts.

Any bazaar chairman will recognize that food like this will be snapped up by eager customers. To collect some extra coin, why not bring your cooking and trimming committees together and package the food in gift boxes? You'll find a number of simple, inexpensive but effective ideas in this section for glamorizing food gifts.

Party Whirls

Attractive addition to gift boxes

1 c. butter
1 c. sugar
2 eggs
½ tsp. vanilla
3 c. sifted flour
½ tsp. salt
½ tsp. ground cinnamon
3 drops red food coloring
½ square semi-sweet chocolate, melted

• Beat together butter and sugar until light and fluffy. Beat in eggs and vanilla; blend well.

• Sift together flour, salt and cinnamon; add to creamed mixture. Divide dough into thirds. Tint one-third pink with red food coloring; add chocolate to the second, and leave the last third untinted.

• Roll each third of dough separately on lightly floured waxed paper into a 13x10" rectangle. Cover baking sheet with waxed paper. Invert untinted dough on baking sheet; remove paper. Repeat with pink and chocolate dough. Cut edges with knife to straighten if necessary. Chill until firm.

• Roll up dough tightly as for jelly roll, using waxed paper to help shape log. Wrap tightly in waxed paper and chill.

• To bake, cut dough in ⅛" to ¼" slices with sharp knife. Place ½" apart on greased baking sheet and bake in hot oven (400°) about 8 minutes. Makes about 7 dozen.

FOR A PRINCELY GIFT, pack old-fashioned cookies in antique containers. Pictured are Party Whirls (in crock), Pecan Lace Roll-Ups (in tin mold) and Fruit Blossom Cookies (in bentwood box). On the table in stacks, Six-in-One Refrigerator Cookies. *To see more of the Mexican tin ornaments, turn to page 82.*

Fruit Blossom Cookies

Old-fashioned fruit-filled cookies

⅔ c. shortening
¾ c. sugar
1 egg
½ tsp. vanilla
2 c. sifted flour
1½ tsp. baking powder
¼ tsp. salt
2 tblsp. milk
Fillings (recipes follow)

• Cream together shortening and sugar. Add egg; beat until light and fluffy. Add vanilla.
• Sift together dry ingredients. Add to creamed mixture along with milk. Divide dough in half. Chill 1 hour.
• Roll dough 1/16 to ⅛" thick. Cut with 3" scalloped cookie cutter. Place about ½ tsp. filling in centers of half the cookies. Place 1½" apart on greased baking sheet. Cut out centers of remaining half of cookies with 1" round cutter; place on filled bottoms and press edges with fork to seal.
• Bake in moderate oven (350°) 10 to 12 minutes. Transfer cookies to racks to cool. Makes about 2 dozen.

Apricot Filling: Combine ¼ c. chopped dried apricots, 1½ tsp. orange juice, ¼ tsp. lemon juice, 3 tblsp. water and 1 tsp. flour in a saucepan. Bring to a boil, stirring constantly. Cook about 5 minutes. Cool.

Pineapple Filling: Combine in saucepan ¾ tsp. cornstarch and ¼ c. crushed pineapple, undrained. Cook until clear, stirring constantly. Cool.

Cherry Filling: Mash ¼ c. cherry pie filling. Add a few drops almond extract, if desired.

Pecan Lace Roll-Ups

Can be filled with whipped cream

2 eggs
⅔ c. brown sugar, firmly packed
1 tsp. vanilla
¼ c. melted butter
¼ c. sifted flour
⅔ c. finely chopped pecans

• Beat eggs until thick. Add brown sugar, 1 tblsp. at a time, beating constantly. Beat in vanilla. Slowly add butter. Fold in flour and pecans.
• Place a tablespoon of batter on well-greased baking sheet, spreading it to make a 4" circle. Cookies should be 2" apart and no more than 4 on a baking sheet.
• Bake at 375° 5 to 6 minutes, or until browned. Loosen cookies with a wide spatula. Place the handle of a wooden spoon on one end of cookie and quickly roll up loosely to make a cylinder. Place on rack to cool. Repeat with other baked cookies. Makes 15.

Six-in-One Refrigerator Cookies

Keep on hand for last-minute guests

2 c. butter
1 c. sugar
1 c. light brown sugar, firmly packed
2 eggs, beaten
1 tsp. vanilla
4 c. unsifted flour
1 tsp. baking soda
½ tsp. salt
½ c. shredded coconut
½ c. finely chopped pecans
½ tsp. ground nutmeg
1 tsp. ground cinnamon
1 square unsweetened chocolate, melted
¼ c. finely chopped candied cherries

• Cream butter. Gradually add sugars; beat until light and fluffy.
• Add eggs and vanilla, mix well.
• Sift together dry ingredients; gradually add to creamed mixture.
• Divide dough in 6 (1 cup) portions. Add coconut to one part; pecans to second; nutmeg and cinnamon to third; melted chocolate to fourth; and candied cherries to fifth. Leave the last portion plain. Chill 30 minutes or longer.
• Shape dough into 6 rolls about 1¾" in diameter. Wrap tightly in plastic wrap or waxed paper and refrigerate overnight.
• When ready to use, slice with sharp knife in ⅛" slices. Place on lightly greased baking sheet.
• Bake in moderate oven (375°) 10 to 12 minutes. Makes 18 dozen.

French Bars

Moist date bars that keep well

2¼ c. brown sugar, firmly packed
4 eggs, well beaten
1½ c. soured evaporated milk (see Note)
1½ tsp. baking soda
2¼ c. unsifted flour
1 tsp. ground cinnamon
½ tsp. salt
1½ c. chopped walnuts
1½ c. cut-up dates
1 c. toasted flaked coconut
Orange Butter Frosting (recipe follows)

• Add sugar to eggs; beat until thick. Stir in soured evaporated milk.
• Blend in dry ingredients. Stir in nuts, dates and coconut. Do not overmix batter.
• Spread dough evenly in two lightly greased 15½x10½x1" jelly roll pans. Bake in moderate oven (350°) about 20 minutes. Cool. Frost and cut in 2½x1" bars. Makes 80.

Note: To sour evaporated milk, pour 1½ tblsp. vinegar into a 2-cup measure. Add evaporated milk until measurement is 1½ c. Stir.

Orange Butter Frosting: Combine 1 lb. confectioners sugar sifted, with ¼ c. butter, ¼ c. orange juice, ½ tsp. salt and 1 tsp. grated orange peel. Beat until creamy. Spread on cooled bars.

Black Walnut Cookies

If you enjoy the flavor of black walnuts, here's your Christmas cookie

6 c. sifted flour
1 tsp. salt
½ tsp. baking soda
1 tsp. cream of tartar
1¾ c. butter
2¼ c. brown sugar, firmly packed
½ c. sugar
2 eggs
2 tsp. vanilla
1½ c. black walnut meats
1½ c. shredded coconut

• Sift flour; measure; sift again with salt, soda and cream of tartar.
• Cream butter, add sugars gradually. Beat until fluffy. Add eggs, vanilla.
• Grind nuts and coconut together in food chopper using medium blade or chop fine in your electric blender.
• Add to creamed mixture. Add sifted flour mixture. Blend well. Chill.
• Shape into 4 rolls about 2 inches in diameter. Wrap in waxed paper or foil. Chill.
• Cut rolls into ⅛-inch-thick slices and place on ungreased cookie sheet.
• Bake in moderate oven (350°) 10 to 12 minutes. Makes 8 to 9 dozen.

Pecan Chews

Easy-to-make cookies with a caramel, toasted-nut flavor

¾ c. butter
1½ c. brown sugar, firmly packed
1 egg
1 tsp. vanilla
½ tsp. salt
2 c. sifted flour
1 c. toasted pecans, chopped

• Cream butter and sugar until light and fluffy. Beat in egg, vanilla and salt. Blend in flour and nuts.
• Spread dough in lightly greased 15½ x10½x1" jelly roll pan. Bake in moderate oven (375°) for about 15 minutes or until lightly browned. Cool on rack for 5 minutes; cut into bars. Remove from pan and continue cooling on rack. Makes 48 bars.

Double Treat Cookies

Better make a triple batch

2 c. sifted flour
2 tsp. baking soda
½ tsp. salt
1 c. shortening
1 c. sugar
1 c. brown sugar, firmly packed
2 eggs
1 tsp. vanilla
1 c. peanut butter
1 c. chopped, salted peanuts
1 (6 oz.) pkg. chocolate chips

• Sift together flour, baking soda and salt.
• Beat together shortening, sugar, brown sugar, eggs and vanilla until fluffy. Blend in peanut butter. Add dry ingredients. Stir in peanuts and chocolate chips.
• Shape into small balls; place on ungreased baking sheet. Flatten with a glass dipped in sugar.
• Bake in moderate oven (350°) for 8 minutes or until brown. Makes 7 dozen.

Almond Moons

Top with icing and colored sugar

2¾ c. sifted flour
1½ tsp. baking powder
¼ tsp. salt
¾ c. butter or margarine
1½ c. sugar
½ tsp. almond flavor
2 eggs, beaten
½ c. ground unblanched almonds

• Sift flour; measure; sift again with baking powder and salt.
• Cream butter and sugar together until light and fluffy. Add almond flavor and eggs; beat well.
• Put almonds through a food chopper or use your electric blender.
• Add flour and almonds. Chill dough.
• Roll dough about ⅛-inch thick. Cut with crescent-shaped cutter.
• Bake in moderate oven (350°) 8 to 10 minutes. Makes about 10 dozen.

Royal Crowns

Serve with creamy lime sherbet

4 hard-cooked egg yolks
½ tsp. salt
1 c. butter or margarine
⅔ c. sugar
½ tsp. almond extract
2½ c. sifted flour
Red or green candied cherries

• Force egg yolks through a coarse sieve with back of spoon. Add salt and mix.
• Cream butter and sugar together until light and fluffy. Add flavoring and egg yolks. Add flour and mix well.
• Place dough in cookie press. Force dough through crown design onto baking sheet. Decorate with bits of cherries.
• Bake in moderate oven (375°) 7 to 10 minutes. Makes 6 dozen.

Heaps and heaps of cookies

We piled cookies sky-high to make the point visually: these are *big* recipes. Each one yields from 6 to 8 to 12 dozen cookies!
In case you don't have time this year to bake a variety of cookies, why don't you and a neighbor make different kinds and trade part of your supply?

Molasses Cookies

The kind of molasses cookies you used to reach for in Mother's cookie jar

1 c. sugar
1 c. shortening
1 c. light molasses
1 tblsp. cider vinegar
6 c. sifted flour
½ tsp. salt
1 tsp. baking soda
½ tsp. baking powder
1 tsp. ground ginger
1 tsp. ground cinnamon
2 eggs, beaten

• Combine sugar, shortening, molasses and vinegar in a saucepan. Bring to boil. Cook 2 minutes. Cool.
• Sift together flour, salt, soda, baking powder and spices.
• Add eggs to cooled molasses mixture. Add dry ingredients. Mix well. Chill.
• Roll out on lightly floured board, about ⅛ to ¼" thick. Cut; put on greased baking sheet.
• Bake in moderate oven (375°) 8 to 10 minutes or until done. Makes about 12 doz. (2½") cookies.

Star Cookies

Sugar cookies cut in a Yuletide star shape. You can frost them if you like

3 c. sifted flour
2 tsp. baking powder
½ tsp. salt
½ c. shortening
½ c. butter or margarine
1¼ c. sugar
1 tsp. vanilla
1 egg
1 tblsp. milk

• Sift together flour, baking powder and salt.
• Cream shortening and butter with sugar until light and fluffy.
• Add vanilla, egg and milk. Beat thoroughly. Add flour mixture. Mix well.
• Chill dough an hour for easy handling.
• Divide in 4 portions. Roll each portion ⅛" thick. Cut with cookie cutters.
• Bake on greased baking sheet in moderate oven (375°) 8 to 10 minutes. Makes 7 dozen (2½") stars.

Fruitcake Cookies

Glamour cookies with gay red and green topknots—rich with fruits and nuts

4 c. sifted flour
1 tsp. baking soda
1 tsp. salt
1 c. shortening
2 c. brown sugar, firmly packed
2 eggs
⅔ c. buttermilk
1 c. chopped pecans
2 c. dates, cut up
1 c. candied cherries, cut in quarters
2 4-oz. cans (1 c.) candied fruits and peels
Red or green candied cherries for top (optional)

• Sift together flour, soda and salt.
• Cream shortening. Add sugar and eggs. Beat until light and fluffy.
• Add buttermilk and flour. Add nuts, cherries, dates and candied fruit.
• Chill dough for several hours.
• Drop by teaspoonfuls about 2" apart, on lightly greased baking sheet.
• Top each cookie with half a candied cherry.
• Bake in moderate oven (375°) 8 to 10 minutes. Makes 8 dozen cookies.

Brazil Nut Bars

A new cookie they'll remember for its rich, nutty flavor. It's easy to make

2 c. sifted flour
2 tsp. baking powder
¾ tsp. salt
½ tsp. cinnamon
½ c. shortening
⅓ c. butter or margarine
1 c. light brown sugar, firmly packed
1 tsp. vanilla
2 eggs
1 c. Brazil nuts, thinly sliced or chopped
1 egg white

• Sift together flour, baking powder, salt and cinnamon.
• Cream shortening, butter and sugar together. Add the eggs and vanilla. Beat until light.
• Add flour mixture and half the nuts.
• Spread in greased 15½ x 10½ x 1" jelly roll pan or two 8" square pans.
• Beat egg white slightly. Brush over dough. Sprinkle with remaining nuts.
• Bake in moderate oven (350°) 20 to 30 minutes. Cut into 1 x 2" bars. Cool on rack. Makes 6 dozen.

Crisscross Cookies

A holiday winner because it has the wonderful lemon-brown sugar taste

4 c. sifted flour
1½ tsp. baking soda
2 tsp. cream of tartar
1 tsp. salt
1⅓ c. shortening
2½ c. light brown sugar, firmly packed
1½ tsp. vanilla
1 tsp. lemon extract
3 eggs

• Sift together flour, soda, cream of tartar and salt.
• Cream shortening. Add sugar gradually. Add vanilla, lemon extract and eggs. Beat until light and fluffy.
• Add flour mixture, mix until smooth. Chill for several hours.
• Roll a level tablespoonful of dough into a ball not quite as big as a walnut.
• Place on greased cookie sheet. Press lightly with tines of fork, making a crisscross pattern.
• Bake in moderate oven (375°) 8 to 10 minutes. Makes 8 dozen.

PICTURED CLOCKWISE from top center: molasses, star, fruitcake, Brazil nut, crisscross cookies.

How to wrap food gifts

Look at all the boxes and cartons you bring home from the supermarket with an eye to recycling them. Some are so decorative they're almost ready to be gift containers—just cut away a brand name or cover it with a gift tag. Others will need slipcovers of paper or tape to disguise them.

Candy Flats

Choose facial tissue boxes with all-over designs. Cut opening on top of box in any desired shape. Glue ribbon or cording on cut edge. Separate layers of candy with cardboard. Cover with plastic wrap and tape it to the bottom of the box. You can see the sweets through the opening.

Cookie Towers

Waxed cardboard milk cartons make sturdy containers and they're easy to decorate. You can cover them with printed gift wrap or colored construction paper by using double-stick tape —it adheres to the waxed surface. Or you can stripe them with self-stick aluminum and cloth tapes.

Peaked-roof containers: Carefully unfold top of carton; wash inside. Cut away triangles on each side of the "peak" (see photo). To get pattern for paper cover: cut away the bottom from one milk carton, unfasten side and lay it out flat. Place pattern on gift wrap or colored paper and draw around it, adding ¼″ foldover allowance at top and ½″ at bottom. Cut out paper and tape it to milk carton on bottom and sides. Fold allowance around roof lines (slashing to corners) and tape in place. Punch holes in top of roof and thread with ribbon to tie up package.

Santa decoration: From white felt, cut an almost circular beard shape plus hat trim and tassel. Lay the felt on a block of wood and scratch it vigorously with a pin or nail, to fluff the edges. Glue to red-covered carton. Draw smile on beard with black felt pen.

Striped tower: Cut away the entire folded top of quart milk carton. Cover sides with shiny self-stick aluminum tape 2″ wide, alternating with red and green cloth tape, ¾″ wide. To make lid, cut one square of cardboard ¼″ bigger than milk carton, plus two squares of thick cardboard just big enough to wedge inside milk carton. Glue the three squares together and cover top with tape. Attach wood bead handle with wire poked through lid and taped underneath.

To pack cookies: If cookies are fragile, stack them in cupcake liners and place the stacks in cookie tower.

Jelly Carrier

Make this sturdy divided basket from two half-pint cream cartons. Cut away folded tops of cartons and staple them together. Cover outside of cartons with self-stick aluminum tape 2″ wide. For handle, cut two strips of aluminum tape 12″ long and about ½″ wide. Peel backing from one strip and stick them together. Tape to basket. For extra strength, cover handle ends with a strip of plastic-coated cloth tape wrapped around top of basket. Line basket sections with colored tissue paper to make nests for jelly jars. Fasten a Christmas ornament to basket handle.

Fireplace Box

Here's a clever way to package a sampling of gifts from your kitchen. Get an empty soup can case from your food store (those holding 48 cans). Turn the box on its long side with open flaps at the back. Pull red brick crepe paper firmly around the box, fasten with cellophane tape at top and inside box. Cover back flaps with red brick paper, leaving them open until the boxes are filled for delivery.

Paste a square of black construction paper on the front to simulate fireplace opening; draw on "fire" with crayon or chalk. Cover top of the fireplace box with several thicknesses of white tissue paper, fold down over front and sides to represent a mantel. Fasten underneath white paper with double-sided cellophane tape.

Decorate top of mantel with bits of pine and ceramic elves or Christmas angels (bought at the dime store). Cut out little felt stockings—same number as children in the family receiving the gift box. Fasten onto front of mantel with double-sided tape or thumbtacks.

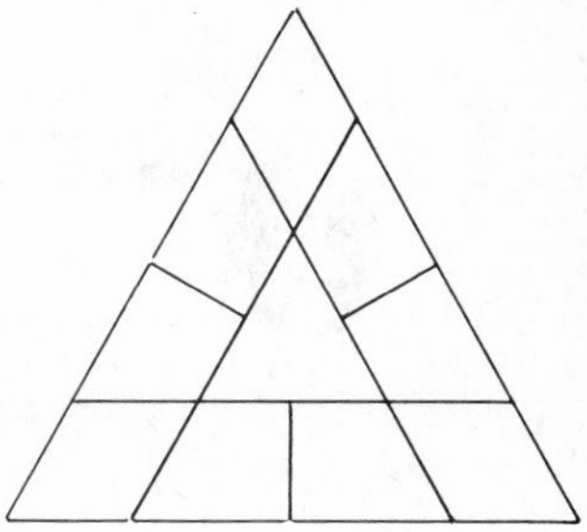

Jelly Jar Tree

Build a tree-shaped display rack for your homemade preserves and put it on the hall table when you entertain. It's a gracious way to invite guests to take home a jar of your good wishes. Tree is an equal-sided triangle (21½″) cut from ⅜″ plywood. Interior partitions for jars are ⅛″ Masonite (see diagram). Glue them in place; paint tree when glue dries. Glue paper flower cutouts to jar lids.

Cookies in a hurry

When time nips at your heels, depend on this recipe. With it, you make cookies that you don't have to roll, or shape, or drop from a spoon. Just spread the rich, buttery dough in a jelly roll pan and slide it into the oven.

For variety (because you'll want to make this recipe often), we give you eight choices for flavoring the basic dough. Also, four choices for the shapes to cut your cookies when they're baked.

After you've tried these variations, you may want to experiment with your own combinations of spices and nuts, to develop a family original. If you bake and freeze several batches, the cookies will be ready to serve when holiday guests drop by.

A. Orange Pecan Flats
B. Brown Sugar/Spice Crisps
C. Lemon Sugar Crisps
D. Austrian Almond Squares
E. Peanut Salties
F. Spicy Nut Triangles
G. Macadamia Nut Gingers

Spicy Nut Triangles

Freeze for the holidays ahead

1 c. soft butter
1 c. sugar
1 egg, separated
2 c. sifted flour
1 tsp. cinnamon
1 c. finely chopped walnuts

• Cream butter and sugar together until light and fluffy. Add egg yolk and beat well.
• Sift together flour and cinnamon. Gradually add to creamed mixture, stirring well.
• Spread dough evenly in a 15½x10½x1" jelly roll pan. Beat egg white slightly and brush over top. Smooth surface with your fingertips. Sprinkle nuts over dough and press in.
• Bake in a very slow oven (275°) for 1 hour. While uncut cookie is still warm, cut into triangles (see directions below).

Variations

Austrian Almond Squares: Substitute 1 tsp. nutmeg for the cinnamon and 1 c. sliced almonds for the walnuts. Cut in squares.

Orange Pecan Flats: Omit cinnamon. Add 1 tblsp. grated fresh orange peel and substitute chopped pecans for the walnuts. Cut in rectangles.

Turkish Cardamoms: (not pictured) Substitute 1 tsp. cardamom for the cinnamon and 1 c. chopped filberts for the walnuts. Cut in rectangles.

Macadamia Nut Gingers: Substitute 1 tsp. ginger for the cinnamon and use finely chopped, roasted and salted macadamia nuts for the walnuts. Cut in diamonds.

Peanut Salties: Omit cinnamon. Substitute firmly packed light brown sugar for granulated sugar and chopped, salted and roasted peanuts for the walnuts. Cut in triangles.

Lemon Sugar Crisps: Add 2 tblsp. grated fresh lemon peel. Omit cinnamon and walnuts. Cut in squares.

Brown Sugar/Spice Crisps: Substitute firmly packed light brown sugar for granulated sugar. Increase cinnamon to 1½ tsp. Add ¾ tsp. nutmeg, ¾ tsp. ginger and ¼ tsp. cloves. Omit walnuts. Cut in diamonds.

Cookie Shapes To Make

Squares: Cut 5 lengthwise strips and 8 crosswise strips. Makes 40 (2") squares.

Rectangles: Cut 4 lengthwise strips and 6 crosswise strips. Cut each in half. Makes 48.

Diamonds: Cut 8 lengthwise strips; then cut diagonally into strips 1½" wide. Makes about 60.

Triangles: Cut 4 lengthwise strips and 6 crosswise strips. Cut each in half diagonally. Makes 48.

Children's corner

Christmas Tradition

Let the children help you make
Currant cookies, Twelfth-night cake,
Anise drops and springerle, Ginger
men to trim the tree. Share with them
each ritual. But teach them, too, the
miracle Of the Christ who came to give
Food by which the soul may live.
DOROTHY P. ALBAUGH

How to Flour Cookie Cutter: Spoon a little flour into a small bowl. Dip the cookie cutter into the flour and tap it gently on the edge of the bowl to shake off the loose flour. Flouring keeps the rolled cookie dough from sticking to the cutter. Flour it as many times as you need to while cutting out cookies.

Rolling cookie dough isn't hard if you chill the dough first and use a pastry cloth and stockinet-covered rolling pin. Rub a little flour into the pastry cloth with your hand. It will disappear into the meshes in the cloth. Roll the stockinet-covered rolling pin around on the floured cloth. When you roll out chilled cookie dough, it will not stick either to cloth or pin. What's more important, the dough will not take up extra flour which would make your cookies tough.

Extra-Good Sugar Cookies

Sprinkle cookies with colored sugar before baking for festive touch

2/3 c. shortening
3/4 c. sugar
1 egg
3/4 tsp. vanilla
1/4 tsp. almond extract
2 c. sifted flour
1 1/2 tsp. baking powder
1/4 tsp. salt
4 tsp. milk

• Beat shortening and sugar together until light and fluffy. Add egg and beat to mix well. Add vanilla and almond extracts. (You can use 1 teaspoon vanilla and omit almond extract.) Mix.
• Place flour-measuring cup on a sheet of waxed paper. Sift flour into cup until it overflows. Level the top by sweeping across it with the straight edge of a knife. Sift measured flour with baking powder and salt. Stir it into sugar-shortening mixture. Stir in milk. Divide dough in half and chill in refrigerator 1 hour or until dough is easy to handle.
• Start heating oven to 375°. Grease a baking sheet with unsalted shortening.
• Roll dough, half of it at a time, from center to edge until it is 1/8 to 1/4 inch thick. (The thinner you roll dough, the crisper the cookies will be.) Cut with Christmas cookie cutters.
• Use a wide spatula to place cookies 1/2 inch apart on greased baking sheet.
• Bake on rack in center of oven 8 to 9 minutes, or until light brown.
• Remove pan from oven at once and use a wide spatula to place cookies on a wire cooling rack. Makes about 24.

Chocolate Sugar Cookies

Frost with confectioners sugar icing

3/4 c. shortening
1 c. sugar
1 egg
1/4 c. light corn syrup
2 squares unsweetened chocolate, melted
2 c. flour
1 tsp. baking soda
1/4 tsp. salt
1 tsp. ground cinnamon

• Beat shortening and sugar together until light and fluffy. Add egg and beat to mix well. Stir in syrup and melted chocolate.
• Stir flour in canister or bag, to loosen it, and spoon it lightly into flour-measuring cup until it overflows. Level the top by sweeping across it with the straight edge of a knife. Sift measured flour with baking soda, salt and cinnamon. Stir into sugar-shortening mixture. Divide dough in half and chill in refrigerator 1 hour or until dough is easy to handle.
• Start heating oven to 350°. Roll dough, half of it at a time, until it is 1/8 inch thick. Cut with Christmas cookie cutters.
• Use a wide spatula to place cookies 1/2 inch apart on ungreased baking sheet.
• Bake 10 to 12 minutes, or until cookies are lightly browned at edges.
• Remove baking sheet from oven at once; use a wide spatula to place cookies on wire cooling rack. Makes about 24 cookies.

Cookies for the Christmas Tree: Cut paper drinking straws into 1″ lengths. Push one into each unbaked cookie on baking sheet.

Bake cookies and remove straws by gently twisting them out while cookies are still hot. Frost cooled cookies and decorate with little candies, or as you like. Pull narrow, bright-colored ribbons through cookies and tie them on the Christmas tree.

Give sweet thoughts for Christmas

Your holiday hostess will beam an even brighter smile of welcome if you come bearing one of these unusual Christmas confections.

When you're deciding which candy to make for gift-giving, think how you'll package it. If you're visiting in the neighborhood, you can easily manage the brimming basket of candy strawberries. For a longer journey, line a box with gold doilies to set off less-fragile sweets. The cornflake wreath (a perfect centerpiece, to be admired first, then eaten) is a good traveler if carefully handled. But do box the candle separately.

Also see page 44 for wrapping suggestions.

Holiday Wreath

Makes a beautiful centerpiece

30 marshmallows
½ c. butter
1 tsp. vanilla
2 tsp. green food color
3½ c. cornflakes

• Combine marshmallows, butter, vanilla and food color (2 tsp. is correct) in top of a double boiler. Heat over water until marshmallows and butter are melted, stirring frequently.
• Gradually stir in cornflakes.
• Drop from spoon onto waxed paper; with hands, shape into a 9" wreath.
• If you wish, decorate with red candied cherries and silver dragées. Makes one 9" wreath.

Miniature Holiday Wreaths: Drop cornflake mixture from teaspoon onto waxed paper; with hands shape into tiny wreaths, about 1½ to 2" in diameter. Decorate with small red candies (tiny red hots or other small candies). Makes 33 (2") wreaths.

Candy Strawberries

Tastes like the real berry, too!

2 (3 oz.) pkg. strawberry gelatin
1 c. ground pecans
1 c. flaked coconut
¾ c. sweetened condensed milk
½ tsp. vanilla
Red decorator's sugar
Blanched almonds, sliced

• Combine gelatin, pecans and coconut. Stir in milk and vanilla; mix well. Chill one hour. Shape into strawberries. Roll in red sugar. If you wish, tint sliced almonds with green food coloring and insert in tops of "berries" to form leaves. Makes 1 lb. 3 oz.

Napoleon Cremes

Rich little morsels with a deep delicious chocolate flavor

½ c. butter
¼ c. sugar
¼ c. cocoa
1 tsp. vanilla
1 egg, slightly beaten
2 c. finely crushed graham cracker crumbs
1 c. flaked coconut
½ c. butter
3 tblsp. milk
1 (3¾ oz.) pkg. vanilla instant pudding mix
2 c. sifted confectioners sugar
1 (6 oz.) pkg. semi-sweet chocolate morsels
2 tblsp. butter

• Combine ½ c. butter, sugar, cocoa and vanilla in top part of double boiler. Cook over simmering water until butter melts. Stir in egg. Continue cooking and stirring, until mixture is thick, about 3 minutes. Blend in graham cracker crumbs and coconut. Press into buttered 9" square pan.
• Cream ½ c. butter well. Stir in milk, pudding mix and confectioners sugar. Beat until fluffy. Spread evenly over crust. Chill until firm.
• Melt chocolate and the butter over simmering water in the top of a double boiler. Cool. Spread over pudding layer. Chill. Cut in 2x¾" bars. Makes about 44 candies.

Decorated Sugar Cubes

So pretty for a tea table

1 c. sifted confectioners sugar
3 tsp. hot water
Food colors
Sugar cubes

• Mix confectioners sugar and water; mixture should be stiff. Add 1 to 2 drops food color to tint frosting in color desired (red for roses, blue for forget-me-nots, green for leaves—or as you prefer). Colors should be dainty pastels.
• With cake decorating tubes, make tiny flower and leaf designs on sugar cubes.

Open House Mints

Ideal mints for holiday entertaining, for receptions and parties

2 tblsp. butter
2 tblsp. shortening
3 tblsp. warm water
5 c. sifted confectioners sugar
2 drops red food color
3 tsp. warm water
2 drops oil of cinnamon
2 drops green food color
2 drops oil of peppermint
2 drops yellow food color
2 drops oil of lemon

• Combine butter, shortening, 2 tblsp. warm water and 2 c. confectioners sugar. Mix thoroughly.
• Add remaining 3 c. confectioners sugar and 1 tblsp. warm water (if necessary, add 1 or more tablespoons confectioners sugar to make mixture stiff enough to roll out).
• Divide mixture in thirds. To one third add red food color, mixed with 1 tsp. warm water and oil of cinnamon; knead thoroughly to mix. Roll out to ⅛" thickness on waxed paper dusted with confectioners sugar.
• To another third of candy add green food color mixed with 1 tsp. warm water and oil of peppermint. Knead to mix; roll out.
• To final third of candy add yellow food color mixed with 1 tsp. warm water and oil of lemon. Knead to mix; roll out.
• Cut with very small hors d'oeuvre cutters in fancy shapes or use the inside of a doughnut cutter. Let the mints stand, bottom side up, on waxed paper at least 2 hours before placing in airtight containers. Makes about 130 mints, or 1¼ pounds.

Success with Christmas candy

From an Iowa homemaker who teaches candy making at her local YWCA, we collected these recipes and tips for making goof-proof candies.

Many women are afraid to make divinity, she says; they think it will flop. The secret of smooth, velvety divinity is plenty of beating. Take a little taste–when it feels velvety on the tongue and the raw syrup taste is gone, it's ready.

And, she emphasizes, it's most important to use a candy thermometer. Temperature plays a basic role in candy making. A few degrees means the difference between a beautiful batch of fudge or a mess that will never set; or a divinity that's hard and tacky instead of soft and creamy.

Here's how to check your candy thermometer:

Place thermometer in a saucepan of vigorously boiling water for a few minutes. Then read the temperature without removing thermometer. It should be at 212° if your thermometer is accurate and you live at sea level. (Water boils at 212° at sea level, at lower temperatures in higher elevations. Subtract 1° for every 500 feet above sea level.) If water boils when thermometer registers 210°, it registers 2° low. This means your candy is done 2°

ROUNDS OF BUTTER-SCOTCH: To form perfect circles when you make butterscotch drops, or any hard round candies, spoon the hot syrup into 1¼" buttered miniature cupcake pans. Cool. To unmold, set bottom of pan in hot water for several seconds. Loosen edges with tip of knife. Butterscotch slides out in beautiful amber disks.

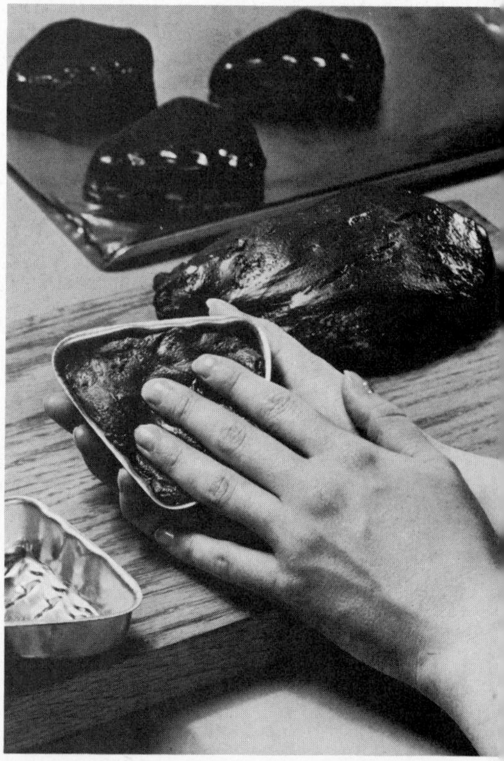

CHRISTMAS TREES OF FUDGE: Press kneaded chocolate fudge into lightly buttered tree-shaped gelatin molds (3½" long by 3" wide at broadest part). Cool. To unmold, gently press knife under edges of tree. Several strong shakes will release it. Decorate simply with white Ornamental Icing. Place a Fudge Tree in center of a plate of candy or a gift-box of sweets.

lower than your recipe calls for. If water boils at 214° on your thermometer, add 2° to the temperature specified in recipe. Checking your thermometer enables you to correct differences due to the inaccuracy of your thermometer and/or altitude.

Old-Fashioned Butterscotch

Butter-smooth with a crunch

2 c. sugar
¼ c. light corn syrup
½ c. butter
2 tblsp. water
2 tblsp. vinegar

• Combine all ingredients in heavy 2-qt. saucepan. Stir and cook over medium heat until sugar is dissolved, then reduce heat and cook at a medium boil, stirring as needed to control foaming and to avoid sticking as mixture thickens. (If sugar crystals form on side of pan, wipe them off.) Cook to the hard crack stage (300°).

• Remove from heat and let stand 1 minute.

• Meanwhile, butter 2 sheets of aluminum foil and place on 2 baking sheets. Quickly drop teaspoonfuls of butterscotch onto foil, making patties about 1" in diameter. Space them ½" apart. If candy thickens so that it will not drop easily, set pan in hot water until it is again workable. Makes about 6 dozen patties or 1¼ pounds.

EASY-DROP DIVINITY: Fill a strong plastic pastry bag half full with divinity mixture. Squeeze out puffs of divinity onto waxed paper. Top each with a walnut or pecan half. Don't waste any: Scrape together the left-over divinity in the bag. Roll into small balls. Dip in melted chocolate.

PEANUT BRITTLE BY-THE-SQUARE: You can form brittle-type candies into squares easily. Pour mixture into a buttered jelly roll pan. Wait 8 to 10 minutes, then mark into square with a knife. When brittle is cool, invert pan over cutting surface. Tap lightly to release brittle. Cut it, using knife marks as a guide. Most squares will be perfect.

Salted Peanut Brittle

To make squares of brittle—see Sweet Tricks on preceding page

2 c. sugar
1 c. light corn syrup
¼ c. water
1½ c. salted peanuts
3 tblsp. butter or margarine
1 tsp. vanilla
2 tsp. baking soda

• Combine sugar, corn syrup and water in a heavy 3-qt. saucepan; mix well. Cook over medium heat, stirring constantly, until sugar dissolves. Continue cooking, stirring frequently to prevent scorching, until mixture reaches 285°. Remove from heat at once.
• Stir in salted peanuts and butter; cook, stirring constantly, until mixture reaches 295°. Remove from heat.
• Add vanilla and baking soda; stir to blend (work fast). Mixture will foam.
• Pour onto well-buttered marble slab or 2 large buttered baking sheets. Spread out as thin as possible with spatula. As soon as brittle is cool enough so that you can work with it (about 5 minutes), turn it over and pull to stretch as thin as possible. (You can use two forks.) When cold, break in pieces. Makes about 2 pounds.

Kneaded Chocolate Fudge

Ideal gift for mailing—pack unsliced rolls in cans or mailing tubes

2 squares unsweetened chocolate, cut in pieces
1 c. milk
3 c. sugar
¼ c. light corn syrup
⅛ tsp. salt
1 tsp. vinegar
2 tblsp. butter or margarine
1 tsp. vanilla
½ c. chopped nuts

• Combine chocolate and milk in 3-qt. saucepan. Cook over low heat, stirring constantly, until milk is scalded and chocolate is melted. Stir in sugar, corn syrup and salt.
• Place over medium heat and stir until sugar dissolves. (If crystals form on side of pan during cooking, wipe off with a damp pastry brush or cloth.) Cook at a steady, fairly low boil without stirring to the soft ball stage (238°). Remove from heat. Very gently stir in vinegar. Add butter—*do not stir*. Cool until lukewarm (110°).
• Add vanilla and beat until candy loses its gloss and starts to thicken. Stir in nuts.
• Pour into lightly buttered pan or large platter. Let stand until cool enough to knead. Knead with fingers about 5 minutes.
• Shape into 2 rolls, each about 2″ in diameter and about 5″ long. Wrap in waxed paper or foil and store in refrigerator or other cool place until ready to use. Slice slightly on diagonal in ½″ slices, wiping knife between cuts if fudge sticks to its blade. Makes 20 to 22 slices, or about 2 pounds.

Ornamental Icing: In a small glass mixing bowl, beat together 1 small egg white (room temperature), 1 c. confectioners sugar, sifted, and ¼ tsp. cream of tartar. Beat until icing stands in peaks, about 10 minutes. Use to trim Christmas Trees of Fudge. Keep icing covered with a damp cloth when not in use, so it does not dry out.

Double Divinity

For pastel divinity—add 15 drops of food coloring to uncooked syrup

2½ c. sugar
½ c. light corn syrup
½ c. water
¼ tsp. salt
2 egg whites
1 tsp. vanilla

• Combine sugar, corn syrup, water and salt in heavy 2-qt. saucepan. Cook over medium heat, stirring constantly, until mixture comes to a boil. If sugar crystals form on side of pan, wipe them off. Reduce heat and cook without stirring until temperature reaches firm ball stage (248°).
• When candy mixture reaches 242°, beat egg whites until stiff, but not dry. Cook candy mixture to 248° and slowly pour about half of it over egg whites, beating constantly with electric mixer at medium speed.
• Continue to cook remaining syrup to the soft crack stage (272°). Beating constantly, pour hot mixture, a tablespoonful at a time, over egg white mixture, beating well after each addition. Continue beating until mixture begins to lose its gloss and a small amount dropped from a spoon holds soft peaks. If mixture becomes too stiff for mixer, beat with wooden spoon.
• Mix in vanilla. Drop by teaspoonfuls onto waxed paper. Makes 27 drops or 1½ pounds.

Chocolate Divinity—If you beat Double Divinity with electric mixer, add 2 squares melted unsweetened chocolate immediately after last addition of hot syrup; beat until mixture starts to lose its gloss. If you beat by hand, beat 5 minutes after last addition of hot syrup to egg white mixture and then add 2 squares melted unsweetened chocolate and beat until mixture holds its shape when dropped from a spoon.

Sweets and sours: gifts in jars

Jewel-Bright Fruit Honeys

Friends will agree you've outdone the bees when you give these new preserves. They're both sparkling combinations of honey and fruit—softer than jelly but not as liquid as honey. Make them now, of winter fruits.

Cranberry Honey

Spoon over pork chops—delicious!

2 c. cranberry cocktail
3 c. sugar
1 tsp. grated orange rind
1 c. honey
½ bottle fruit pectin

• Bring first 3 ingredients to a boil; simmer 10 minutes. Add honey. Bring to a rapid boil; boil 1 minute. Remove from heat.
• Add pectin; skim. Pour into sterilized jelly glasses. Seal. Makes 5 six oz. glasses.

Citrus Honey

Drizzle over piping hot popovers

3 medium-size lemons
1 medium-size orange
1 c. sugar
2 c. honey
½ c. water
½ bottle fruit pectin

• Pare rind from fruit; reserve fruit sections. Cut rind into ½" thin strips. Combine rind, sugar, ½ c. honey and water in a small saucepan. Bring to a boil. Cover. Simmer 10 minutes, stirring occasionally.
• Meanwhile, remove all membrane from fruit sections: dice fruit. Add fruit and juice to cooked mixture; bring to boil. Simmer, covered, 20 minutes. You should have 2 cups of fruit mixture; if not, add enough water to make 2 cups.
• Turn into large saucepan; stir in 1½ c. honey. Bring to to a rapid boil, stirring constantly. Boil 1 minute. Remove from heat.
• Add pectin; stir and skim 5 minutes. Pour into sterilized jelly glasses. Seal. Makes 4 six oz. glasses.

LAST MINUTE hostess gifts

When you go visiting, you feel so cheery offering goodwill in a jar, all tied up in red ribbon and jingle bells. Right now, you're probably wishing you'd put up more relishes when your garden or roadside stand was loaded.

But it's not too late to get out your canning kettle and jars. You'll find all the makings for these relishes and conserves in supermarkets. Maybe not at bargain prices, but available!

Some of the recipes require heat processing while others are refrigerator relishes—gifts you can make overnight. The Slaw-Stuffed Peppers need a week to marinate; packed in a large glass container, they make a spectacular gift. If you can Mincefruit Pie Filling, be sure your gift includes our suggestions for its use.

Pink Grapefruit Jelly

For variety, tint some jelly green

3 c. canned or bottled grapefruit juice
1 (1¾ oz.) pkg. powdered fruit pectin
4 c. sugar
6 drops red food color

• Pour juice into a 6 qt. saucepan. Add pectin and stir until dissolved. Place over high heat and bring to a full boil.
• Add sugar all at once and stir until dissolved. Bring to a full rolling boil. Boil for 1½ minutes, stirring constantly.
• Remove from heat. Stir in food color. Skim with metal spoon. Pour into sterilized jelly glasses. Seal. Makes 5 (½ pint) jelly glasses.

Tangy Beet Relish

Its peppy flavor perks up pork, beef

4 c. chopped raw beets
4 c. chopped cabbage
1 c. chopped onion
1½ c. chopped red peppers
1 (4 oz.) jar prepared horseradish
2 c. sugar
3 c. vinegar
1 tblsp. salt

• Combine all ingredients in 4 qt. saucepan; simmer 10 minutes. Ladle into hot, sterilized jars; process in hot water bath 10 minutes. Makes 6 pints.

Golden Glow Relish

A gold-tinged potpourri of colors

2 qt. cucumbers, peeled and seeded
2½ c. ground carrots
2 c. ground onions
1 c. ground red peppers
1½ c. ground green peppers
1 (4 oz.) jar pimientos, chopped
3 c. water
2 tblsp. salt
3 c. cider vinegar
2 c. sugar
½ tsp. turmeric
1 tsp. dry mustard

• Grind cucumbers; combine with carrots, onions, red and green pepper, pimientos, water and salt; let stand 3 hours. Drain off brine and discard.
• Combine vegetables, vinegar, sugar, turmeric and mustard in a 6 qt. pan. Bring to a boil; simmer 10 minutes. Ladle into hot, sterilized jars; process in hot water bath for 10 minutes. Makes 6 pints.

Slaw-Stuffed Peppers

Beautiful for gifts, too

12 whole green peppers
4 qt. water
¼ c. salt
2 medium heads cabbage, finely shredded
¼ c. salt
1 (4 oz.) jar pimientos, diced
5¼ c. sugar
6 c. water
6 c. cider vinegar
1½ tsp. whole cloves
5 sticks cinnamon
1½ tblsp. whole allspice
1½ tsp. salt

• Slice tops off peppers and remove seeds. Soak overnight in solution of 4 qt. water and ¼ c. salt.
• Combine cabbage and ¼ c. salt; let stand overnight. Drain well. Mix pimientos and cabbage; fill peppers with mixture. Tie tops on with thread; put in 8 qt. crock.
• Combine sugar, water, vinegar and spices in 6 qt. pan. Bring to a boil; cook 10 minutes. Pour on hot solution and weight down peppers. Marinate at least one week. To serve, cut peppers in quarters. For smaller amount, halve recipe and use 4 qt. crock. Makes 12 peppers.

Rich and buttery, light as down—
these pastries look like jewels
when they are glazed with a sweet icing
and filled with sparkling jams or jellies.

A. Crescents B. Butterflies C. "S" Shapes D. Whirls

Turnip and Onion Relish

Makes a zippy frankfurter relish

5 c. shredded white turnip
2 c. chopped onion
4 tsp. salt
4 c. sugar
3 c. white vinegar
¾ tsp. paprika
1 tsp. yellow food coloring

• Combine turnip, onion and salt and let stand for 1 hour. Drain.
• Combine sugar, vinegar, paprika and food color and bring to a boil. Add drained turnip mixture and simmer for 1 minute. Ladle into hot, sterilized jars and seal. Process in boiling water bath for 5 minutes. Makes 3 pints.

Potpourri Relish

Double the recipe for the holidays

¾ c. red wine vinegar
½ c. olive oil
¼ c. water
2 tblsp. sugar
1½ tsp. salt
1 tsp. oregano
¼ tsp. pepper
½ medium cauliflower, cut in flowerets
2 carrots, cut in 2" strips
2 stalks celery, cut in 1" slices
1 green pepper, cut in 2" strips
1 (4 oz.) jar pimiento, drained and cut in strips
½ c. sliced pimiento-stuffed olives
2 medium onions, sliced
1 clove garlic
1 bay leaf

• Combine vinegar, oil, water, sugar, salt, oregano and pepper in a large skillet or dutch oven. Add cauliflower, carrots, celery and green pepper. Bring to a boil, stirring occasionally. Reduce heat; simmer, covered, for 5 minutes. Cool. Combine cooked vegetables with pimiento, olives and onions.
• Place garlic clove and bay leaf in mixture and refrigerate at least 24 hours so vegetables can marinate. Remove bay leaf and garlic clove. Makes about 6 cups.

Christmas Relish

Festive, colorful vegetable relish

1 (10 oz.) pkg. frozen French-style green beans
1 (10 oz.) pkg. frozen whole kernel corn
1 (10 oz.) pkg. frozen peas
1 cup diced celery
1 medium onion, sliced
½ cup chopped green pepper
1 (4 oz.) jar pimiento, drained and chopped
½ cup sugar
¾ c. white vinegar
½ c. salad oil
1 tsp. salt
⅛ tsp. pepper

• Cook the green beans, corn and peas separately, following package directions, until vegetables are tender-crisp. Drain. Combine all vegetables in a large bowl.
• In a small pan, heat sugar and vinegar until sugar is dissolved. Cool. Add salad oil, salt and pepper. Pour over vegetables in bowl and refrigerate at least 24 hours. Makes 6 cups.

Pear Jubilee

Make extra jars for Christmas gifts

1 c. dried apricots, cut in thin strips
1 lemon, cut in thin slices
¾ c. water
5 c. peeled and finely diced ripe pears
4 c. sugar
1 tblsp. rum extract

• Combine apricots, lemon and water in saucepan. Cover, and simmer 5 minutes. Set aside.
• Combine pears and sugar in heavy 4-qt. kettle. Cook over low heat until clear and thick, about 1 hour. Stir often to prevent scorching. Add apricot mixture; stir well. Add rum flavoring.
• Ladle into hot sterilized jars. Seal. Makes 4 half pints.

Mincefruit Pie Filling

Big treat for pie lovers. Can some now to use in winter

4 lbs. pears
3 lbs. apples
4 medium oranges
2 (15 oz.) pkgs. seedless raisins
5 c. sugar
1 tblsp. salt
4 tsp. ground cinnamon
1 tsp. ground cloves

• Cut unpeeled pears, apples, and oranges in quarters. Remove cores and seeds. Run through food chopper, using medium blade.
• Add raisins, sugar, salt, cinnamon and cloves; stir to combine. Bring to a boil over medium heat. Simmer until thick, about 1 hour. Stir frequently.
• Pack at once in hot pint jars. Adjust lids. Process in boiling water bath (212°) 25 minutes.
• Remove jars from canner and complete seals unless closures are self-sealing type. Makes 8 pints.

Note: Use 4 c. filling to make 2-crust 9" pie; bake in hot oven (400°) 25 to 30 minutes. Or, use it as a filling for rolled cookies, sometimes adding chopped nuts, as a filling between cake layers, and as a hot topping for ice cream sundaes.

Pear Relish

Especially good with ham or pork

6 lbs. ripe pears (18 medium)
3 c. sugar
2 c. white vinegar
½ c. yellow mustard
2 tblsp. salt
2 c. diced onions
1 c. diced green pepper
1(4 oz.) jar pimientos, diced
¼ c. raisins

• Pare pears and cut into eighths lengthwise.
• Combine sugar, vinegar, mustard and salt in a 6-qt. kettle. Bring to a boil and add pears, onions, green pepper, pimientos and raisins. Bring to a boil; reduce heat and simmer 10 minutes or until pears are tender. Ladle into hot sterilized jars. Seal. Makes 6 pints.

Butter-bright pastries

You can use your imagination when it comes to shaping and filling the pastries. Try canned cherry, blueberry or pineapple pie filling. Or use apricot halves to make Apricot Nest Rolls—the golden center set off with white icing.

Homemade pastries as delectable as these command premium prices at bazaar sales—10¢ or 15¢ apiece. And friends will exclaim over them, whether you present them in a gift box or on a serving tray, warm from the oven. Make several batches the first week in December and tuck them away in your freezer.

Butter-Bright Pastries

Keep these lovely pastries in the freezer for brunch and breakfast

2 pkgs. active dry yeast
¼ c. warm water (110° to 115°F)
⅓ c. sugar
⅛ tsp. salt
1 c. cold milk
4 to 4½ c. sifted flour
2 eggs
1 c. butter
Glaze (recipe follows)

• Dissolve yeast in warm water. Combine yeast mixture, sugar, salt and milk. Beat in 2 c. flour; add eggs, beating well. Stir in enough flour to make a soft dough. Cover and refrigerate for 15 minutes.

• On a lightly floured surface, roll dough into an 18x15" rectangle. Cut ⅓ c. butter into small pieces. Dot surface of dough with butter, leaving a 1" margin. Fold 18" side into thirds and then fold 15" side into thirds. Wrap in floured aluminum foil; chill 15 minutes. Repeat rolling and folding procedure twice, using remaining butter. (When you roll dough second and third times, turn dough so narrow side faces you.) Chill 15 more minutes.

• Divide dough into fourths. Roll and cut into desired shapes. Let rise until doubled. Bake in hot oven (400°) 8 minutes or until golden. Cool.

° Glaze with an icing made by combining 1 c. sifted confectioners sugar, 2 tblsp. butter, 2 tblsp. evaporated milk and ½ tsp. vanilla. Fill with assorted jams or jellies. Makes 24 pastries. Wrap and freeze pastries. To reheat: Wrap frozen pastries in foil; heat in hot oven (400°) for 10 minutes.

Crescents: Combine ¼ c. brown sugar, firmly packed, ¼ c. chopped nuts and ¼ tsp. cinnamon. Melt 2 tblsp. butter. Cut dough into 5x2x⅛" rectangles and spread with butter. Sprinkle with filling. Roll like a jelly roll. Shape into crescent with seam side down. Snip at 1" intervals.

Butterflies: Cut into 3x¼" squares. Fold opposite corners to the center and press down.

"S" Shapes: Cut into 8x1x¼" strips. Roll back and forth to form evenly shaped sticks. Shape into an "S" with sides of "sticks" touching.

Whirls: Cut into 8x1x¼" strips. Roll back and forth to form evenly shaped sticks. Place one end in center and wind dough pinwheel fashion. Tuck loose end under.

Twists (not pictured): Cut into 8x1x¼" strips. Roll to form evenly shaped sticks. Fold in half; cross ends over each other to form twists.

Slick Trick

Notch your bread board by inches. When you roll out dough, you'll know exactly when you have the size pastry you need.

Apricot Nest Rolls

Hostess gift with a homemade touch

6 to 6½ c. sifted flour
½ c. sugar
2 tsp. salt
2 pkg. active dry yeast
1 c. milk
1 c. water
½ c. butter or margarine
2 eggs, slightly beaten
2 tsp. grated lemon peel
2 (1 lb.) cans apricot halves, very well drained
Icing (recipe follows)

• In a large bowl, mix 1½ c. flour, sugar, salt and yeast.

• Combine milk, water and butter in a saucepan. Place over low heat until liquid is warm. Gradually add warm liquid to dry ingredients and beat 2 minutes at medium speed of electric mixer. Add eggs, lemon peel and enough flour to make a thick batter. Beat at high speed 2 minutes. Stir in enough flour to make a soft dough. Place in greased bowl. Cover and let rise in a warm place until doubled, about 1 hour.

• On lightly floured surface, roll ⅓" thick. Cut with 3" cookie cutter. Cut holes in centers, no larger than a thimble. Place on greased cookie sheets. Let rise in warm place until doubled, about 1 hour.

• Place well-drained apricot halves, cut side down, in center of each roll. Brush dough with beaten whole egg, for extra color.

• Bake in moderate oven (350°) for 14 minutes or until golden brown. While warm, spread with Icing. Makes 3 to 3½ dozen rolls.

Icing: Mix 2 c. confectioners sugar, ½ tsp. vanilla and about 2½ tblsp. hot water.

Fancy shapes for dinner rolls

Fixing bread with a festive flourish takes only a few minutes more than making plain pan rolls. Our photos show you seven ways to cut and shape them–take your pick, or try them all! The recipe is our best dough for light, tender, rich and delicious yeast rolls; each batch makes 24 good-size rolls.

Bake them ahead and freeze them for the holidays. Wrap the rolls, as soon as they are cool, in aluminum foil or plastic wrap or bags; seal, label, date and freeze. Recommended storage time: 3 months to a year.

To serve cold, thaw in package at room temperature about 1 hour. To serve hot, place foil-wrapped frozen rolls in hot oven (400°) 20 minutes. If wrapper on rolls cannot be heated, place in paper bag and heat in moderate oven (350°) until hot, about 15 to 20 minutes.

Rich Hot Rolls

Freeze these lovely dinner rolls and reheat in foil before serving

¾ c. milk
½ c. shortening
½ c. sugar
1 tsp. salt
2 pkgs. active dry yeast
½ c. warm water (110 to 115°)
4¼ to 4¾ c. sifted flour
2 eggs

• Scald milk; add shortening, sugar and salt. Cool to lukewarm.
• Sprinkle yeast on warm water; stir to dissolve.
• Add 1½ c. flour to milk mixture; beat well by hand or with electric mixer at low speed 1 minute. Beat in eggs and yeast.
• Gradually stir in enough remaining flour, a little at a time, to make a soft dough that leaves the sides of bowl. Turn onto lightly floured board; knead until smooth, satiny and no longer sticky, 5 to 8 minutes.
• Place in lightly greased bowl; invert to grease top. Cover and let rise in warm place until doubled, 1 to 1½ hours. Punch down and turn onto board. See photos and directions for how to divide and shape dough.
• Place rolls on greased baking sheets; brush tops with egg wash made by combining 1 egg yolk and 1 tblsp. water. Let rise until doubled, 30 to 45 minutes.
• Bake in moderate oven (375°) about 15 minutes, or until golden brown. Makes 24 rolls.

CRESCENTS: Divide dough into halves. Roll each half into a circle 12" in diameter. Brush with melted butter. Cut into 12 pie-wedge pieces. Roll up from wide edge to point and curve into crescent shape. Place on baking sheet with point underneath.

(Note: If you'd rather work with smaller portions of dough, you may divide dough into quarters; roll into 8" circles and cut into 6 pie-wedge pieces. Or divide dough into thirds; roll into 10" circle and cut into 8 pie-wedge pieces. Any one of these methods will yield 24 rolls.)

SQUARE KNOTS: Divide dough into quarters. Cut each quarter into 6 equal pieces. Roll each piece of dough into a strip 12" long; cut it in half. Shape each half to make a U; place one U on top of the other, ends pointing in opposite directions. Pull ends of top U through loop of bottom U.

BOWKNOTS: Divide dough into quarters. Cut each quarter into 6 equal pieces. Roll each piece of dough into a strip 7 to 8" long. Tie into a single knot as you would a piece of string.

BRAIDS AND CIRCLE BRAIDS: Divide dough into quarters. Cut each quarter into 6 equal pieces. Cut each piece into 3 equal pieces (you'll have 18 pieces from each quarter of dough). Roll each piece into pencil-thin strips 6" long. Pinch 3 strips together at one end and braid. Leave braid straight or form into a circle. (For slightly smaller rolls, pinch only 2 strips together and twist instead of braiding.)

SWIRLS AND DOUBLE SWIRLS: Divide dough into quarters. Cut each quarter into 6 equal pieces. Roll each piece of dough into a strip 12" long. To form single swirl, wind the dough pinwheel style (front row on baking sheet). For double swirl, roll into 18" strip and form into a reverse "S".

CLOVERLEAF: Divide dough into halves. Roll each half out to make a flat oblong about 9x18". Brush with melted butter; roll up like a jelly roll, on the long side. Slice into 12 equal pieces (about 1½" wide). With shears, make two parallel cuts across each piece, but don't cut completely through. Lay roll flat and fan out slices to make cloverleaf.

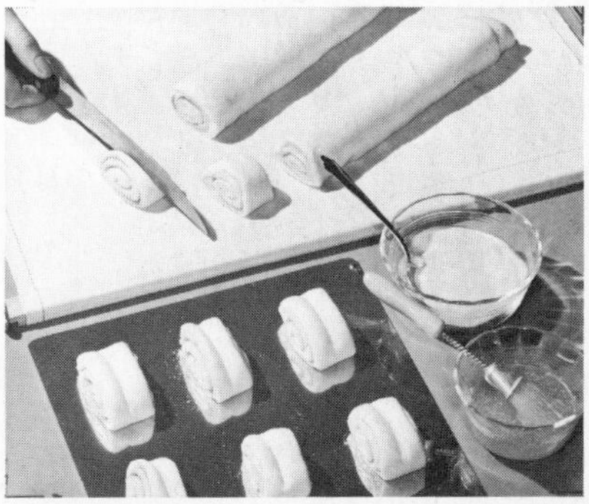

BUTTERFLIES: Divide dough and roll up in jelly roll shape, as for cloverleaf rolls. Slice each roll into 12 equal piece (about 1½" wide). Crease each pieces heavily across center with dull edge of knife.

Downright delicious doughnuts

Glazed Potato Doughnuts

Don't expect to eat just one

1 pkg. active dry yeast
¼ c. warm water
1 c. milk, scalded
¼ c. shortening
¼ c. sugar
1 tsp. salt
¾ c. mashed potatoes (instant may be used)
2 eggs, beaten
5 to 6 c. sifted flour
1 lb. confectioners sugar
6 tblsp. water
1 tblsp. vanilla

• Dissolve yeast in warm water.
• Combine milk, shortening, sugar and salt. Cool until lukewarm. Stir in yeast, potatoes and eggs. Gradually add enough flour to make soft dough. Turn onto floured surface; knead until smooth and satiny. Place in lightly greased bowl; turn over to grease top. Cover. Let rise in a warm place until doubled, 1 to 1½ hours.
• Roll to ½" thickness; cut with 3" doughnut cutter. Cover; let rise until doubled (about 30 minutes).
• Meanwhile, stir confectioners sugar, water and vanilla together. (Mixture will look like very thick cream.)
• Fry in deep hot fat (375°F). Drain on absorbent paper. Drop hot doughnuts into glaze. Place on cooling rack until glaze is set. Makes about 3½ dozen.

German Twists

Serve with cups of hot cocoa

1½ pkgs. active dry yeast
¼ c. warm water
½ c. boiling water
½ c. shortening
⅓ c. sugar
1 tsp. salt
½ c. evaporated milk
2 eggs, beaten
5 to 6 c. sifted flour
Granulated sugar

• Dissolve yeast in warm water.
• Combine boiling water and shortening; blend well. Add sugar and salt. Stir until lukewarm. Blend in yeast, milk and eggs. Gradually stir in enough flour to make a soft dough. Turn onto lightly floured surface. Knead until smooth and satiny (about 7 minutes). Place in lightly greased bowl; turn over to grease top. Cover. Let rise in a warm place until doubled, about 1 to 1½ hours.
• Turn dough onto floured surface. Roll to ½" thickness; cut into 8x½" strips. Place fingers on ends of each strip and gently roll back and forth to form evenly shaped 12" sticks. Fold in half; cross ends of stick over each other to form twist. Pinch to secure ends well. Cover; let rise until doubled (about 30 minutes).
• Fry in deep hot fat (375°F). Drain on absorbent paper. Roll in sugar. Makes about 3 dozen.

Applesauce Doughnuts

These doughnuts are so easy to make

4½ c. sifted flour
3 tsp. baking powder
1 tsp. ground cinnamon
1 tsp. ground nutmeg
½ tsp. salt
½ tsp. ground cloves
1 tsp. baking soda
1 (1 lb.) can applesauce (2 c.)
4 eggs
1 c. sugar
1 c. brown sugar, firmly packed
3 tblsp. cooking oil
1 tsp. vanilla
½ c. milk
Sugar

• Sift together flour, baking powder, cinnamon, nutmeg, salt and cloves; set aside. Stir baking soda into applesauce.
• Beat eggs well. Gradually add both sugars and oil, beating well. Beat in applesauce mixture and vanilla. Add dry ingredients alternately with milk, mixing well.
• Drop by tablespoonfuls into hot oil (375°). Fry until golden brown. Drain on paper toweling. Roll in sugar. Makes 5 dozen.

Golden miniatures

Bake fruitcakes in soup cans for your friends—our recipe is deliciously different and economical, too. You candy the pineapple and cherries yourself. They cost much less than commercially glacéed fruit and retain their fruit flavors and colors better, too. Nor is there need to mellow these cakes; they're last-minute. If you bake ahead, wrap and freeze them right in the cans.

Golden Miniatures

These beautiful fruitcakes are perfect for Christmas bazaars

4 c. sifted flour
2 tsp. baking powder
1½ tsp. ground nutmeg
2 tsp. ground cinnamon
½ tsp. salt
2 c. butter
2 c. brown sugar, firmly packed
12 eggs
1 tblsp. grated lemon peel
3 c. coarsely chopped pecans
Candied Pineapple, cut up (directions for candying fruit follow)
Candied Cherries, halved

• Sift together flour, baking powder, nutmeg, cinnamon and salt. Reserve ⅓ c. of this mixture.
• Cream butter and brown sugar. Add eggs, one at a time, beating well. Gradually add flour mixture, mixing well. Add lemon peel.
• Toss ⅓ c. flour with fruit-nut mixture. Stir into batter.
• Spoon into 12 greased and floured 10½ oz. cans, filling 1″ from top. Bake in slow oven (275°) 1 hour 15 minutes or until cake tests done. Cool.
• Before serving, you can frost fruit cakes with an icing made by combining 2 c. sifted confectioners sugar, 1 tblsp. soft butter, 1 tblsp. milk and ½ tsp. vanilla. Blend well. Drizzle over cakes. Decorate with candied fruit.

Candied Pineapple and Cherries:
• Drain 2 (1 lb. 14 oz.) cans sliced pineapple; reserve syrup. Combine 2 c. sugar, ½ c. light corn syrup and 1⅔ c. pineapple syrup in a heavy 10″ skillet. Cook over medium heat, stirring constantly, until mixture boils. Cook until temperature reaches 234°.
• Add a third of the pineapple slices; bring to a boil. Reduce heat; simmer 25 minutes or until pineapple is transparent around edges. Remove; drain on wire rack. Repeat with remaining pineapple. Then add 3 (8 oz.) jars maraschino cherries, drained. Simmer for 25 minutes. Let dry 24 hours at room temperature.

Perfect to serve with coffee

Pineapple/Pecan Loaf

A "must" for the holidays

½ c. brown sugar, firmly packed
¼ c. shortening
1 egg
2 c. sifted flour
1 tsp. baking soda
¾ tsp. salt
⅓ c. frozen orange juice concentrate, thawed
3 tblsp. water
1 (8½ oz.) can crushed pineapple, undrained
1 tsp. vanilla
½ c. chopped pecans

• Cream sugar and shortening. Add egg; beat until light and fluffy.
• Sift flour, soda and salt. Combine concentrate and water. Add alternately with dry ingredients to the creamed mixture, stirring well after each addition.
• Stir in crushed pineapple, vanilla and pecans. Pour into a greased 9½x5¼x 2¾" pan. Bake in moderate oven (350°) for 40 to 50 minutes.
• Remove from pan immediately. Cool on rack. Makes 1 loaf.

Lemon Squares

A superb cookie everybody raves about

1½ c. unsifted flour
½ c. brown sugar, firmly packed
½ c. butter or margarine
2 eggs
1 c. brown sugar, firmly packed
1½ c. coconut
1 c. chopped nuts
2 tblsp. flour
½ tsp. baking powder
¼ tsp. salt
½ tsp. vanilla
1 c. confectioners sugar
1 tblsp. melted butter
Juice of 1 lemon

• Mix the 1½ c. flour, ½ c. sugar and butter. Pat down well in buttered 9 x 13 x 2" pan. Bake in very slow oven (275°) 10 minutes.
Filling: Beat eggs; stir in sugar, coconut, nuts, flour, baking powder, salt and vanilla. Spread on top of baked mixture. Bake 20 minutes at 350°.
• While warm, spread with frosting made by combining confectioners sugar, melted butter and lemon juice. Cut in squares. Makes about 24 (2") squares.

Chocolate-Orange Torte Gingerbread

This is unusual; a conversation piece dessert. Use your own basic gingerbread recipe if you prefer it

1 (14 oz.) pkg. gingerbread mix
1 tsp. ground ginger
1 tsp. ground cinnamon
2 tblsp. melted butter
Orange-sliver Chocolate Icing (recipe follows)

• Stir together the gingerbread mix, ginger and cinnamon. Then prepare the gingerbread according to package direction *except* add the 2 tblsp. melted butter along with the water called for in the package directions.
• Pour into greased 9" round layer cake pan. Bake according to package directions.
• Cool in pan for 10 minutes, then remove from pan and cool on rack. When cake is cool, place on serving platter; spoon Orange-sliver Chocolate Icing over top, allowing it to drizzle down cake sides. Makes 8 servings.
Orange-sliver Chocolate Icing: Combine ½ c. orange marmalade, ½ c. semi-sweet chocolate pieces and a few grains of salt in top of double boiler. Heat over hot water, stirring occasionally until chocolate melts and mixture is shiny.

Banana Doughnuts

Children will love these doughnuts

5¼ c. sifted flour
4 tsp. baking powder
1 tsp. baking soda
2 tsp. salt
½ tsp. ground nutmeg
¼ c. shortening
1 c. sugar
3 eggs, beaten
1 tsp. vanilla
1 c. mashed ripe bananas
1 tblsp. lemon juice
½ c. buttermilk or sour milk

• Sift together first five ingredients. Set aside.
• Cream shortening and sugar thoroughly. Stir in eggs, vanilla, bananas and lemon juice.
• Add dry ingredients alternately with buttermilk to batter mixture.
• On well-floured surface, knead dough lightly for about 1 minute. Roll dough about ⅓" thick and cut with floured 2½" doughnut cutter.
• Fry doughnuts (a few at a time) in hot fat (375°) for 1 minute or until golden; turn and fry on other side. Drain on paper towels.
• Coat with granulated sugar while hot. (Shake doughnuts, a few at a time, in sugar, in paper bag). Makes 3 dozen.

Slick Tricks

When you forget to soften butter for baking, shred it on a grater—use the large holes. The thin shreds can be used immediately or softened to creaming consistency in several minutes.

Underline unusual ingredients in your recipes so you can check the cupboards before you begin to cook.

When a recipe calls for a sharp Cheddar cheese and you have only a mild one, add a bit of pepper, dry mustard and Worcestershire sauce. You will then have a sharp cheese flavor.

Treat the birds to a Christmas feast

When you're writing down your Christmas gift list, don't forget to include a large chunk of suet and several bags of seeds to feed the hungry birds that will gather round the tree branches or shrubs in your backyard.

In fact, if you make the least effort, you can enjoy the cheerful companionship of birds outside your window all winter long. In the "Gifts to Make" section of this book, you'll find a pattern and directions for building a clear plastic see-through bird feeder which a former Farm Journal crafts editor, now living in Massachusetts, has fastened to her window sill. Birds from the woods a few hundred feet away come daily to enjoy the feast she sets out—and her children have learned to call them all by name.

There are simpler constructions, too, that you can put up to attract birds and provide a Christmas gift. Richard C. Davids, nature enthusiast, describes his methods (and his joy) in attracting and feeding birds in *How to Talk to Birds**:

Few birds feel safe if they are all alone at a feeder. But they need room to take off swiftly without batting their wings against a neighbor. For this reason, the best seed feeders are big. The one outside my living room window is four feet long and almost a foot wide. A dozen evening grosbeaks can eat at once, while a hundred others wait their turn in the trees.

Siskins, sparrows, juncos and goldfinches prefer feeding on the ground, which is fine until snow comes. After that you can feed inside a big cardboard box lying on its side, which will be free of snow and sheltered from the wind. (Where rats are a problem, better feed well off the ground.)

The best feeder for those who want lots of action and who don't mind a somewhat unsightly structure outside the window is one made with a window screen for the floor and a storm window a foot or two above it for the roof, held up by four strong posts. Where snow isn't much of a problem, you can simply use the screen.

Suet feeders are simpler. All you need is something to hold the suet out of reach of dogs. A mesh onion bag is as good as anything. There are dozens of tricky littte suet feeders on the market, all of them fine for winter feeding if you don't mind the messy job of replenishing them every day or so, smearing peanut butter or suet into tiny holes. Coconut shells filled with suet are attractive, and so are big pine cones. But as more and more birds start coming, you'll want increasingly bigger feeders.

Woodpeckers, nuthatches, titmice and chickadees seem to prefer a vertical feeder, but for warblers, bluebirds and most perching birds, you need a horizontal one. Paul Fluck, well known ornithologist, uses a cedar log supported horizontally between 3-foot posts, which revolves on metal pins. He gouged out holes an inch deep to hold suet. When starlings are around, he can rotate the log so the holes are underneath, out of reach. As many as 15 downy and hairy woodpeckers use it at a time.

What to Feed

Kidney suet is probably the favorite of birds, but with so many people feeding birds today, most of us are content with any beef suet. A little meat mixed through it won't hurt. In fact, chickadees prefer it now and then for variety's sake. Just make sure there's none of it in your feeder when warm weather comes. The fragrance gets pretty high. Stocking the suet feeder costs little or nothing. Feeding seed eaters is another matter.

The prime food is sunflower seeds. If you really want to play Santa Claus, crack the sunflower seeds. There's no easy way I know, but a rolling pin works. For coaxing birds to eat out of your hand, there's probably no better bait.

You can save considerable on sunflowers by buying the small-seeded kind, by the sack or in 100-lb. lots. Buy buckwheat if you can; it's almost as good and generally costs quite a bit less. Flax seed attracts some birds. Few seem to care about wheat or oats or barley. Corn, either whole, cracked or on the cob, is popular with jays, titmice, cardinals and red-bellied woodpeckers. Milleted sorghums are fine and inexpensive. Birds much prefer white to red millet according to a wholesaler of bird seed.

There are dozens of other foods that birds like. Dog biscuits pulverized with a rolling pin make a fine food. Nutmeats of any kind are good. Pumpkin, squash and cantaloupe seeds attract some birds. My window ledge feeder holds a smorgasbord of odds and ends. It's fun to see how birds vary their diet, given a choice. Sometimes there's a run on suet-peanut butter mix. Another time it might be cornbread leftovers.

Most popular with a number of birds are doughnuts. We string them on a wire one above the other and suspend them from a branch to thwart squirrels. It's not long before only a thin white skeleton of the doughnut remains.

For most birds, winter and winter nights are critical. They must have full crops when night falls. A bird's metabolism is so rapid that many can barely keep alive overnight. Cardinals in Minneapolis, for instance, seem barely able to survive the long winter nights of the north. They are usually the last at the feeder in the evening and the first there in the morning.

Gourmet Fare to Lure Birds

Now for the feeding secrets—the tricks that will lure your neighbor's birds to your yard. Peanut hearts, buckwheat and canary seed will do it. So will hemp seed—marijuana by another name, and only seed that has been sterilized to prevent germination can be legally sold. This means ordering it from a bird supply company at about 30¢ a pound. While you're ordering, get a sack of Niger thistle, about $18 a hundred. It draws goldfinches like a magnet.

A secret ingredient of cage-bird feed is the seed of a member of the lowly cabbage and turnip family with the exotic name gold of pleasure. For generations, old hands at canary breeding used it to gloss up plumage and promote singing. It does the same for wild birds, Paul Fluck tells me. Goldfinches color up and sing. So do redpolls and cardinals. The price is around $40 for a 100-lb. sack, which should last a long while. Little research has been done on the effect of this seed on wild birds. There seem to be no harmful results.

* Reprinted by permission of Alfred A. Knopf, Inc., copyright © 1960, 1972 by Richard C. Davids.

Festive Christmas

Softly spotlighted, a miniature Nativity scene reminds everyone who sees it to stop for a minute and think what Christmas is all about.

To duplicate this crèche setting, build or buy a wooden shelter for exquisite porcelain figures. Or cover cardboard construction with wood grain plastic. Spread golden straw on the floor for kneeling Wise Men and animals, and hang a sparkling star above. Natural greens around the setting will hide wires if you want to light a star.

Decorations

No matter how many trimmings you have tucked under the eaves, to "deck your halls with" at Christmas time, you'll still want to add a new ornament or two. Something's missing if you're not busy making and doing this time of year—caught up in a project, giving yourself wholeheartedly to Christmas.

Browse through the next 20 pages for ideas. You'll find some projects that are quite ambitious—long-lasting decorations you'll bring out each year with increasing pride and sentiment. Like the spectacular five-foot embroidered felt tree to hang, like a tapestry, on the wall. Or a blow-up of "Silent Night"—the notes picked out with miniature lights—to place over piano or mantel. You'll see door decorations, tree ornaments, wall hangings and table centerpieces, many easy to do but no less festive. Get the family involved, creating a setting for your Merriest Christmas yet.

Christmas Card Montage

Choose the most beautiful cards you've saved and spread them out on a large piece of heavy black cardboard, overlapping them and rearranging them until you have a pleasing design (see photo below).

To make the arrangement "come out" from the background in a 3-D effect, remove the overlapping cards and set them aside. Cut off backs of remaining cards and glue them to the cardboard background, using rubber cement.

To stiffen overlapping cards, mount the face of each on a piece of heavy cardboard, using rubber cement. Trim cardboard flush with edge of card; paint edges black or white.

Cut small cubes of Styrofoam and glue to back of mounted cards; then glue cubes to background, following the design you planned originally.

For another crèche design which you (or the children) could make from modeling clay and cardboard boxes, please turn page.

Crèche

Roadside weeds look like trees in a crèche setting only 9 inches high and easy to make from cardboard boxes. Pile up a few different-size box lids to make the platform and glue them together. The building behind is made from two boxes the same size, about 8x9½″ and 2″ deep. Cut a 6″ round window a little off center in the top of one box, and a 5″ window in the bottom of the first box and top of second box. Paint boxes white inside; glue and tape them together, with package sealing tape. Use same tape to attach towers made from cardboard tubes topped with Styrofoam balls. Domed roof of building is cut from a large Styrofoam ball. Coat entire building and platform thickly with white gesso or latex paint; let it set for a few minutes, then texture it with a sponge. Poke holes in platform with ice pick to insert dried weeds; or hold with florist's clay, cover with sand.

The white stucco building makes an effective setting for bright painted clay figures that your children make . . . or for figures you might bring home from Mexico or the Southwest.

To make each figure pictured, use modeling clay that dries hard. Shape a cone about 2½″ high and 1¼″ at the base. To make arms, roll a bit of clay into a tube shape about 4″ long; flatten it in the middle and lay across shoulders (top of cone) and position arms. Head is a clay oval about ¾″ long; attach it with a bit of toothpick to top of cone. Shape head covering with fingers from clay pinched flat; place on head and trim edges with scissors. Insert about 7 glass-tipped straight pins to make halos. Shape Joseph's staff of wire, or a twig.

Model Babe in one piece; make crib separately, texturing sides to look like straw. Let figures dry thoroughly and paint.

Form sheep (about 1½″ to 2″ from head to tail) in one piece, texturing body to look like wool. Use ends of small wood matchsticks for legs. Paint legs dark gray, sheep light gray. Let dry; then dry brush sheep lightly with white.

Advent Calendar

Count the days to Christmas by opening the little doors on this decorative poster. Behind each door is a small Christmas scene or motif, clipped from Christmas cards.

Materials: *2 pieces of heavy cardboard 20x30″ (we used corrugated cardboard); Christmas cards or other sources of Christmas art; white paint; felt pens in an assortment of colors; white glue; gold braid; gold glitter.*

• Cut out 24 designs you like from old Christmas cards—different shapes and sizes. Lay them out in a random pattern on one of the cardboards; glue in place.

• Lay tracing tissue over pasted-down cutouts and trace outlines; draw a little door around each one.

• Paint second sheet of cardboard white. Trace doors on white surface and cut through cardboard along 3 sides of each outline so door will open over each piece of art below when you paste the cardboards together.

• With colored felt pens, decorate all the doors (see photo for suggestions). Number the doors from 1 to 24, but mix up the sequence, so the children will have to look for each door.

• Fill in between doors with more little decorations; also trace garlands around doors with white glue, sprinkle glitter.

• Glue cardboards together (be sure doors match art below) and add braid.

The first greeting...

at your front door

Regal Christmas Columns

Hang these brilliant red-orange-hot pink boards to mark your entrance. You may want to leave them up all year!

Materials: *Clear pine ½" thick, cut 4 boards 7½" wide and 6' long; and 2 boards 3½" wide and 6' long; enamel undercoat; red, orange and hot pink enamel or enamel spray paint; 9 tongue depressors (or similar thin wood); white glue; 18 small screws.*

• Enlarge patterns for top-of-board designs (see Appendix), or cut your own scrollwork from folded paper, the same width as boards.
• Trace around patterns on one of the wide boards, making 12 of the wide designs and 2 of the narrow. Cut out with coping saw or electric jigsaw.
• Sand all wood—boards and cutouts—and paint with enamel undercoat.
• Spray or paint with colored enamels. Note that cutouts at top of boards are same color; those glued to surface of wide boards are contrasting color.
• Mount cutouts ½" above top of each board with tongue depressors glued and screwed to backs (see detail in sketch).
• Glue cutouts to face of boards as shown, hang on nails.

Angel Greeter

With your whimsical friend out front, you're sure to find guests on your doorstep wreathed in smiles.

Materials: *Softboard (such as Celotex) 20x22½"; 6" Styrofoam ball; white glue; white latex paint; colored felt.*

• Enlarge pattern (see Appendix) and trace design on board; cut with jigsaw.
• Cut Styrofoam ball in half and glue to softboard to make head. Paint the entire figure with latex paint.
• Cut features and decorations from felt and glue in place. Banner may be felt or ribbon; thread it through the hand of the angel and hang on door.

Tissue Santa

Ask your youngest to draw a Santa for the door—here's how to make a permanent piece of art from it. The 6-year old who drew the Santa pictured is now 16—and still pleased when Mom hangs it.

Materials: *Masonite; white paint; tissue paper, light and dark red, light and dark pink, orange, teal blue, yellow; acrylic polymer medium.*

• Paint masonite white. Use a child's drawing of Santa for a pattern (enlarging it if necessary) or let the child draw directly on the masonite. Cut the figure out with a coping saw or electric jigsaw.
• Cut or tear tissue paper into small pieces. Apply to white surface this way: Brush a small patch with polymer medium, lay the bit of tissue on and brush over with polymer medium. Use light pink for face, dark pink for nose, orange for mouth, teal blue for eyes, yellow for tassel and gloves. For suit, start with lighter reds first, building up color by overlaying darker reds. Polymer medium acts both as glue and varnish. Paint boots and belt black.
• When finished and dry, trim away excess tissue at edges; put a hanger on the back and hang on door.

GREETINGS

DECORATIONS FOR

an old-fashioned Christmas

If holiday time at your house means the perfume of bayberry candles mingling with resin-scent of pine and spruce . . . and gingerbread boys and popcorn strings on a tree that grazes the ceiling . . . you'll surely have just the right spot for a quaint Calico Angel. She's two feet tall, aproned and ruffled in the old-fashioned way.

Calico Angel

Materials: *Corrugated cardboard 24 x 17"; natural color burlap; ½" yard each yellow calico and plain muslin; 1 package red rickrack; red iron-on tape (for heart trim); pink felt (for face); black embroidery floss; rubber cement; ½ yard red package-tie yarn; stapler.*

• Enlarge pattern (see Appendix). Cut entire outline in cardboard, plus 2 cardboard wings.
• Add ¾" to outside edges of pattern (allowance for wrapping fabric around cardboard) and cut the following pieces: Calico sleeves; calico underskirt. Muslin apron, muslin wings. Burlap hair and topknot; pink felt face. Calico neck ruffle (bias strip 2½x7"); Calico hem ruffle (bias strip 1½x14");
• Brush sleeve area on cardboard lightly with rubber cement, press sleeve fabric in place; fold ¾" allowance to back of cardboard and staple. Secure underskirt same way.
• Turn neck, sleeve edges and hem of apron under ¼"; press and hem. Position rickrack and stitch in place. Cut hearts from iron-on tape and apply to apron following manufacturer's instructions. Lay apron in place, lapping to back at shoulders and sides below arms; staple.

• Fold neck ruffle lengthwise, right sides together; stitch and turn. Gather to fit neck and rubber cement in place.
• Press and stitch ¼" hem on both edges of hem ruffle; gather to fit lower edge of underskirt and rubber cement in place.
• Stitch rickrack to muslin wings and rubber cement to cardboard, folding ¾" allowance to back; staple. Position wings and staple to body.
• Embroider eyelashes to felt face and cement to cardboard. Cement and staple burlap hair in place; tie yarn trim to topknot.
• Glue a fabric-type picture hanger to back of angel for hanging.

Swedish Wall Hanging

Scandinavians are fond of embroidered wall hangings, and most families have one especially for Christmas—they call it a *Jul Vaggbonad.* This one is typical showing the Scandinavian housewife at holiday time: hanging her *Jul Vaggbonad,* serving fancy coffee bread and taking children to Julotta services.

Materials: *1 yard heavy green fabric (such as sailcloth); 2 yards red piping tape; felt (red, yellow, orange, white); embroidery floss (orange, black, red, white, yellow, flesh color); hardware or wood strips for hanging.*

• Cut 2 pieces of green fabric, 34x12″ (one will be liner).

• Enlarge patterns and cut from white felt 3 aprons, 1 cat, 1 cup, 3 head scarves; from red felt 2 skirts, 1 heart, 1 rectangle, 1 child's coat; from yellow felt 2 stars; from orange felt 1 skirt, 1 child's coat.

• Arrange patterns on green fabric as shown in photo and trace those parts of pattern to be embroidered—faces, children's feet, bread, etc. Note that housewife pattern is reversed for center figure.

• Appliqué felt pieces to hanging using straight stitch. Using 3 strands of floss, embroider faces, housewife's bodice and arms, children's hands and feet, coffee bread, umbrella and apron strings in satin stitch. Using couching stitch to make stripes on aprons, and squares on scarves. Outline windows with chain stitch.

• When embroidery is completed, lay lining over hanging, right sides together, insert red piping in seam and stitch. Turn right side out and press.

• You can buy hardware for hanging at many needlework shops. Or cut and stain two wood strips, same width as hanging, and tack at top and bottom, pulling fabric around to back of wood.

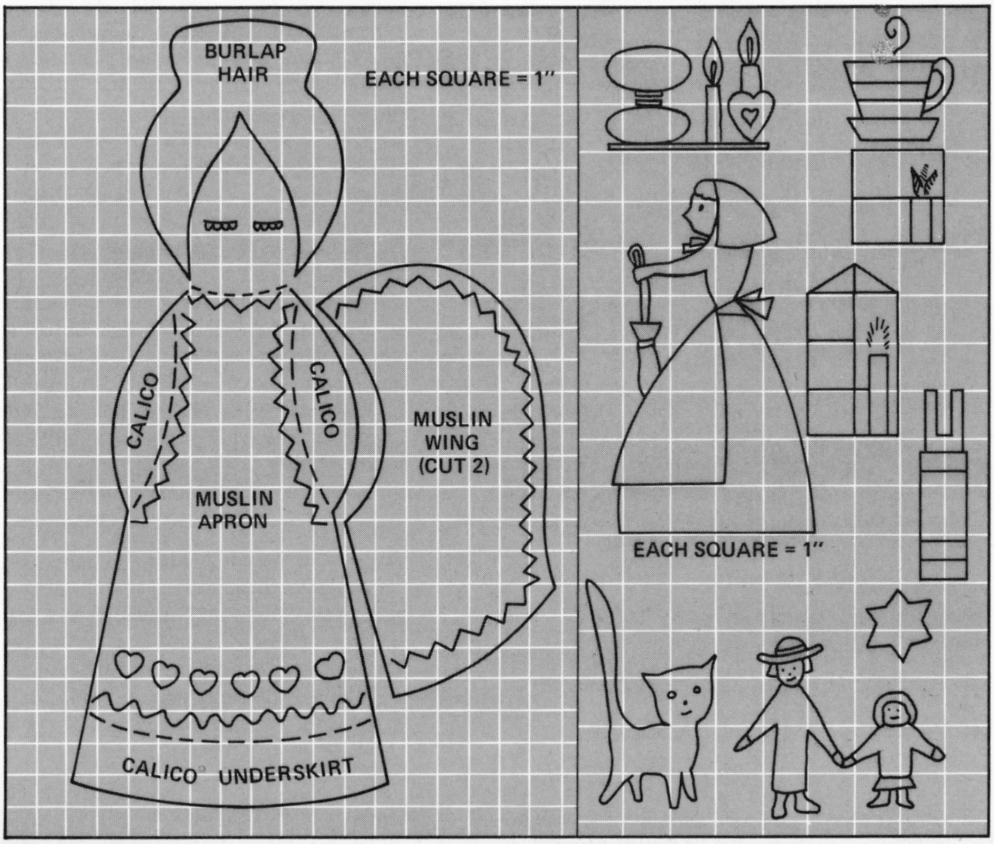

WHEAT TREE (about 30"): Ingredients are wheat heads dyed green, spruce cones, with red velvet ball and birds.

NUT WREATH (about 24" in diameter): Varnished nuts—pecans, almonds, Brazil nuts, filberts—with sweet-gum balls, yarrow, rabbit tobacco, cedar.

WICKER BASKET BIRD FEEDER (about 33"): Heads of grain sorghum with pine cones. Bow is made of burlap.

CORN SHUCK WREATH (about 30" in diameter): Corn shucks (left natural) yarrow (dyed red) and pine cones —dramatized with a big burlap bow.

DRYING, DYEING AND WIRING

decorations of natural materials

You can make beautiful decorations for your door, wall or table top if you have access to such natural materials as grain heads (wheat, barley, rye); creeping cedar, rabbit tobacco (also known as fragrant everlasting), yarrow, nuts or seed pods, spruce and pine cones, corn shucks, grain sorghum and of course, evergreens of all kinds.

A welcome change from the ubiquitous plastic greenery, these well-made wreaths and trees would fetch a fine price at bazaars. As a money-raising project, your club might even set up committees for mass production and market your wares to city stores.

Besides the natural materials, you will need these supplies from a florist: wood picks, fine copper wire, florist's tape, plastic foam cones, triangles and wreath bases, ribbons and other special trims as described.

Prepare natural foliages (such as boxwood, creeping cedar, cunninghamia or other evergreens) by submerging them for 10 days in a mixture of one-third anti-freeze and two-thirds water. It must be a high-grade anti-freeze–the cheap kind won't work. This keeps the foliage pliable and it won't shatter. After it is completely dry you can dye it if you wish.

Wheat Tree: You can use wheat, bearded wheat, barley or rye. Cut the heads before they mature and dry them in the shade. Next dip them in a hot solution of bright green fabric dye (follow package directions for making dye solution). When heads are dry, wire 4 or 5 together on a 3″ pick–you will need about 75 clusters for the table tree. Space them uniformly over an 18″ plastic foam cone. Wire the cone to a pedestal of cherry wood, or substitute a section of an old banister as a base or a compote. Look for the red velvet balls and small velvet redbirds in a city dime store.

Nut Wreath: This wreath should not be used outside, but looks handsome in a large family room. It is tedious to make but will last several years if you store it properly. Foundation foliage is creeping cedar dyed brown, plus rabbit tobacco and yarrow (some natural and some dipped in green and yellow dyes). Let it dry thoroughly before you wire it to 3″ picks. With a small bit, drill a hole in each nut (pecan, filbert, almond and English walnut). Insert in the hole the end of a chenille stem or pipe cleaner which has been dipped in glue. When dry, this is attached to a pick. Clusters of 3 small spruce cones are wired to picks, also cones of Norway pine. The picks are then inserted in a plastic foam base (about 30″ in diameter). The entire wreath is sprayed with a coat of clear plastic or varnish. You might also add a touch of walnut or mahogany stain you buy in a spray can. Finishing touch is a huge bow of green velvet ribbon. For nuts you can substitute native seed pods.

Wicker Basket Feeder: Make this door-tree design for the birds of grain sorghum cut when it is quite immature, and dried in the shade so it remains light green. Stems should be no longer than 3″. Wire 3 or 4 heads into a bundle and put them on 3″ picks. Other natural ingredients are 3 dozen gilded pine cones. The foundation is a triangle of plastic foam 2″ thick, 12″ wide at the bottom and 18″ high. Wire it to a wicker mail basket sprayed gold. Use a green burlap bow at the base and attach streamers to the back of the basket to add length (see photo).

Corn Shuck Wreath: This decoration for a large area is made primarily of shucks (from mature corn) cut in strips 6″x1″. Double four or five of these strips and wire them to a 3″ pick. It takes about 125 picks of shucks for a wreath with a 24″ plastic foam foundation. In the same wreath you'll also use about 4 dozen small pine cones wired and put on picks. The red is wild yarrow dipped in dye. Cut the yarrow stems to a 3″ length and wire them to a 3″ pick. Add about 18 tiny green burlap ribbon bows (also on picks) to add a little color. The large bow at the top is made of 6″ burlap ribbon. You can buy this waterproofed or you can waterproof your own by spraying it with varnish, shellac or clear plastic.

Decorating with lights

Of all the people who trim trees this year, only the grandmas and grandpas will remember the first tree lights . . . those strings of 8 lights all on a circuit which meant that if one bulb blew, all the lights went out.

We're grateful for today's independent light strings—each bulb its own boss. But even more, we welcome the advent of the *miniature* lights. So tiny that you see the light, not the bulb, the miniatures look like fairy lights sparkling on your tree . . . or wherever you want to use them.

Never a year goes by but someone thinks of a new way to use miniatures for a big decorating effect. Here are some suggestions.

Glass Tree of Lights

Topiary tree is shaped by gluing together glass grape molds (from hobby stores—molds are used to cast plastic fruit). Miniature lights shine through glass globes. You can make the tree taller than the one pictured—just cut a longer aluminum pole. Plant it outside in a garden bed or planter, if you wish.

Materials: *69 (1¾") glass grape molds; a string of miniature lights with white cord (or spray cord white); ¾" aluminum tubing 17" long; white glue; flower pot; plaster of Paris; wood circle ½" thick and 4" in diameter; ⅝" dowel, 1" long; 1 wood screw.*

• Glue 16 glass molds together with white glue to make a ring, stems pointing to center. (Apply glue to both surfaces and let it partially dry before pressing molds together; then hold for a minute until glue sets.) Let dry. Glue a second row of 13 molds to first row; then rows of 10, 6 and 1, to complete top half of globe. Let each row dry before adding next.
• Turn globe over; glue 13 molds in place—all stems should point to center of globe.
• Insert lights in molds—you will not have enough lights for every mold.
• Glue on a last row of 10 glass molds.

• Cut a slit in the wood circle for light cord, 1½" from edge. Screw piece of dowel to center of circle. Place glass globe on the other side of the circle (opposite dowel), slide cord into slit and glue wood to glass.
• Plant aluminum tube in pot of plaster. Set globe on tube, fitting dowel into tube —pad dowel, if necessary for snug fit.

Hanging Flower Vase

Here's another idea for using the glass grape molds. Hang a group of them in a window or a corner, filled with water and fresh daisies. You'll like the effect.

Materials: *Glass grape molds; clear nylon fishing line; white glue.*

• Cut one piece of fishing line 12" long and one piece 24" long. Glue both ends of the long piece and one end of the short piece to the neck of the grape mold. Try to space them evenly. Use a rubber band to hold ends in place until glue dries.
• When dry, remove rubber band and wrap another piece of fishing line around the neck, covering glued ends; tie a knot and clip loose ends.
• Hold lines at the top to see that vase hangs evenly; knot the lines about 1" from the top and clip off loose end. Fill mold with flowers.

A Christmas Carol In Lights

If you have a piano, this is the perfect decoration to hang over it.

Materials: *Page of music (see qualifications below); untempered masonite or ¼" plywood 24x36" (or size dictated by your music); rubber cement; wood for frame, ¾" x 1½", about 10'; white glue, Skotch cleats, 1" nails, 1" black tape; miniature tree lights.*

• Look for a favorite Carol with melody notes separate from piano score. Cut away piano score; rubber cement the title, melody notes and words to white cardboard, using care to line up music staffs and verses accurately.
• Allow a generous margin around the printed material and order a negative photostat blow-up from a photo copying firm, the width you want the finished picture to be, including the margins, plus an extra inch all around to wrap around the frame. Our "Silent Night" is 36x24" overall, with 3" margins at sides and top, 4½" at bottom.
• Cut masonite or plywood to dimensions of picture and make a simple butt-joint frame to brace it on the back. Nail picture board to frame and countersink nails; edge of board should be flush with edge of frame.
• Use rubber cement to mount photostat on face of board, following this procedure carefully to get a wrinkle-free surface. Lay photostat over board and, with a pin prick, mark each corner. Turn photostat over and draw outline of picture on back by connecting pinmarks. Coat this area evenly with rubber cement; also coat entire surface of board with rubber cement. Let dry.
• Lay two large sheets of tracing paper over the dried cement on the photostat, leaving about 2" uncovered down the middle. Hold the framed board over the photostat, lining up corners with the pencil outline; then press to bond the center strip (cemented surfaces will bond tightly when they touch).
• Turn over *both* board and photostat, so photostat is now on top. One side at a time, start pulling out the tracing paper—slowly—smoothing the photostat to the board as you go. Protect surface from fingermarks by rubbing with cloth.
• Cement photostat to sides of frame, too, cutting corners at a 90° angle. Cover sides of frame with black tape.
• Drill holes through notes to fit miniature light sockets. Pull lights out of sockets; push sockets in to holes from back; insert lights through holes from the front. If you have more lights than notes, wind the extras through an arrangement of greens under the picture.

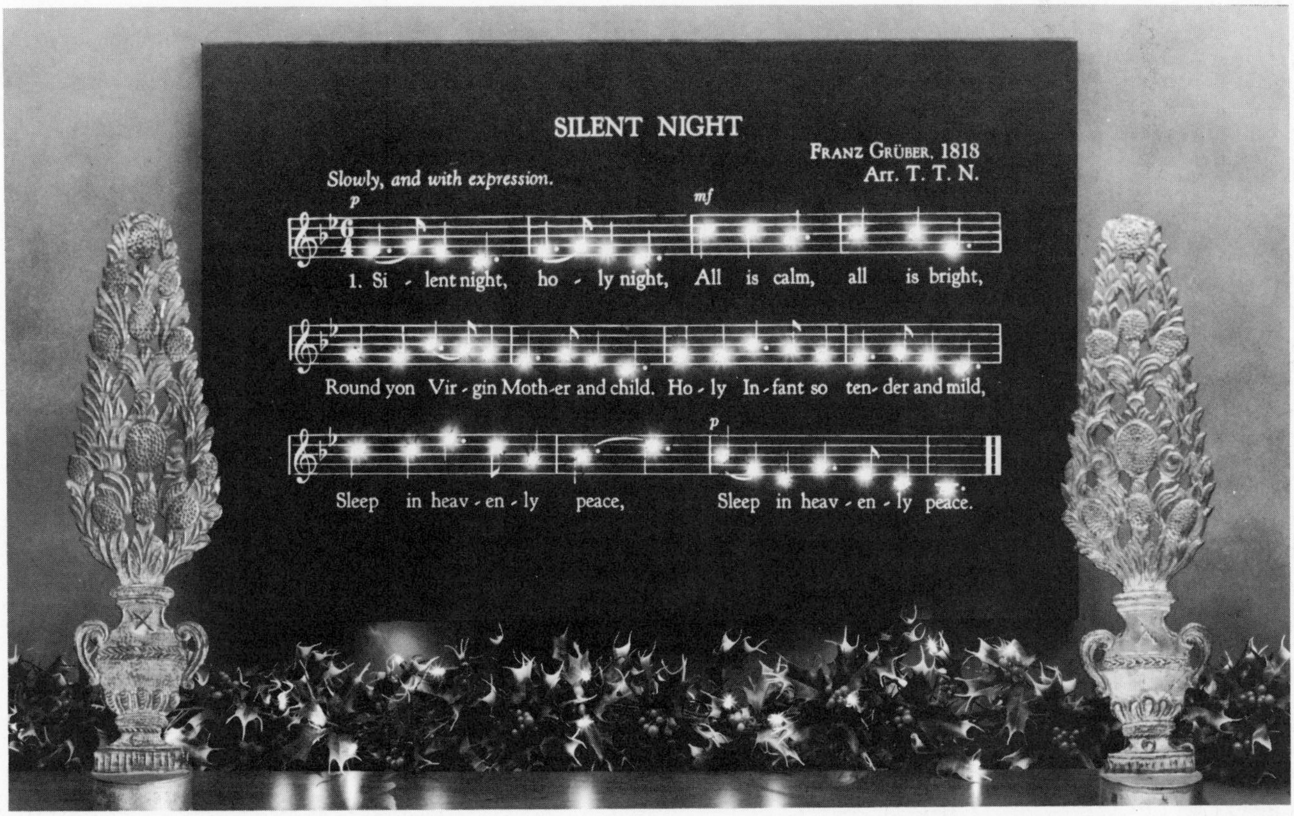

Christmas tree on a wall

Big as life, five-and-a-half feet tall, this tree fills a room with color but takes not one square inch of floor space. And it never drops a needle.

If you're traditionalist about trimming a real tree for the living room, you could hang the felt panel in the entry, hallway, dining room—wherever you'd like a dramatic display of Christmas color.

When it's time to put away your decorations, wrap the felt around a carpet tube and overwrap with brown paper or a dry cleaner's plastic; your tree will stay fresh and clean for years to come.

Materials: *White felt panel 40x68″ (or substitute any* heavy *white fabric); firm white fabric for lining (faille is ideal); felt and floss in assorted colors.*

• On the felt panel, outline a triangular tree shape about 62″ tall, 38″ wide at base. Mark it with pins or pencil dots 2-3 inches apart.

• Enlarge patterns and cut tree trunk, evergreen boughs and felt ornaments. Use 5 shades of green for evergreen—dark, bright and light. Bright green tree trunk is about 36″ long, 2-2½″ wide at base. Cut lots of circles in different sizes for ornaments, plus other simple shapes as you wish—trace them from cookie cutters or Christmas cards.

• Position the colored felt pieces quite close together inside the outlined area on the white felt panel. Attach them with French knots. Use two strands of floss to embroider the knots, and choose a contrasting color to secure each ornament or bough—for example, attach a pink circle with a purple French knot. Cover the dotted line with small felt circles and scatter more French knots in assorted colors all over the tree between applique pieces.

• Fold hems at top and bottom of panel; stitch lining at top and bottom, leaving an open space at the top to insert a rod for hanging. Catch-stitch side.

Make trimmings for your table

You can put together some of these centerpieces in 5 minutes flat. Even those that take a little time to "build" are very easy to make.

1. RED FOREST. From shiny red glazed paper, cut semicircles ranging from 18 to 24" in diameter. (See Appendix, how to draw large circles.) Form them into cone shapes and tape with double stick tape. Arrange a forest of them in the center of your table. In among the trees, place figurines or Christmas ornaments.

2. SUSPENDED CENTERPIECE. If you need every inch of the buffet for food service, hang your decoration from the ceiling. Buy gold paper ornaments, or cover Styrofoam balls with tissue paper petals. To do this, cut petals 2½x3½" (see pattern) and gather them, 4 at a time, with a wire twisted tightly around the middle. Fluff out petals. Cut wire to ½" and stick into 1½" balls. Cover entire ball with petals; you'll need about 60 tissue paper cutouts for each.

3. SNACK TABLE. Cut away the red wax coating on the top of a big Gouda cheese to make a star pattern. Decorate felt circles with sequins and gold braid to look like Christmas ornaments. Glue them to wood dowels and stick them into the cheese. Place on a serving tray and surround with crackers and cheese slices.

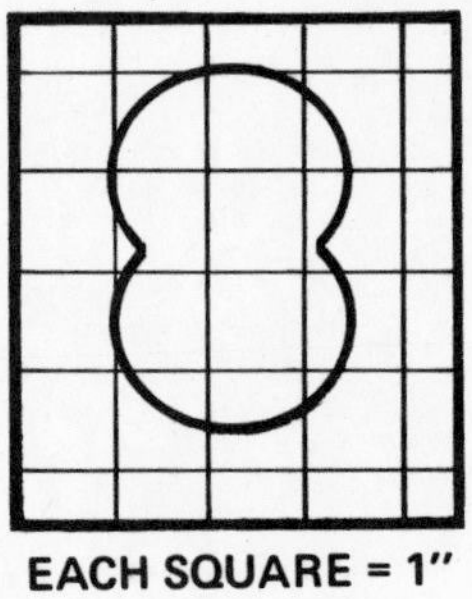

EACH SQUARE = 1"

4. WHITE EGG NOG TABLE. Wind a string of miniature lights around a tall white Styrofoam cone (use lights with a white cord, or spray cord white). Then poke white painted or flocked branches into cone and decorate the tree with plain blown white eggs.

5. FIVE-MINUTE TREE. Skewer cherry tomatoes on picks and poke them into a bouquet of fresh parsley. One of these would be just the right size for a cardtable centerpiece.

6. FLOWER POT SERVER. Build a last-minute tiered server for your buffet by stacking trays on upended flowerpots. If you don't have trays in graduated sizes, cut plywood rounds and paint them in Christmas colors.

7. BOUQUET-IN-MANY-VASES. Collect glass bottles in different shapes and heights. Put one red flower in each and mass them together on your table. Or use greens and colored Christmas balls on wire stems.

8. BASKET STACK. Gild pint-size wood berry baskets or make them from metal-faced cardboard. Fill with artificial currants or candy strawberries, and pile them in the center of the table.

Enchanting tree trims

THEY'RE TIN!

In Mexican villages, artisans emboss, cut out and color these bright ornaments from tin, a favorite craft material south of the border. As tin is not the easiest thing to find in hobby or hardware stores, you may very well substitute aluminum sheets which you can obtain from print shops. These will be just fine, once you've cleaned off the ink.

You can also buy sheets of "do it yourself" aluminum at the hardware store. Or, if you can limit yourself to relatively small ornaments, you can use the bottoms of TV dinner trays—this weight metal is easy to cut (use old scissors) and easy to emboss. Tin cans are not suitable for embossing —they're too hard; kitchen foil is too soft.

A hard rubber mat on which to do the embossing will be most satisfactory, but you can substitute a layer of felt topped with a piece of smooth leather or vinyl (or a padded notebook cover).

If you have modeling tools and metal styluses, use them to tool your designs; otherwise try both ends of a large metal crochet hook, a blunt-point yarn needle or a knitting needle.

The colors are easy to apply with felt pens; just be sure you get the *permanent* colors that "mark on anything"; water color pens will rub off. For extra shine, coat the color with clear nail polish. Or paint the metal with transparent glass stain, available in hobby stores. Colors are brilliant and shiny.

Materials: *Metal as described; felt pens in permanent colors as desired, plus clear nail polish; or glass stain.*

• Ornaments pictured are half actual size; see Appendix for directions on enlarging designs, or draw your own.
• Lay the paper pattern on metal, with the hard rubber mat beneath. With a modeling tool, hard pencil or ball point pen, go over the design lines, using enough pressure so lines show up.
• Remove pattern and work carefully with tools to emboss metal. Go over the design lines again, to groove them into metal. Then turn the metal over and, with a broader instrument, work on the metal between the lines—this will round it out, making the lines more emphatic.
• Cut out the ornament with old scissors or tin snips.
• Color ornament with glass stain or with felt pens and, if desired, coat with clear nail polish.

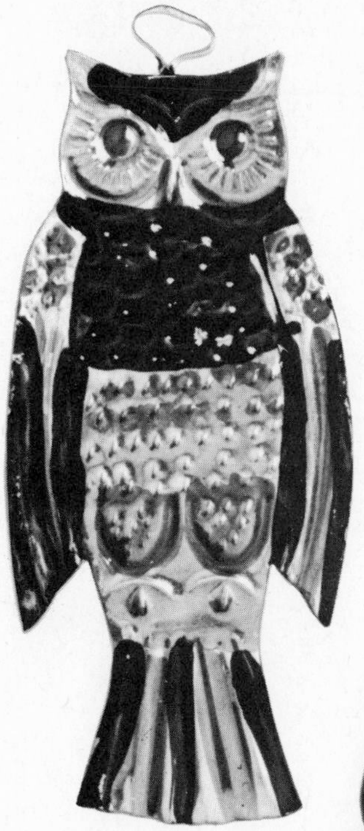

CORKS

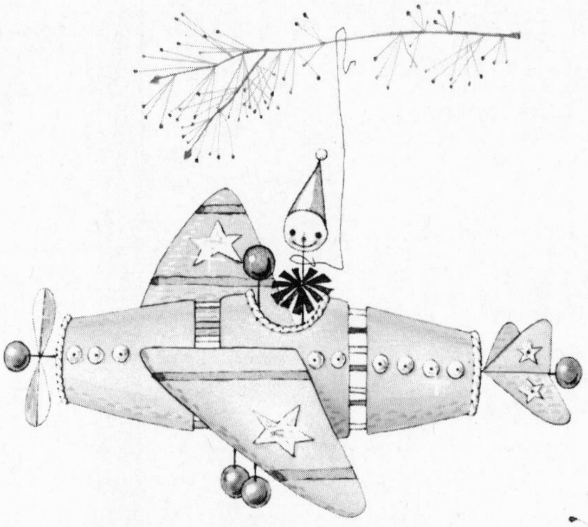

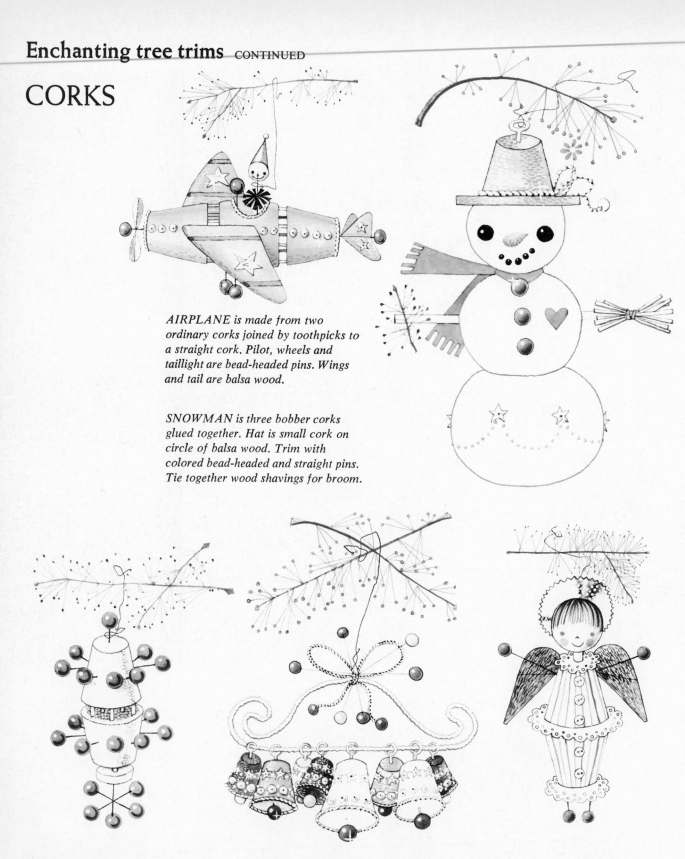

AIRPLANE is made from two ordinary corks joined by toothpicks to a straight cork. Pilot, wheels and taillight are bead-headed pins. Wings and tail are balsa wood.

SNOWMAN is three bobber corks glued together. Hat is small cork on circle of balsa wood. Trim with colored bead-headed and straight pins. Tie together wood shavings for broom.

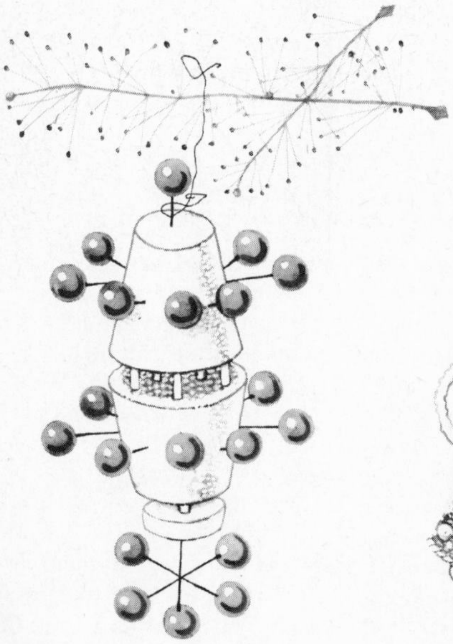

MOBILE ORNAMENT is formed of two corks painted white and fastened with toothpicks sharpened at both ends. Bead-headed pins make a design around middle, top and bottom.

CHRISTMAS BELLS are small corks decorated with paint, cord, sequins and bead-headed pins for clappers. Top with screw eyes and slip onto pipe cleaner tied with a bow knot.

LITTLE ANGEL has body of corks with a bit of paper doily glued between. Trim with doily frills, tiny pearl buttons, balsa wood wings, tree ball head and metallic paper halo.

EGGS

Egg Tree

Cut pieces of wood lath (1³⁄₁₆″ wide) as follows: 30″ (for tree trunk), 9″, 15″ and 21″. Nail the short piece 1½″ from top of trunk. Measure 5½″ from middle of top branch and nail second branch. Nail third branch 6½″ below middle branch. Wind green gift-tie yarn around trunk of tree and staple artificial plastic boxwood to branches. Plant tree in a bucket of sand and tie on eggs.

Paisley Eggs

Blow out large white eggs and decorate them with "commas" cut from bright fabric. Draw comma patterns 1 to 2¼″ long, some fat, some thin. Trace onto tightly-woven fabric, reversing half of them. You'll need 9 to 10 cutouts for each egg. Paint cutouts on back with white glue/water mixture and press to egg. Knot a thread through one comma and put it over blow-hole, to make hanger for ornament. When glue dries, spray decorated eggs with clear glaze.

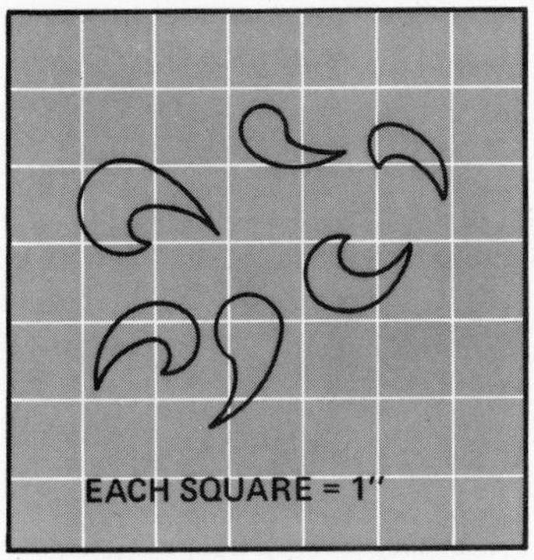

Spools and beads and curtain rings

What a cheerful afternoon you'll have, painting, pasting and stringing these colorful ornaments.

Materials: *Spools of thread (new or empty); wood handles which department stores give you for carrying home large parcels; bits of gift wrap and ribbon; large beads (wood or plastic); yarn, felt and paint in assorted colors.*

• Remove wires from wood handles and paint. Paint empty spools and cover with ribbon or scraps of gift wrap. (Or select colors of new thread—a collection of thread ornaments would be an unusual gift for someone who sews a lot.) Paint beads. Cut felt flowers about 1" in diameter; make holes in centers with an eyelet punch.

• String the colored spools, beads and felt flowers on contrasting colors of yarn. If yarn needle is too big to go through beads, make a "needle" from a twisted wire. Pull yarn through long

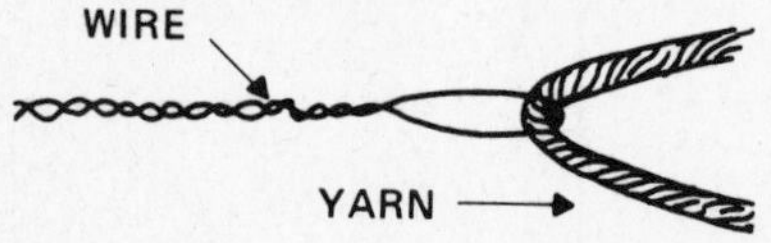

wood handles with a crochet hook. Doubling yarn gives you a loop at the top to hang ornament. Tie on yarn tassels at bottom.

Painting beads: *The trick is to paint them all over and dry them without smearing. Thread beads on string and hook string from one end to the other across the open top of a cardboard carton. Paint beads with a paint brush, or spray paint. Or put smaller beads on*

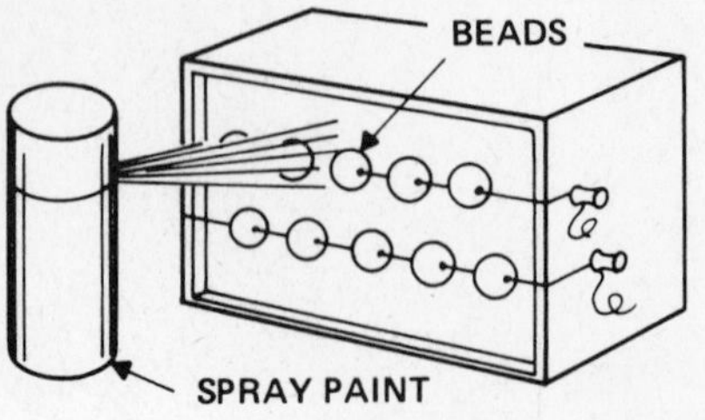

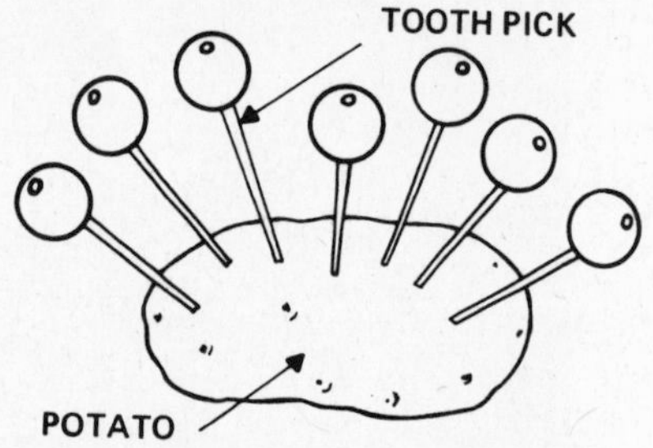

round cocktail picks and poke them into a piece of plastic foam or an old potato.

Curtain Rings

Turn curtain rings into swings for Santas, elves, angels and owls, or lace them with a spider's web of colored yarn.

Materials: *Wood curtain rings, 2¾" outside diameter (about 20¢ each in drapery departments); fabrics (felt, double-knit, whatever scraps you have, red, green, white, pink, black); embroidery floss; ⅝" wood bead; lightweight wire; purchased wood angel figure; flat stone; paint; yarn; carpet tacks or brads; white glue.*

Santa: Draw rounded teardrop shape about 2½" long; cut 2 teardrops from red felt. Sew together, stuffing lightly. Cut semi-circle face from pink fabric; embroider blue eyes and red nose (French knots). Glue to body. Cut beard and trim for cap from white felt; tack over face so eyes and nose peek out. Cut black felt boots and sew to bottom edge of red body. Glue Santa to curtain ring swing.

Elf: Cut wire 12" long and form stick figure, twisting on arms from wire 5½" long. Use stick figure to make pattern for green felt tights and red turtleneck sweater; cut 2 of each. Sandwich wire form between front and back of sweater and tights and glue; overcast edges if not using felt. Thread wire neck through ⅝" wood bead to make head; paint on

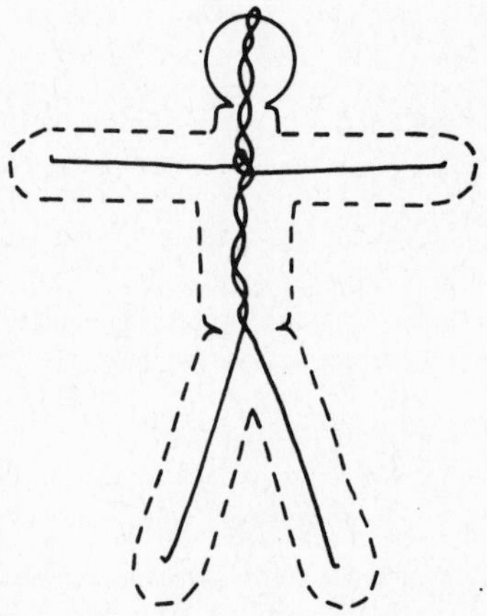

eyes and a smile. Cut triangle of red felt and sew to make cone-shaped hat. Glue hat to head and bend figure to sit in curtain ring swing.

Other swingers: Paint owl eyes and feathers on a flat stone and glue to inside edge of curtain ring. Or glue purchased angel figure 1⅜" tall to ring. Or make a tiny tree by painting a pine cone green and trimming it with strawflowers or Indian beads.

Yarn Webs: Draw circle same size as curtain ring on paper to locate nail positions. For perfect spoke design (pink-purple ring), you must have an odd number (19 or 21) of nails equidistant from each other. Mark curtain ring with pencil at nail positions; pound in tiny brads or upholstery tacks. Paint ring and nails color desired. Lace with contrasting yarn. To secure yarn, put a dot of white glue on starting and finishing nail and tie yarn tight; hold until dry; then trim end close to nail. You can pound nails into both sides of curtain ring and lace with contrasting yarns.

Greeting card designs

If you send out a handmade card, you are very likely to get a letter back—people are impressed when you design your own cards. Do shop for envelopes first. You'll find blank cards with matching envelopes in art supply stores, ready to decorate. Or you can cut construction papers to fit standard-size envelopes from the stationery store. See Appendix for tips on cutting paper neatly.

Plastic Sandwich Cards

Materials: *Clear adhesive plastic; leaves and evergreen sprigs (you can use either fresh or pressed greens); paper doilies; construction paper; rice paper.*

• You need two pieces of plastic for each see-through card. Peel backing paper from one piece, place design material (greens or doilies) on sticky surface; peel backing from second piece and layover design. Press together.
• Cut out frames from construction paper and sandwich plastic designs between.
• Instead of making a see-through card, you can arrange a snow scene on colored paper (juniper sprig, rice paper hill, paper doily snowflakes) and simply cover it with clear plastic.
• To make hanging snowflake, sandwich two paper doilies in clear plastic. Using a long stitch on your sewing machine, stitch them together down the center. Write your name and greeting on a tag and tie to snowflake card.

Paper Cutout Cards

Materials: *Colored construction papers; blank cards with matching envelopes; rubber cement; thread.*

• For Holly and Tree cards, cut holly leaves or tree "slivers" from colored construction paper; bend each piece down the middle by pressing paper against the edge of ruler.

• Paste the left side of each piece to card following design layout; leave right side free to bend forward slightly, giving the design a dimensional look.
• For Angel card, sketch design for flying angel with arms outstretched; trace parts onto appropriate colors of construction paper and cut out robe, head, hair, wings, hands and feet. Glue to card with rubber cement. Cut out stars

(or stick gummed stars back-to-back) and string them on a needle and thread; knot to angel's hands.

Marbled Paper Cards

Materials: *Artist's oil paints, turpentine, wallpaper paste, paper for printing and for mounting prints.* Or *fingerpaints and fingerpaint paper.*

• Mix some wallpaper paste with enough water to make a smooth, but thick mixture and put it in a foil tray or pan big enough to accommodate the paper you want to color. Mix paint colors with turpentine in small paper cups.
• Using a paint brush or stick, shake a few drops of paint on the surface of the paste. You can use one color, or two or three, depending on the effect you want. The oil paint will not mix with paste—it remains on the surface.
• Now, with the tip of a small brush, stroke through the drops of paint to make a marbled pattern. Move the brush in circles, making a swirl (see "Peace" card) or zigzag back and forth.
• Carefully place a piece of paper on the paste-and-paint mixture and pat it so the paper makes complete contact with the surface—no air bubbles.
• Peel off the paper; the colors will stick to it and the surface of the paste will be clean, ready for your next drops of paint. Some of the paste will cling to the paper—rinse it off in a second tray of clear water. When paper dries, it can be ironed flat.
• Another way to print your own paper is with fingerpaint (see Candles card).
• To assemble cards: Trim printed paper to desired shapes and paste onto cards. The "Peace" card has dark paper with circle cutout laid over printed swirl. Rice paper dove is pasted on.

Fabric Cutout Cards

Materials: *Bright printed fabrics; blank cards with matching envelopes; felt pens; stencil paper or light-weight cardboard.*

• For Madonna card, cut a long, arch-shaped piece of printed fabric, plus two circles of heavy plain fabric for faces. Draw features on faces with a finepoint black felt pen. Paste faces to fabric, and fabric to card.
• For Angel and Tree cards, trace design on the front of a blank card; cut out design area with X-acto knife. Lay fabric inside card and glue front to back, sandwiching fabric between.
• Cut a stencil for Angel head and wings and use felt pens to color.

NEEDLEWEAVING GOES FAST. You work on a simple cardboard loom or inside an embroidery hoop to make these colorful gifts: a 3-hoop mobile, Christmas ornament, placemat, striped pillow, stuffed doll mobile.

Gifts to make – new crafts to try

When you enfold a handmade gift in tissue paper and tie it up with Christmas seals and ribbons, you pack a bit of yourself inside. Your pleasure in making the gift becomes as much a part of it as the yarns or fabrics you stitched into it, the wood you painted and decorated, the plastic or clay you formed.

This year, why not double your pleasure by learning a new craft or experimenting with materials you've not used before? We promise you a creative adventure—resulting in handsome and useful gifts for family or friends, or for sale at your bazaar.

Beginning here, you can learn to weave with a needle on a simple cardboard loom. In pages following, you'll find ideas, patterns and directions for doing patchwork (try a fake fur pillow, or a suedecloth tote); sculpting weedholders from plaster bandages; forming acrylic plastic (begin with jewelry—then graduate to the see-through birdfeeder); embroidering or knotting wall hangings; sewing stuffed dolls; pasting seed mosaics; making and painting wood toys, mobiles, bookends, pictures and picture frames; sandcasting candles; even making rugs from felt, rope and rags.

Needleweaving

One of the most flexible and inexpensive of creative crafts, needleweaving is not to be confused with stitchery or embroidery which are applied to a fabric that has already been woven. Weaving starts with a set of threads called warp, which are stretched, in our method, across cardboard (or across an embroidery hoop). Weft is the thread that crosses and is woven into the warp with a large-eyed needle. This is the simplest possible way to weave and offers the weaver great freedom in manipulating the yarn.

Detail showing effect of light versus dark warp, same weft. At right: preparing cardboard loom.

Materials

Yarn: For warp yarn, choose some kind that does not have much stretch. Carpet warp is a good cotton warp. Linen is excellent and goat hair with a fuzzy texture gives an overall "bloom" to the finished work. Weft threads can be anything: leftover yarn from knitting projects, colored cords or gift wrap ties, thick, thin, shiny-smooth or fuzzy. It's a good idea to collect a "library" of yarns in which to browse as you select colors and textures you want to use together.

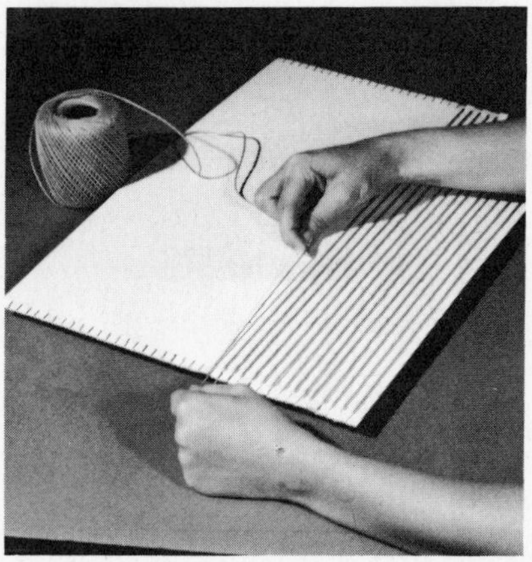

Cardboard: Stiff cardboard makes an adequate loom for a small weaving. A larger cardboard loom should be reinforced on the back with a second piece of cardboard cut slightly smaller than the first. Glue them together. For very large projects, substitute untempered masonite for cardboard, cut or notched with a handsaw or power saw. Paint it white to make it easier to see what you are doing as you weave.

Needle: If you cannot find a needle with a big eye and blunt point which is also curved, you can bend one about ¾″ from the tip with a pair of pliers—it bends more easily if you heat it with a torch.

Dog comb: You may need a tool for pushing the woven thread into place—weavers call this a beater. A dog comb or any large-toothed comb will do; often your fingers or the weaving needle will be all you need to compact the yarns.

Scissors and X-acto knife.

Preparing Loom

Cut cardboard slightly larger than you want finished weaving to be (cardboard 14x20″ will make a placemat about 13 x19″). Cut slits ¼″ deep and ¼″ apart on the narrow edges of a rectangular loom (or opposite edges of a square loom) with scissors or X-acto knife.

Knot the end of warp thread at the back of the loom in the first slit near one corner. Bring the warp across the face of the loom to the first slit in the opposite end, leading it to the back of the loom, then to the front again through the next slit. Continue leading the warp back and forth across the face of the loom, keeping warp in parallel rows and of even tension. Fasten warp in last slit with another knot at the back.

Detail of weaver's knot.

Weaver's Knot and Chain Stitch

Cut the weaving yarn (weft) about 2 yards long. Anchor it to the warp with the weaver's knot, placed at one corner of the loom. Do a few rows of chain stitch—this useful stitch helps space the

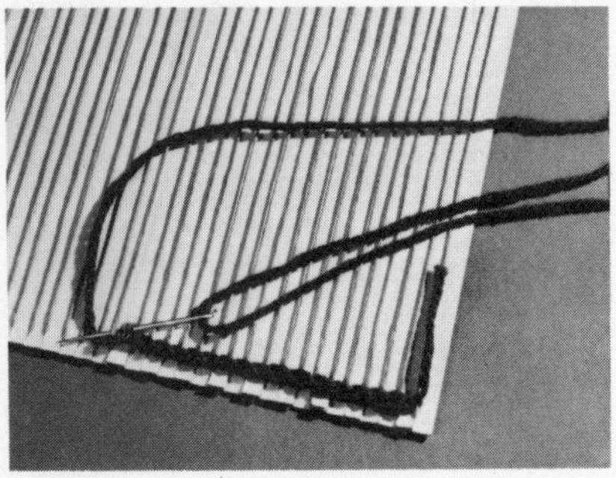

Close-up of chain stitch.

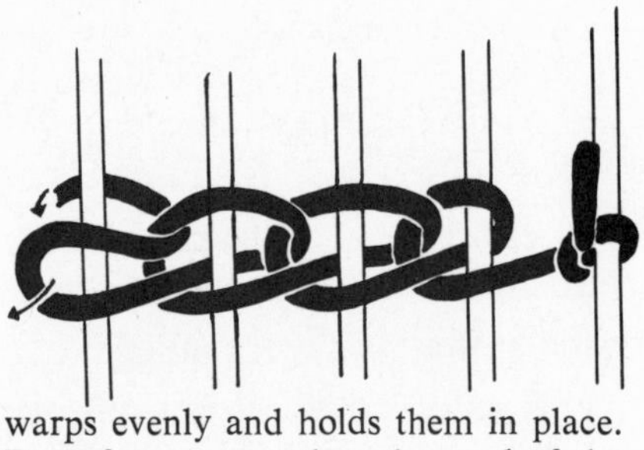

warps evenly and holds them in place. Do a few rows at the other end of the loom, too.

Caution: *It is important, in doing any of the stitches, not to pull the weft too tight. Keep your eye on the warps, especially at the selvages; if they're pulling out of line as you weave, loosen up!*

The Plain Weave

Some call this the darning stitch; it is the basic stitch for needleweaving. Just take your needle over and under the warp threads; turn around and come back under the warps you first went over and over those you first went under. Placemat, pillow and doll are all

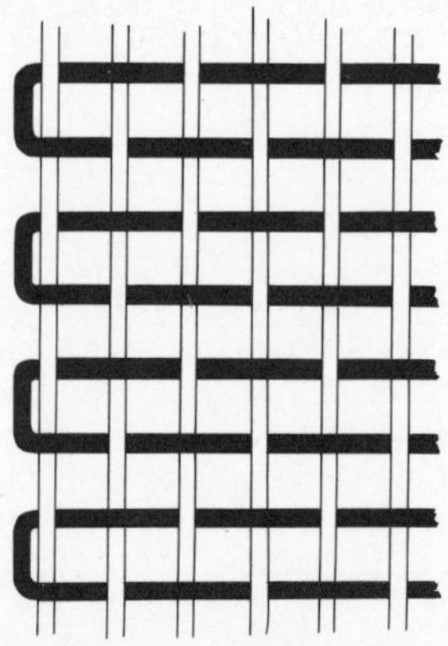

woven like this; changing the color and texture of weft yarn every few rows provides the pattern.

The Egyptian Knot

When the weft loops around the warp, the result is a knot-type of weave; you can see in the photos how the needle dips each time under two warps—the warp being wrapped and the next one to be wrapped. The tricky part is turning around—study the close-up photo

Egyptian knot close-up.

which shows how you wrap the outside warp twice; then dip under and around the next warp; then continue as before. When the Egyptian knot is well done, every wrap looks like a beautiful little

Weaving the Egyptian knot.

bead of yarn. When several rows follow one another, they produce a rib in the direction of the warp.

Removing Weaving from Loom

With a crochet hook, gently lift the loops out of the slits on the back of the loom. You can push the weaving out to occupy these little loops at the ends. Poke any ends of yarn to the back side and weave them into the body of the weaving before snipping them off. To make pillow, weave front and back separately and sew them together, stuffing with a standard pillow form.

Simple Hatching

The method of moving from light to dark or from one color into another gradually is called hatching. In simple hatching, the lines of light yarn run parallel to the dark that they penetrate.

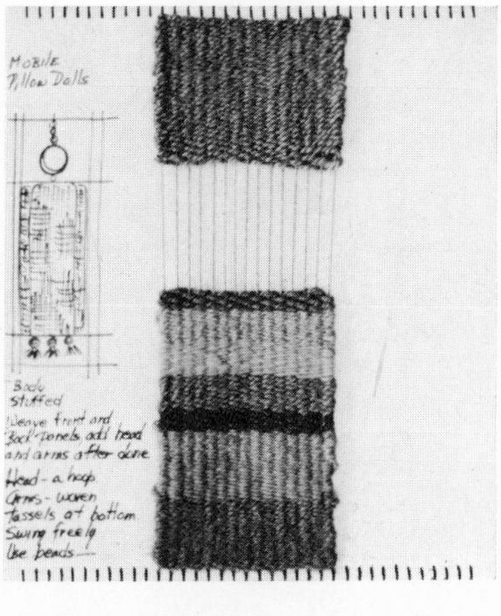

Special Directions for Doll

Cut loom 10″ long and warp it with 15 warp threads. Weave front of doll using different color yarns to make stripes; remove from loom. Rewarp loom and weave back. Weave arms separately on 5″ loom, using 4 warps. Sew doll together and stuff lightly. Tack on arms; add tassels for legs. Head is a wire hoop wrapped with yarn in buttonhole stitch; heart decoration is embroidered felt. Hang the doll as a mobile.

Hoop Loom

When you finish a weaving you usually dispose of the loom. But sometimes you will want to work on a hoop which becomes a permanent part of your design. It might be a metal hoop, a little heavier than coat hanger wire. Use the buttonhole stitch to cover the metal with yarn and run warp threads through this stitchery. Or use a wood embroidery hoop and notch or drill it to hold warp.

Three-hoop Mobile

Interlock three hoops in graduated sizes together and wrap each one with yarn, using buttonhole stitch. Look at color picture and note that each hoop will be warped differently.

Top hoop: Thread 4 or 5 warp threads from one side of hoop across the center to the other side. Weave. Then thread another set of warps at an angle to the first, but crossing in the center. Weave in a contrasting color. Continue adding warps and weaving in more colors until you're pleased with the design.

Middle hoop: This time, run the warp threads in bands from side to side, but not through center of hoop. Weave each band as you warp it; then warp the next band. Square them off, some bands running across, some up-and-down. The puffy spots are extra-thick or fuzzy yarns, or weft threads that are allowed to loop at the selvages.

Bottom hoop: Instead of running parallel to each other, warp threads can be laced into a loom in a pattern called *eccentric warping.* After leading the warp across the loom, you bring the second warp to the *right* of the first. Then take it across the loom to the *left* of the starting warp. This makes the warps cross each other in the center—the effect will look something like the spokes of a bicycle wheel. Weave colored yarn through the warps to make an airy tracery of color.

Christmas Ornament

Fasten a pair of embroidery hoops at right angles to each other with glue and cover them with white yarn, using buttonhole stitch. Run 2, 3 or 4 warp threads from one hoop edge to another and weave loosely with a soft white yarn, weaving each set of warps before stringing in the next. Let the warps cross each other in random patterns, to fill center of sphere. Decorate outside edge of hoops with green and red braid.

More Weaving Techniques

Needleweaving does not have to go back and forth, in straight rows. You can begin to weave in the middle of the loom, making curves and loops, letting your needle roam freely among the warps.

But it takes more courage than most beginners have to start a large project with the weaving thread wandering at whim. To give you confidence in doing a *meandering weft,* you might make a small needleweaving on a 5x7″ cardboard. Pictures show how to begin; finished piece could be a clutch bag, a pocket for a dress, even a picture.

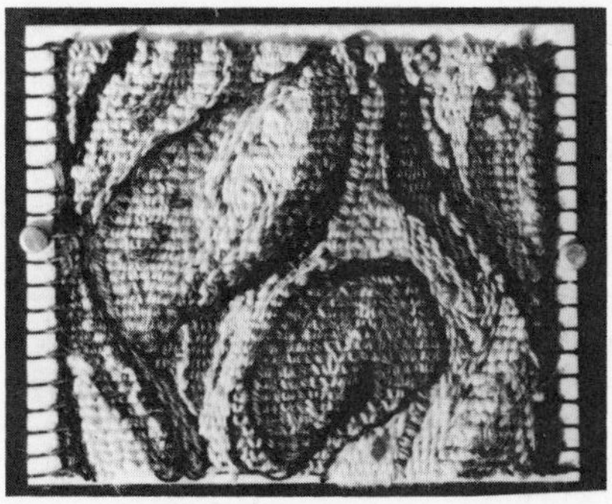

Adapted from *Needleweaving, Easy as Embroidery,* copyright © 1971, 1972 by Esther Warner Dendel; published by Farm Journal, Inc., Philadelphia, Pa., distributed by Doubleday & Co., Inc., Garden City, N.Y.

GIFTS TO MAKE IN
patchwork

With authentic old quilt block patterns for starters, you can design almost anything imaginable for friends to wear or use in their homes. Likely, your scrapbasket will yield the materials to make your gift. And since most patchwork patterns are straight cuts and straight seams, you can piece them on your sewing machine—the work goes fast. But the results are indelibly, satisfyingly, handmade . . . gifts you'll be proud to give.

You don't even have to like needlework. Sketches show how the block designs translate as easily into paint or cut-and-paste as in fabric.

Cutting the Pattern

Trace patterns (see pages following) for the design you've selected onto lightweight cardboard or fine sandpaper. (If you're working with slick-surfaced fabrics, use sandpaper—it won't skid.) For greatest accuracy, use a straight-edge ruler to trace the patterns. And cut out each piece with exactness for a perfect fit.

Lay pattern cutouts on the wrong side of fabric, with the grain as marked (unless you're using a non-woven or vinyl material). Trace around patterns with a pencil, directly on fabric. Leave ½″ space between each outline to allow for seams (¼″ is a satisfactory seam allowance for most fabrics).

Cut fabric pieces ¼″ out from tracing line. Try to keep this seam allowance even—it makes piecing easier.

The pencil line is the seam line. Place right sides of fabric together and stitch through pencil lines on wrong sides.

Note: Accuracy in stitching pencil line to pencil line is important. If you're off as little as 1/16″ per seam, it adds up to 1″ after 16 seams! Always match corners and points first (pin or baste) before stitching. For complicated patterns, it is safest to baste pieces together before you machine stitch to make sure that seams are accurate.

Piecing the Blocks

As a general rule, stitch the center pieces together and work out to the edges. But not always. Arrange the pieces for the block and decide how you can put sections together. For example: Flying Geese.

1. Sew the small triangular pieces together to make rectangles.

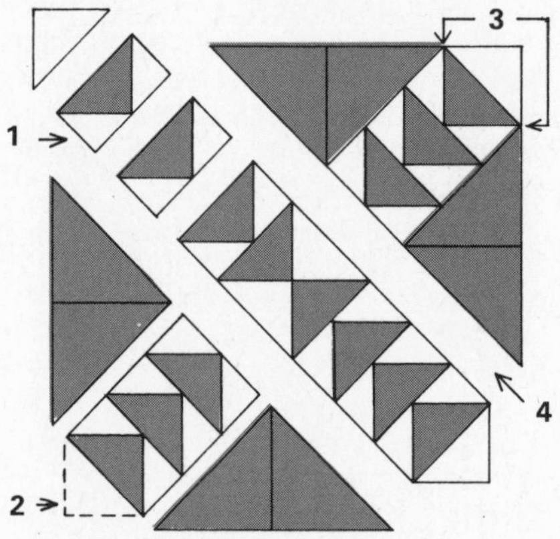

2. Piece rectangles together to make two short strips and one long center strip (these form an X).
3. Stitch large triangles to short center strips.
4. Finally, stitch triangular corners to the long center strip.

The more long seams you can set up, the faster the work will go. Look at Pinwheel, for example (below). It's easier to sew strips; then join the strips together with one long seam.

To keep the work flat and avoid puckering, press each seam open as you go. If you have a lot of seams coming together in one point (as in the center of Morning Star), taper seams to about ⅛″ before you cross them with another seam.

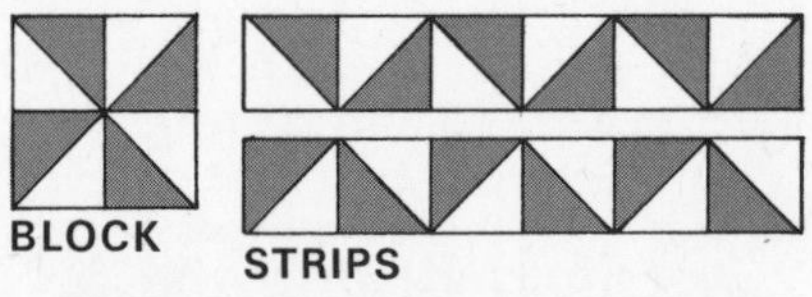

If fabric tends to ravel, finish edges as you go—overcast by hand or machine (stitch, press, trim, finish edges.)

Sewing Clothes

To make the man's vest (sketched) or other garments from patchwork, look for dress patterns with few pieces, straight lines and easy fit—avoid intricate seaming and darts. Piece quilt blocks and lay them on pattern pieces before you join blocks together. Your object: to distribute colors evenly and to match left and right sides at front and back. Shift blocks around until you have the best effect. For professional results, match blocks at seam lines, too —as with plaids.

Double Knit Poncho

Here's how to enlarge the Starry Path block to poncho size:

The pattern divides into four equal segments in both directions (dotted lines). Each one of these squares measures 3″; when joined they make a 12″ block. To make the 40″ poncho, make each square 10″; draw diagonals to correspond to the design. Cut cardboard pattern to match triangle sizes.

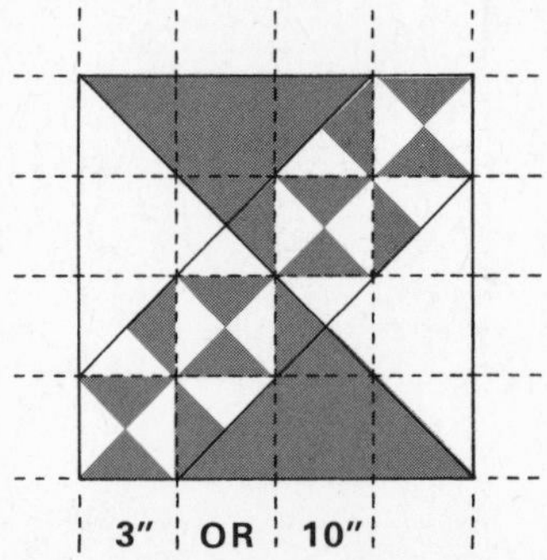

To cut fabric, lay long side of large triangle on straight of goods; cut 2 light and 2 dark. Lay short side of small triangles on straight of goods and cut 14 dark and 14 light (or as you wish—see sketch). Cut fabric ¼″ from pattern line for seam allowance.

Because knit fabrics stretch, stitch them with a slight zigzag. Newer machines have special discs or dials for stretch-stitch sewing. Some machines also stitch and overcast knits in one operation. For this, the seam allowance will be less than ¼″.

Stitch preshrunk woven seam binding around neck opening for stability.

VARIATIONS ON PATCHWORK: Man's vest pieced from several blocks; Optical Illusion design painted on cube table; Starry Path poncho; Twelve Triangles wall hanging; Bow Tie area rug. Blocks below, left to right: Starry Path, Forest Paths and Twenty-four Triangles.

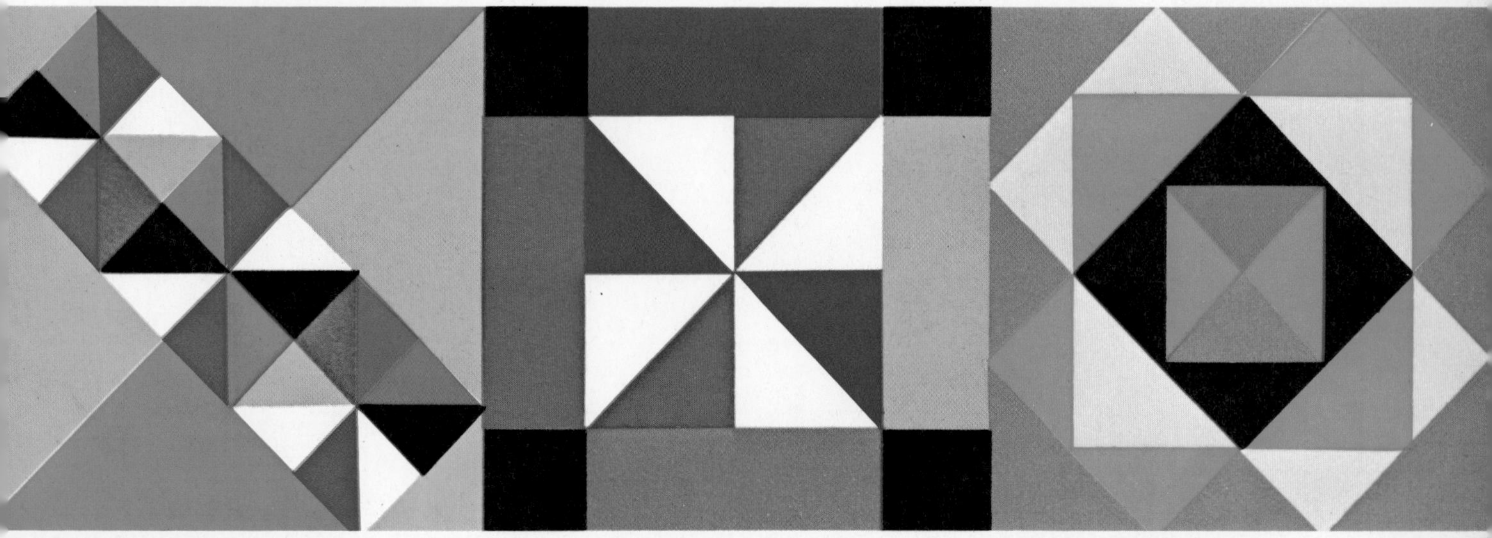

TWELVE TRIANGLES WALL HANGING

Cut pattern pieces as indicated to make a 15″ block; the wall hanging sketched in color on preceding page is 45″square —nine blocks. When you reverse lights and darks in alternate blocks, the repeat design seems to move—an optical illusion. Duplicate pattern in felt, paint, metallic foil or colored paper. If you sew the wall hanging, we recommend lining it. Topstitch the blocks along seam lines onto felt or non-woven interfacing, to give the finished piece "body".

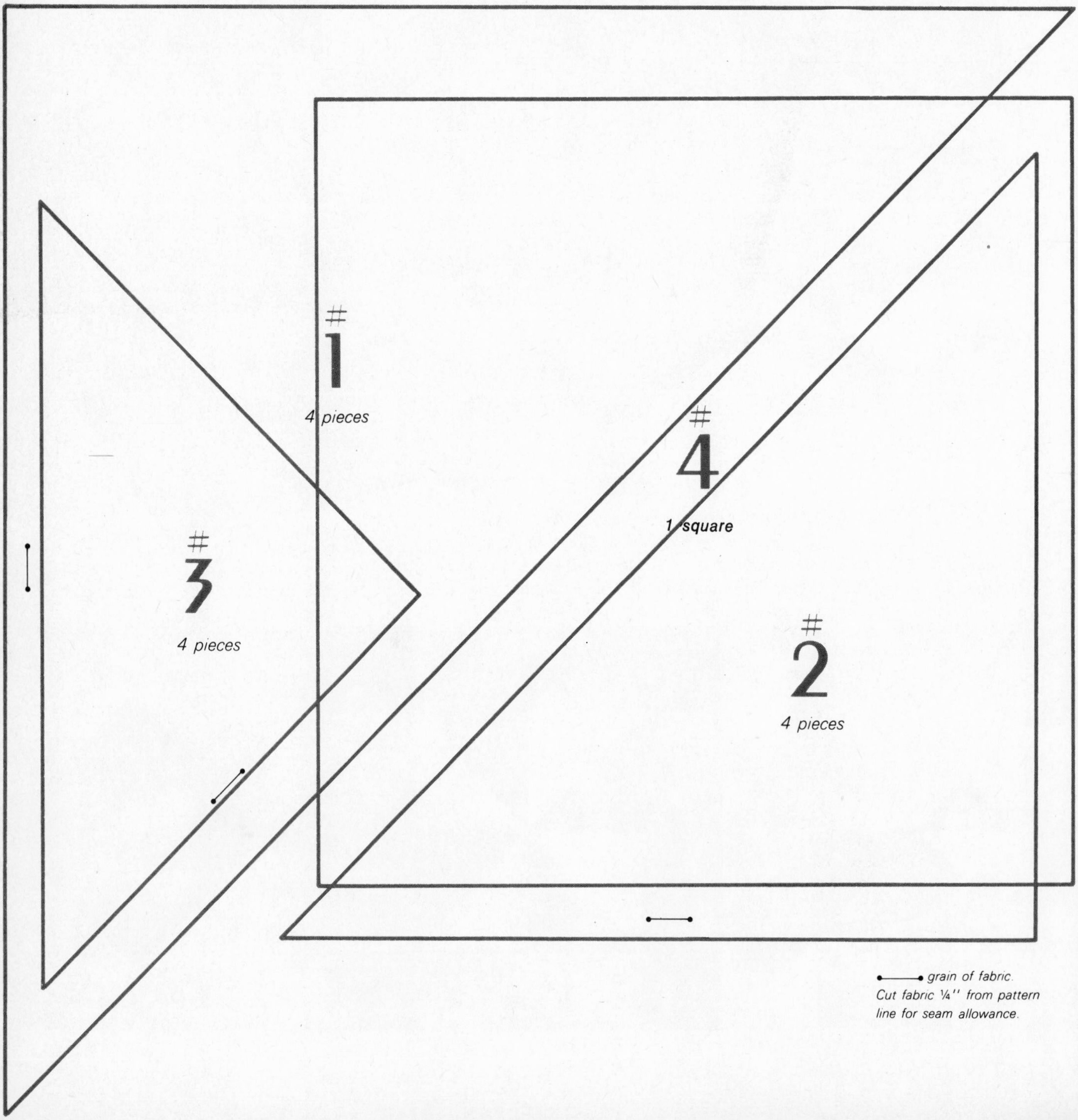

grain of fabric.
Cut fabric ¼″ from pattern line for seam allowance.

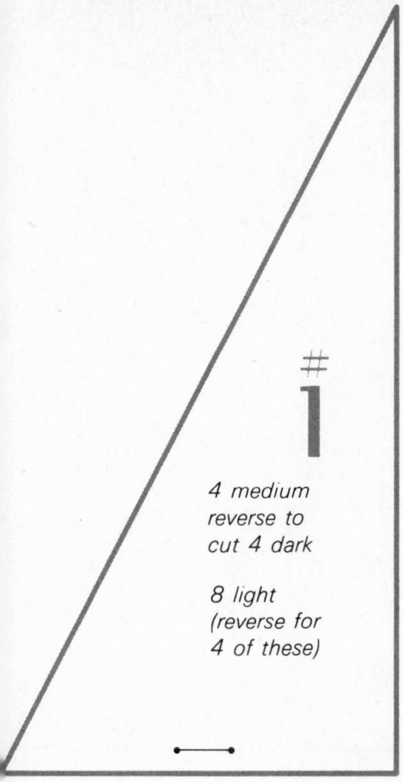

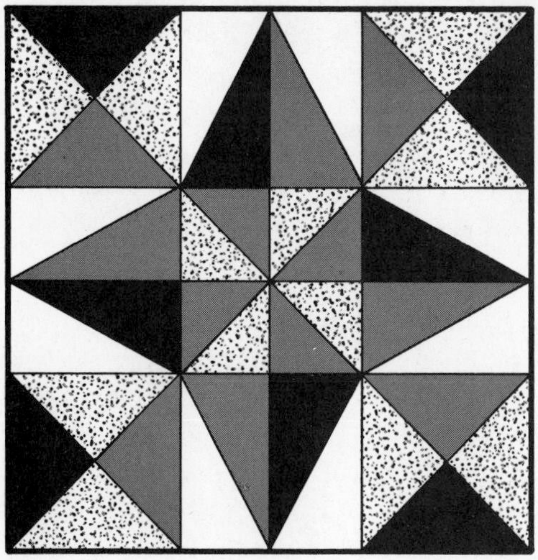

12½" square

OPTICAL ILLUSION CUBE TABLE

Block is 12½" square; enlarge pattern, if necessary, to fit your table (see directions with Poncho). Using ruler and measuring carefully, draw pattern block on each surface of cube. Paint table in four colors, applying one color at a time. Let paint dry before applying next color. Use masking tape to keep lines sharp. Or cut triangles from colored paper, glue to table and protect with several coats of shellac or varnish.

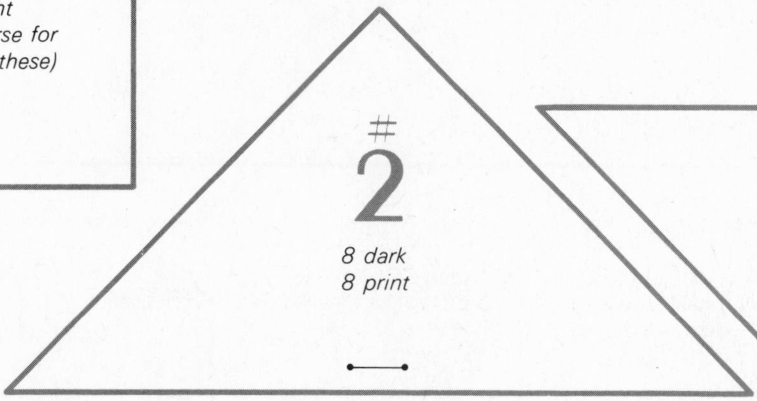

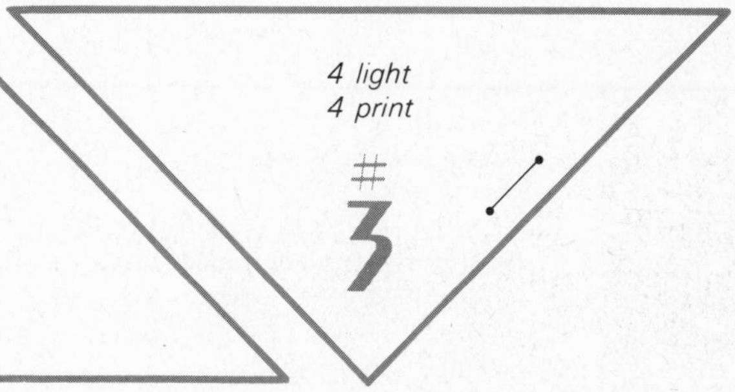

BOW TIE AREA RUG

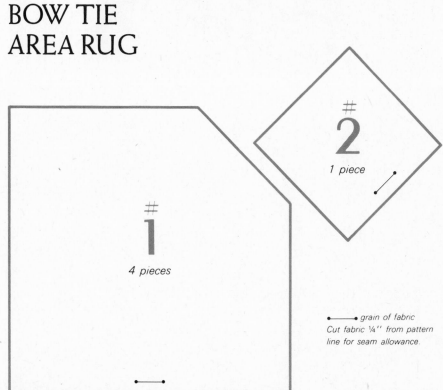

For a 36x48" area rug, double the size of Bow Tie pattern, to make 12" blocks. Collect up to five colors of scrap carpet and cut enough of the pattern pieces to make 12 blocks. Glue carpet to jute burlap backing with white glue.

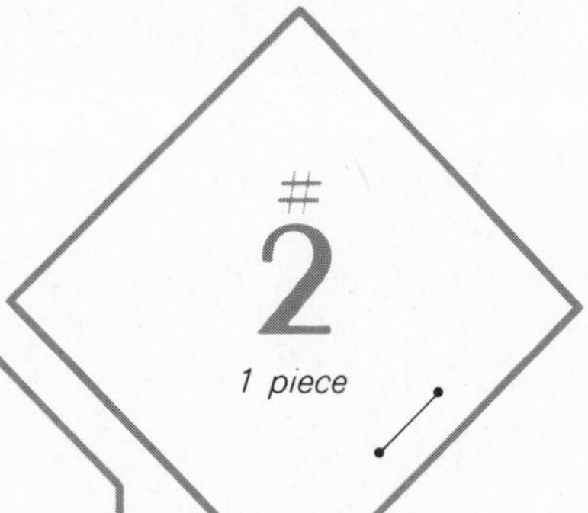

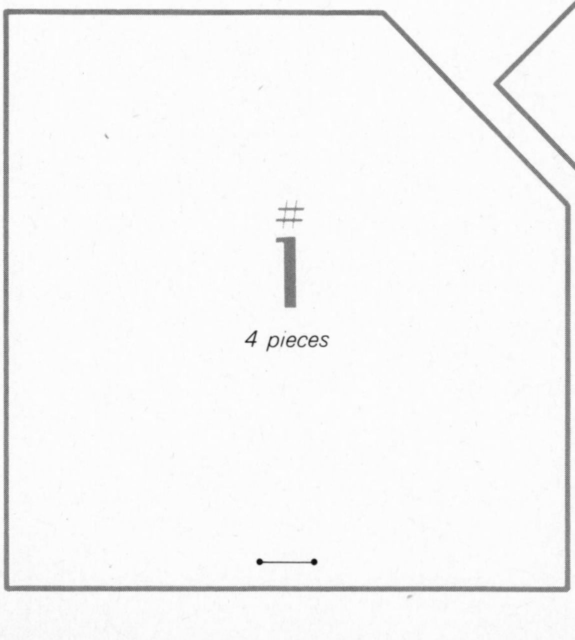

grain of fabric
Cut fabric ¼" from pattern line for seam allowance.

6" square

FRAMED X TOTE

To make tote pictured, you'll need suede cloth in three colors, beige, brown and dark green. For each block (front and back of tote), cut 4 small triangles of beige and 4 brown. Cut 6 large triangles in green and 6 brown. Sew pieced blocks together, adding fringe cut from brown suede at bottom; a brown cuff and shoulder strap at top. Fabric-backed vinyls that look like snakeskin, suede, crushed leather or shiny patent are lightweight and supple, easy to stitch by machine. They're perfect for totes, belts, vests, skirts—even pillows or floor cushions.

How to Sew Vinyls

Vinyl fabrics have no grain to worry about for patchwork. Allow the usual ¼″ seam allowance. Since pinholes show in some vinyl fabrics, use paper clips. Or pin pieces together in the seam allowance. We recommend basting before you machine stitch—ripping out incorrect machine stitching also leaves holes.

After stitching, finger-press the seams open. If the fabric doesn't respond to finger pressing, you can get these seams to "lie down" by topstitching with your machine—zigzag or feather-stitch. Or use a double needle stitch with two different color threads. Put in any hems with handstitching through the knit backing only.

10″ square

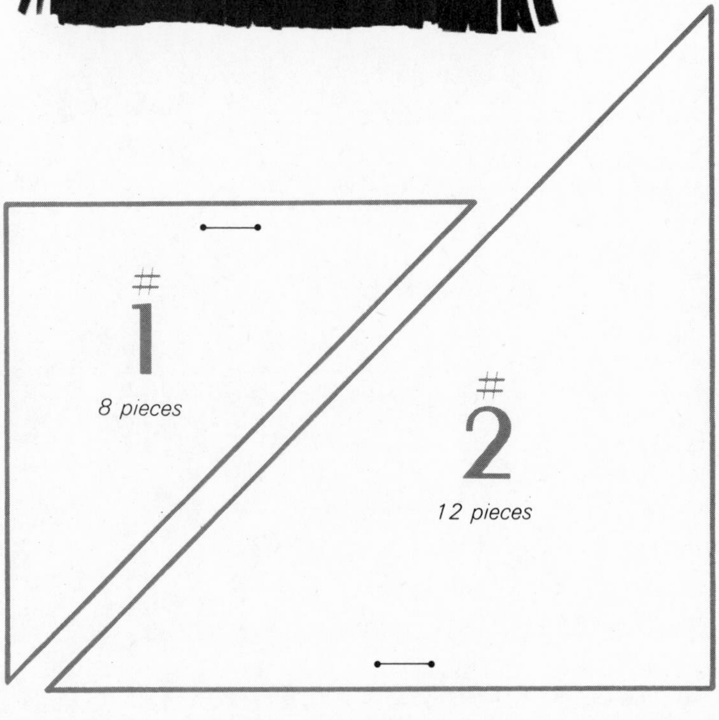

•——• *grain of fabric.*
Cut fabric ¼″ from pattern line for seam allowance.

ROCKY ROAD BABY'S BIB

The Rocky Road quilt block is just the right size for a bib. Sew it in Christmas colors for an eye-catching item at your church bazaar. From pattern #1, cut 3 red, 2 green and 1 white. From pattern #2 cut 1 green and 1 white. Embroider French knots on white piece #1, in shape of Christmas tree, using green floss. Stitch pieces together (see photo). Cut lining from plain white fabric. Stitch lining to bib around neck circle (right sides together); clip, turn and press. Press ¼″ seam allowance all around edges of bib and lining and slip stitch lining to bib. Sew snap at neck closing.

You can enlarge the Rocky Road pattern for other uses, if you wish. Draw the square any size you want; put compass point in one corner and set radius ⅔ the size of the square. Draw the curve.

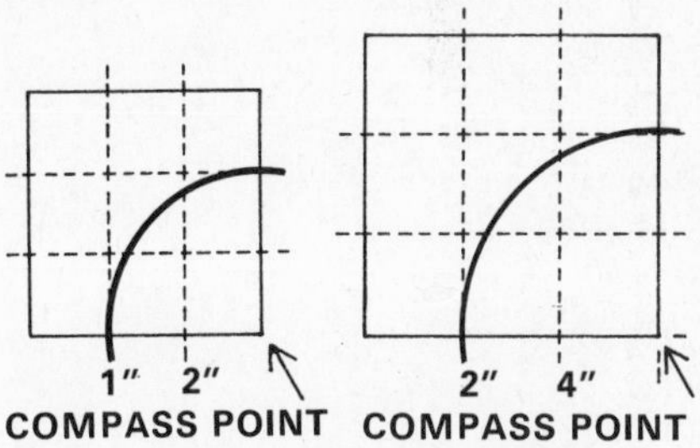

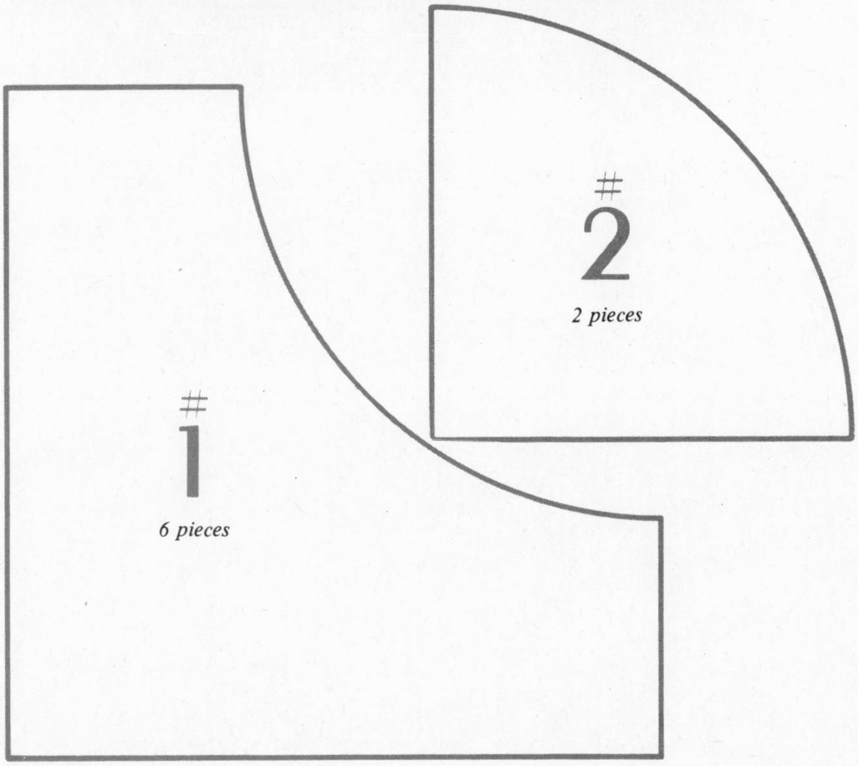

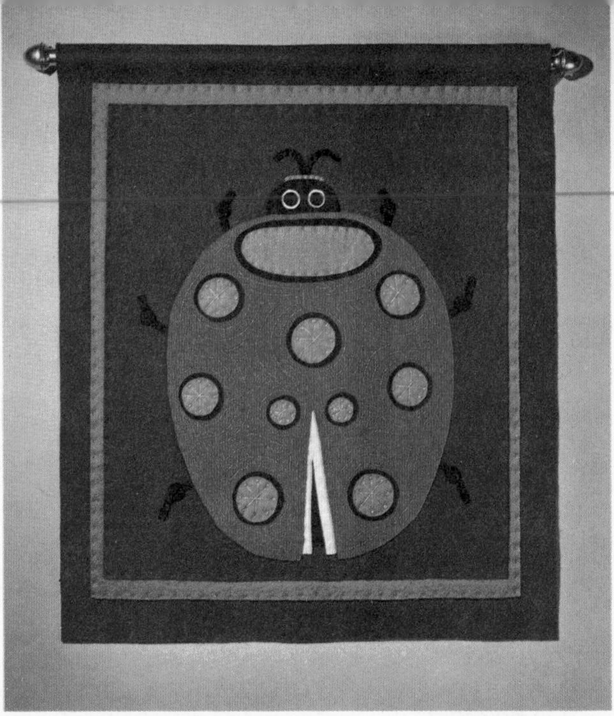

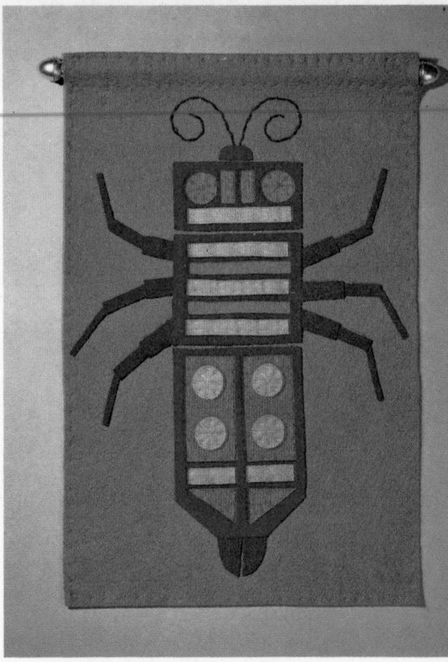

Storybook wall hangings

Every child has a favorite story he wants you to read him at bedtime. Why not choose one of the illustrations he loves, enlarge it to make a wall hanging, and place it over his bed? He'll feel that friendly eyes are keeping watch over him, even when you tiptoe out.

You'll find directions for enlarging patterns in the Appendix; they explain how to convert any art to a different size.

Rapunzel

The princess's golden hair seems almost real: long braids of yellow yarn.

Materials: *Dark green felt panel 21x 18½"; felt scraps in various colors; yellow yarn; red ribbon; brown embroidery floss.*

• Enlarge patterns and cut felt pieces as shown (you can cut castle in two or three pieces–stone embroidery will hide piecing). Arrange pieces on background panel and attach with running stitch. Use embroidery floss and couching stitch to make stone lines on castle.

• For hair, cut six (4′) lengths of yellow yarn; fold in half and tack to front and top of head and at neck. Braid ends into two long braids and tie with ribbons.

Flower Tree

A tree of flower petals is easy to make.

Materials: *Dark green felt panel 22x 14½" plus red, green and brown felt pieces.*

• Cut tree trunk 11" long and 1½" at base; appliqué to felt panel with running stitch. Cut leaves 1 to 1½" long and round centers about ⅜" in diameter. Appliqué leaves in groups of 6, beginning at top of trunk and working toward outside.

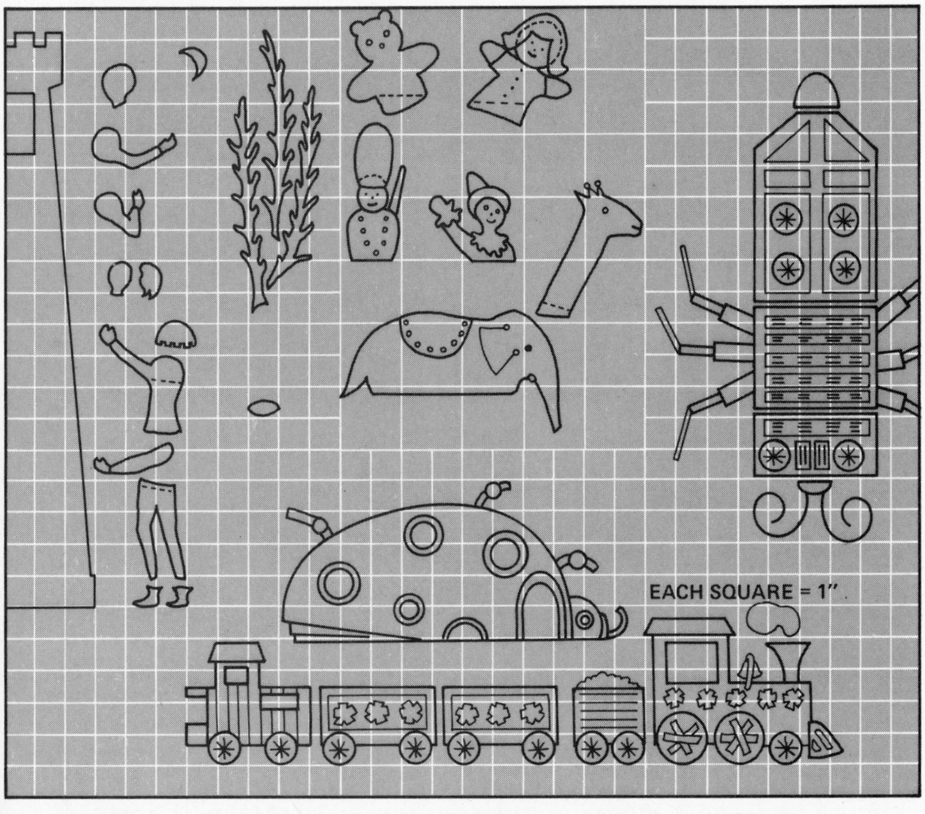

Ladybug

"Ladybug, ladybug, fly away home." You can make your home her home.

Materials: *Two dark green felt panels, 13½x12" and 21x14½"; gold felt 14¾ x12¾"; red felt 8½x12" plus felt scraps and colored threads.*

• Cut ladybug shape 12" long and 8½" wide from red felt; attach to smaller rectangle of green felt with running stitch. Add detail: felt spots, outlined with gold stitch; legs, eyes, antenna.

• Sew green panel to gold panel and then to larger green panel; fold over 1½" hem at top of large green panel; insert curtain rod for hanging (lining not necessary).

Beetle

Look into children's nature books for bugs and beasties—they translate into colorful designs like this.

Materials: *Bright green felt panel 17½ x11½"; felt scraps and threads in various colors; navy embroidery floss.*

• Cut felt rectangles as shown to make beetle 15" from antenna to tail, 4¼" wide. Cut legs in segments to measure about 4" long, plus felt markings. Tack to panel with French knots and running stitch; decorate markings with same simple embroidery. Make antenna from embroidery floss using couching stitch.

Little Engine

"I think I can" puffs the brave little engine, starting down the track.

Materials: *Dark green felt panel 9x24"; felt scraps and threads in various colors; brown and red embroidery floss.*

• Enlarge patterns and cut felt pieces as shown. Attach to background panel with French knots and running stitches. Add details with colored threads: spokes on wheels, French knot spots on giraffe, facial features, trim lines on cars. Hook cars together with red embroidery floss and tack down brown track with couching stitch.

To hang panels:

Cut cotton broadcloth 1" bigger all around than felt; fold ½" under on each side and press. Place on back of felt. Stitch two lines about 1" apart across top—this is for curtain rod hanger. Stitch around remaining three sides. Insert rod.

Dolls for any age

Hundreds of years ago, dolls served less important functions than comforting little girls. Kings and courtiers presented elaborately dressed dolls to each other—that's how the Paris fashion news got around before people had magazines to look at.

By the 17th century, though, play dolls were being scolded and spanked, soothed and rocked to sleep by little mothers everywhere. Boys, too, joined the play with doll families, while real mothers and fathers invented homemade dolls for their children from whatever materials were available: corn husks, dried apples, carved wood, molded paper, leather and—most often—rags.

Lovable rag dolls live on quite comfortably in our mechanized world and enchant youngsters even though they don't actually speak and can only cry pretend tears. And they keep up with fashion changes, too. Just look at the new shapes and patterns we have for you to sew and stuff this year. There's gangly George, demure Annabelle wearing a Granny dress, and a Mother and Baby bright enough to masquerade as a decorative pillow for someone who'll never be too old for dolls.

And for novelty, or for Christmas decorations, make a few of our Clothespin Angels. They're not cuddly, but they're awfully cute, and quite easy to make.

(Turn page for stuffed doll patterns)

Clothespin Angels

Dolls like these will be collector's items if the old-fashioned clothespins disappear.

Materials: *Straight wood clothespins (not spring type); marking pen; cotton cording or pipe cleaners; scraps of fabric and yarn; white glue; needle and thread; ribbons and trimmings; felt for wings (or substitute fabric stiffened with starch or iron-on interfacing).*

- Draw face on clothespin with marking pen—be sure you center face over clothespin "legs". If you ruin a face, try again on back side; cover first face later with hair, or use sandpaper to remove drawing.
- Make arms of cotton cording, pipe cleaners or folded cotton fabric and glue at shoulder line; tack hands together at front. Wrap fabric over upper half of body to make dress top; sew or glue in place. Gather a skirt and sew or glue it on; cover raw edges with a belt of ribbon.
- Enlarge wing patterns; cut 2 wings for each angel from felt or stiffened fabric and sew in place.
- To make hair: Use a very light weight, somewhat fuzzy yarn. Cut several 4" strands to make a swatch; tie at one end and glue to top of doll's head. Let dry. Then wrap yarn around head and glue or stitch in place. Or tie yarn strands in center, glue to head; when dry, pull into pony tail or pigtails (see sketches).

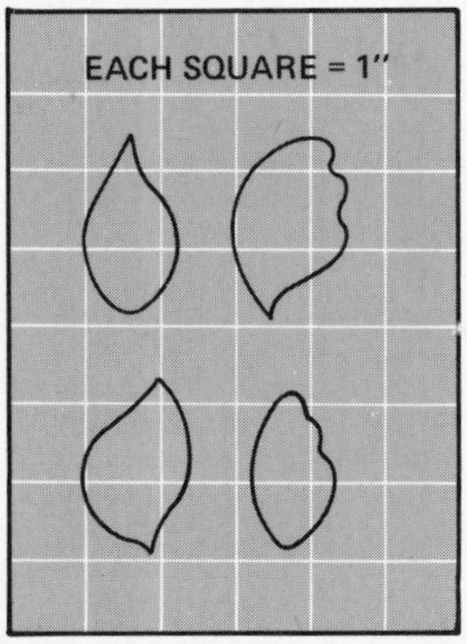

George

Like Humpty-Dumpty, George can perch on a wall dangling his big feet. Somewhere inside he jingles when you pick him up.

Materials: *Red/white striped fabric 11 x20"; deep blue fabric 9x24" (we used heavy duck); heavy pink fabric for face; dark pink for cheeks, light blue for eyes; red for hands; black for shoes; 14" of red-edged white ruffle and white yarn for hat trim; jingle bells; kapok or shredded foam for stuffing.*

• Enlarge patterns (see Appendix). From striped material cut hat (stripes run up and down) and legs (stripes run across). Cut body and arms from blue fabric. Cut face, eyes, cheeks hands and shoes as noted.
• Appliqué eyes and cheeks to face with sewing machine using zigzag stitch. With dark red thread, zigzag mouth from cheek to cheek. Appliqué face to blue front of doll.
• Pin back of doll to front, right sides together, and stitch all around doll except for about 4" at bottom, where you will insert legs. Turn and stuff doll.
• To make legs and feet: Use heavy fabric for shoes, or stiffen shoe top with iron-on interfacing. Embroider gold shoelaces on shoe top, using zigzag stitch on sewing machine (or satin stitch by hand).
• Right sides together, stitch front leg to shoe top and back leg to shoe bottom.
• Right sides together, stitch shoe top and shoe bottom together around toe; trim seam to ⅛".
• Right sides together, sew front leg to back leg. (A)
• Fold excess fabric on shoe bottom to make heel and stitch in a curved line to shape heel. Trim. (B)
• Turn leg and shoe right side out and stuff foot and leg up to knee. Stitch across knee; then stuff rest of leg.
• Place stuffed legs in open seam in doll's body and stitch securely, closing seam, too.
• Stitch hands to arms; then stitch front of hand and arm to back, right sides together. Turn, stuff hand, stitch at wrist line; stuff arm. Fold top edges in and slip-stitch to body.
• Stitch cap, adding ruffle at bottom edge and yarn tassel at point. Sew jingle bells securely to George's head; cover with cap and slip-stitch cap in place.

Mother and Baby

Baby nestles in a pocket sewn to Mother doll.

Materials: *½yd. bright print fabric; pink fabric for faces; yarn for hair; embroidery thread for features; kapok or shredded foam for stuffing.*

• Enlarge patterns (see Appendix); add ¼" seam allowance but add ½" to face outlines. Cut both dolls and pocket from print fabric; cut faces, baby's hands and feet from pink fabric. Embroider features on faces and tack yarn hair in place, using couching stitch.
• Lay face pattern on front of mother doll and trace around it. Cut hole for face ¼" inside tracing line; place embroidered face underneath hole. Clip edge as necessary to turn under ¼" hem and blind stitch print fabric to face.
• Stitch the two pocket pieces together along the curved top, right sides to-

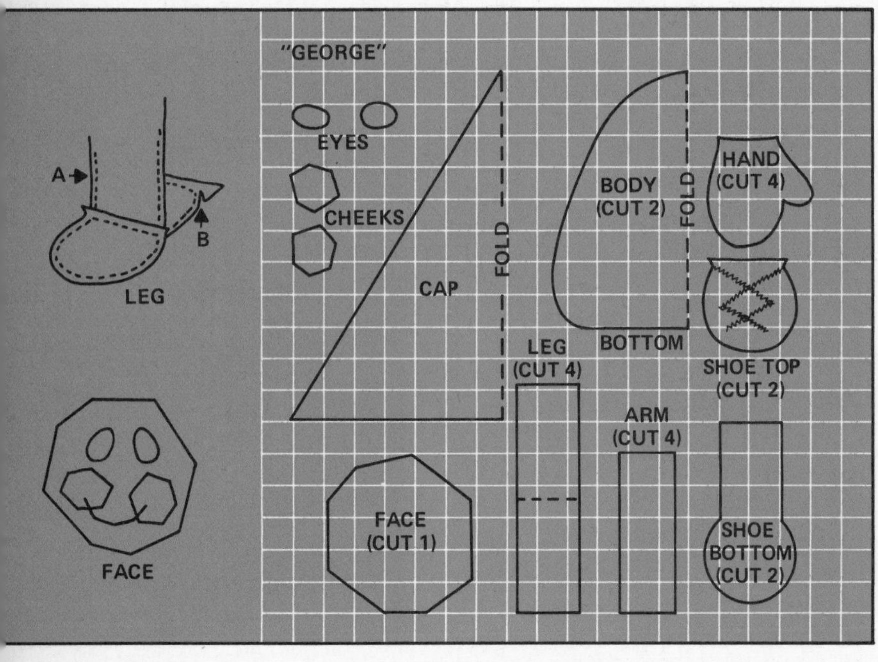

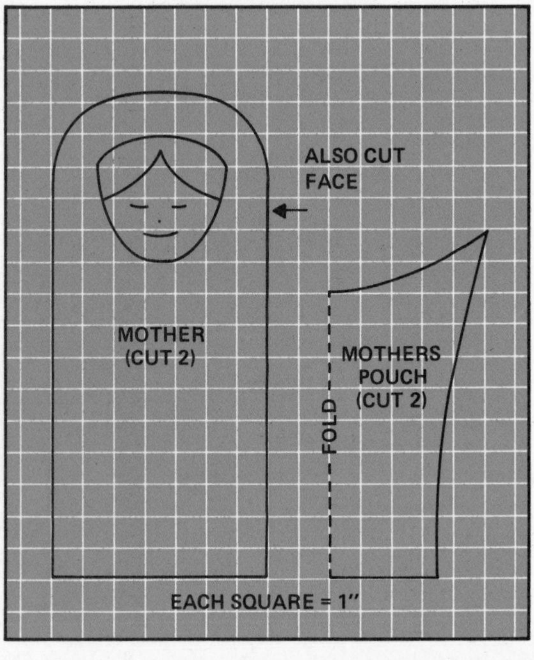

gether. Turn, clip and press.

• Pin pocket to front (right side) of mother doll; pull excess pocket fabric to the center and pin it flat to keep it out of the way while you stitch doll together. Lay back of mother doll on top of front, right sides facing. Stitch all around doll except for 3" opening at top, for stuffing. Turn and stuff doll. Slip-stitch to close opening.

• Cut hole for face in front of baby doll and sew face into print fabric, same as mother.

• Stitch baby's hands and feet, leaving opening at wrists and ankles for stuffing. Turn and stuff.

• Pin hands and feet to right side of front of baby, pointing in (see sketch); lay back of doll over front, right sides together. Stitch all around doll except for 3" at side for stuffing. Turn and stuff. Slip-stitch to close opening.

Annabelle

Demure Annabelle has a cluster of ringlets at the back of her head.

Materials: *Orange fabric 12x28"; print fabric 6x28"; eyelet ruffle 24"; lace for trim; embroidery thread; yarn for hair; drinking straws; white glue; narrow ribbon; kapok or shredded foam for stuffing.*

• Enlarge patterns (see Appendix). Cut 6 body pieces, 4 head pieces and 4 hands from orange fabric; cut 6 bodice pieces, 4 arms and a skirt 24x6" from print fabric.

• Stitch body pieces together, leaving 2" of last seam open. Turn and stuff. Slip-stitch to close opening.

• Stitch bodice pieces together except for last seam. Pull bodice around body and slip-stitch final seam at center back.

• Sew ruffle to edge of skirt; join back seam. Gather skirt around waist and fit to doll. With skirt pulled up over top of body, hand stitch skirt to bodice and body (when skirt is pulled down, seam will be inside).

• Stitch hands; turn and stuff. Stitch lace trim across bottom (small end) of sleeves. Right sides together, stitch sleeve seam to form tube; turn. Tuck hand into end of tube and stitch, closing seam. Stuff arm lightly. Fold top edge of sleeve in and slip-stitch arms to body at shoulder line. Tack hands together at front.

• To make head: Embroider face with embroidery floss. Stitch ends of long piece (side of head) together to make a ring. Fit face into face side of ring and stitch. Stitch 2 pieces for back of head together and fit them into other side of ring, leaving 2" open at bottom. Turn; stuff head; slip-stitch to close opening.

• Embroider yarn hair smoothly to stuffed head, following seam line across forehead and around ears (stitching should outline "ears"); and downward in a graceful curve to base of neck. Sew loops of yarn to form bangs. Use long stitches to the center of back of head to make a smooth hairdo. Make ringlets separately—cut drinking straws about 2" long, coat with white glue and wrap with yarn. When dry, sew curls to back of head, starting with bottom curls and working up. Tie ribbon around curls.

• Sew head to top of body. Hide seam with collar of lace. Tack pinafore straps over shoulders and into a V in the back. Cover edges and waist seam with ribbon belt.

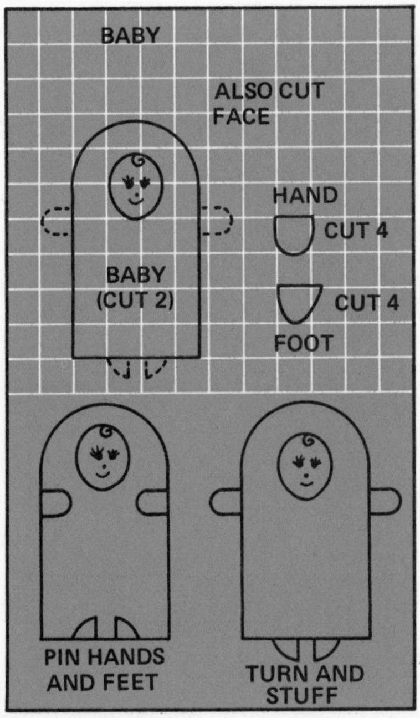

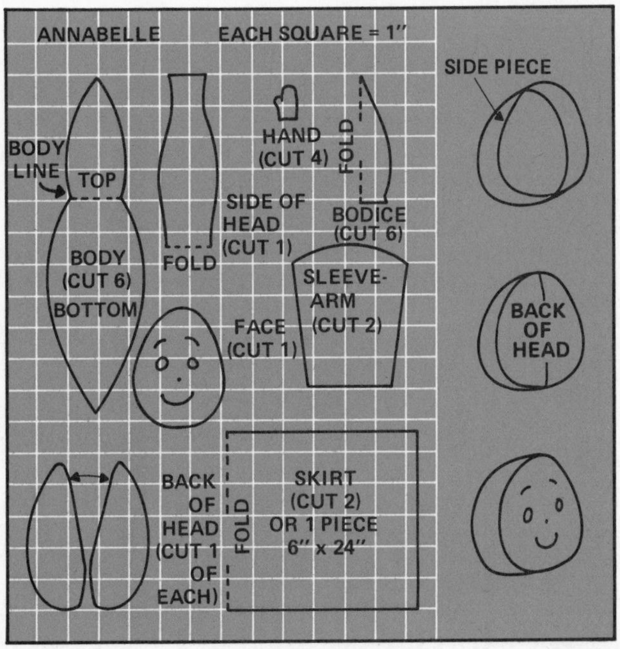

1

Holiday slick tricks

Before children play with new games they receive for Christmas, tape directions inside the lid.

Use a tray under your holiday centerpiece—easy to move when you want to change tablecloths or freshen the arrangement.

Empty egg cartons make excellent storage boxes for your small Christmas tree ornaments.

2

3

4

5

Make a Christmas switchplate for your child's room. Select the front from one of last year's cards and cut a hole to fit the switch. Secure with masking tape.

Attach hand grips to both ends of a sturdy box that will fit in your car trunk. Fill the box as you shop; everything can be carried into the house at once.

When you take down your Christmas tree, wrap it in an old sheet and carry outside. You'll spend much less time cleaning up needles.

Save plastic dry cleaning bags for packing things to be mailed. They are lightweight, space-filling and hold items in place.

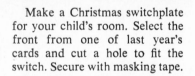

6

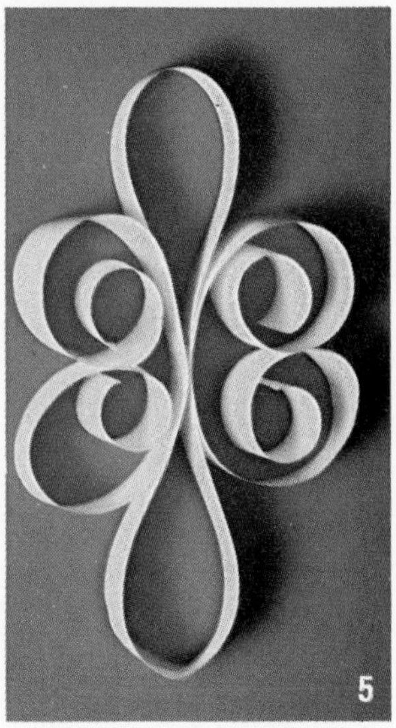
5

Put your heart into these handmades

Christmas presents that you make yourself carry with them a special message of caring and thoughtfulness. Make any one of these to give as tree trims or as a decoration for around the house. Young and old will love them.

1. Tortoiseshell Basket

Use a propane torch to get darkened effect on wicker or reed baskets—avoid holding flame close to surface for any length of time. Then shellac basket for a glossy, protective finish. Fill with fresh or dried posies—a colorful thought for a shut-in.

2. Angel

Materials: *Pellon, metallic gold thread and cord, felt, large wood bead, tiny pearl beads, lightweight paper-backed gold foil, white glue, food coloring, pipe cleaner, fine wire.*

To make dress: Cut a 12x12″ piece of Pellon. Mix food coloring with 1 cup water. To test color strength, dip Pellon scraps in dye; hang to dry. Add more color if needed; dye 12″ square. Cut a 9″ diameter foil circle; fold in half and glue paper sides together. Apply glue along foil edge and center Pellon in place; trim Pellon. When dry, form into cone shape and glue edge to hold shape. Use a fine needle and gold thread to create running stitch design on Pellon. Glue or sew on pearl beads; glue on felt or sequin trims.

To make head: Wrap and glue gold cord around wood bead for hair; tie in back George Washington style. Push bead on knotted pipe cleaner you insert in cone. For a halo, string pearl beads on fine wire; glue on top of hair. Cut and glue on foil wings. Paint face. Tie on a cord for hanging.

3. Wise Men

Cut and glue felt to fit around cardboard tube about 4″ high; glue on decorative trims. For the head, paint a ping-pong ball white. When dry, paint facial features.

To attach head: Cut and glue a cardboard ring across top of tube (head rests on inner edge – glue to hold in place); or glue head on felt you drape across tube as part of a cape. Drape a felt square, rectangle or triangle over head to make the cape. Push straight pins through felt and tube to hold cape in place.

To make felt inner crown: Fold felt around a ball of paper and secure with a rubber band, or cup a small square of felt around paper and glue on cape top. Cut and glue gold metallic cardboard to fit around felt inner crown; glue on sequin jewels.

4. Stained-glass Snowflakes

For each snowflake, cut two equal size circles from medium-weight gold metallic cardboard. Sketch your design on tracing tissue with a pencil. To transfer sketch onto circles, center tracing tissue over one circle—retrace design outline; repeat for other circle. Use a sharp X-acto knife to cut out design. Place colored tissue paper between circles and rotate so design outlines do not match—this makes another pattern. Place a fine string or thread loop between circles for hanging and glue circles together. Add extra color with felt or paper dots.

5. Sculptured Paper Curls

Cut 1″ wide strips of medium-weight (smooth) paper in varying lengths up to 12″. Use the sharp edge of your scissors to curl the paper in different directions. Glue loops and curls together. Thread cord with knotted end through one end of curl to hang from tree. Leave white or color with spray paint.

6. Wreath of Hearts and Bows

Cut and glue pink and magenta felt hearts (about ¼″ apart) on ring you cut from cardboard. Glue pink yarn border around each heart; glue small yarn loops between hearts to make bows. Cut magenta felt berries with paper punch; glue on yard loops.

For wreath of leaves and heart: Cut a ring and heart shape of cardboard. Cut and glue white felt to fit both sides of ring; cover the heart the same way with magenta felt. Cut leaves and berries from felt and glue in place; add magenta sequins for sparkle. Glue on green yarn border.

Slick Tricks

Stack spools of Christmas ribbon in an oatmeal box. Cut a slit in the box for each spool; tape ribbon ends to the outside. You have a dispenser—and all the ribbons are in one place.

Decorate a shopping bag for each member of the family. Letter a name on each. Collecting gifts in bags will help keep order around the Christmas tree.

Plaques, sconces and weed holders

This is a great modeling project for kids. You use a sculpture material which dries rock-hard in minutes, doesn't need firing, can be painted and is easy to clean up after (den mothers, take note). Called Pariscraft, the material comes in rolls like surgical gauze, 3″ wide; the gauze is impregnated with plaster of Paris. To use, simply cut off the length you need, dip in water and apply to your base form. You can make these plaques with paper-maché strips, but we think you'll like the weight and the real plaster/ceramic look you get with this new art material, available in craft and hobby stores.

Materials: *Heavy cardboard (heavy weight chipboard at art supply houses is the heaviest and least expensive; you may use corrugated cardboard); Pariscraft art material (or substitute strips of paper dipped in wheat paste or white glue mixed half and half with water); gesso (a painting base available at art stores); paint (for lasting craft work, we find acrylic polymer paints the most satisfactory; tempera paints may be used); polymer medium (optional); antiquing foam glaze (optional); spray-on glaze, shellac or varnish; plus incidental supplies needed for individual plaques, as described.*

General Directions

• Cut cardboard to size you want for plaque design. Cover it on both sides with Pariscraft, to minimize warping. Rub the fabric with your finger to smooth it, or leave it be if you want a textured weave. Apply flower or weed holders as described for individual plaques. Decorate, as you wish, with braids, lace or cutouts glued on with white glue—cutouts may be cardboard or cut from egg cartons. When dry, coat entire plaque with gesso; if you want a very smooth surface, sand, coat again with gesso and sand again.

• Paint, antique and varnish plaque as you wish. Cut felt to cover back. To hang plaque: Sew the eye half of a dressmaker's hook-and-eye at one end of felt and glue felt to back.

Butterfly Plaque

• Cut cardboard 4x15″. Cut out a 3″ section in a frozen orange juice can; fold cut edges forward, trim metal bottom of can and staple the resulting half-can to the cardboard.

• Cover can and cardboard with Pariscraft strips. Trim can with cotton braid. Paint and antique plaque.

• Apply butterflies this way: Brush some polymer medium on the plaque where you want the butterfly. Immediately lay butterfly in place and press firmly with a pad of facial tissue. Use a soft artist's paint brush to apply a coat of polymer over the butterfly, brushing gently from body to edge of wing. When dry, give butterflies another coat of polymer. You could also decorate plaque with butterflies cut from gift wrap or cards, glued on with white glue.

• Fill holder with dried starflowers.

Weed Holders

• Cut cardboard about 7″ long and 3-3½″ wide and coat on both sides with Pariscraft. Cut drinking straws or wire spirals from a stenographer's notebook to lengths desired; wrap with strips of Pariscraft and press to coated plaque. Apply more Pariscraft, as needed, to secure the flower holders. When dry, coat with gesso, paint and fill with interestingly shaped weeds.

Candle Sconce

Make candleholder from chipboard 4x 15″ and the top or bottom of a soup can. Cut a slit near bottom edge of chipboard, push can lid through just far enough to bend and tape to back of chipboard. Cover can lid and both sides of plaque with Pariscraft.

• Cut a strip of thin cardboard 1″ wide and coil to make a holder for candle; glue to can lid and secure with more Pariscraft.

• To make lattice design, cut strips of thin cardboard and interlace, gluing strips where they overlap. Glue lattice to plaque. Coat plaque with gesso; let dry. Paint and antique if desired.

• To reflect candlelight, glue giant silver sequins in spaces between lattice with clear silicone glue (available at hardware stores).

Pennsylvania Dutch Plaque

The "window box" is a half-pint cream carton. Cut cardboard for plaque 4½x 8″ and trim top to make arch. Cut top from cream carton and cut carton in half; glue to cardboard and coat carton and plaque on both sides with Pariscraft.

• Sketch design on plaque; cut out bird, flower and leaf shapes from pressed-pulp egg cartons and apply with white glue. Stems are string, glued to design.

• Coat entire plaque with gesso. Paint, antique, fill box with strawflowers.

Rough Plaster Plaque

Cover a 3½x7¼″ cardboard on both sides with Pariscraft. Mold pouch for flowers from a double strip of Pariscraft about 6″ long. Press it tightly to plaque at sides and bottom and use your fingers to shape pouch—it dries in minutes.

• Cut long strips of Pariscraft about ¾″ wide, dip in water and apply to surface of plaque and pouch in a scrunched-up design.

• When dry, paint plaque and pouch with gesso. To get two-tone stone color, paint entire surface with a mixture of raw umber and white acrylic paint; then add more white to the mixture and brush over the raised parts of plaster to give it a frosty look.

Rough Plaster Vase

Find a cardboard tube big enough to hide an olive bottle. Cut a cardboard circle for base, and glue tube to base. Cover with Pariscraft, following directions for Rough Plaster Plaque to get the rough ceramic look.

• Coat with gesso. Paint first with a mixture of burnt sienna, burnt umber and white; then add more white to mixture and brush raised parts of plaster.

Clear plastic bird feeder

...shelters the birds

...lets you watch

Give the family a clear view of all the birds who come to feed this winter. You attach the back of the feeder to your house so that it stands up in front of the window. Birds enter through holes drilled in the front of the feeder. The hinged top protects food from weather and squirrels—also makes it easy for you to refill. For what to feed, see suggestions at end of food section in this book.

If you've never worked with acrylic plastic sheet, you'll find it both easy and interesting. You can cut it with standard power tools or by hand, drill it and cement it with solvent to produce strong transparent joints. For specific directions, see Appendix.

We have these additional suggestions: Handle the plastic as little as possible; it scratches easily. In fact, it's a good idea to keep the protective masking paper on the pieces you're working with as long as you can. You can sand and buff edges before removing paper.

What gives a plastic construction "class" is a clear, transparent edge. This takes patience and experimentation, but the effect is worth it. After sawing, rough sand edges—you can even hold pieces against a belt sander. A file does a good job of smoothing out rough saw marks or nicks. Finish sand with a fine grade of emery paper used wet. Then use a muslin buffing wheel with buffing

compound to get the clear edge. Buffing wheel can be used on lathe chuck or electric drill. Be sure to use *white* buffing compound (the colored grit is difficult to remove from plastic).

Materials: *Plexiglass, ¼" thick, 20x 24"; two ¾" brass hinges; ¼" wood dowel; solvent cement; screws.*

- Cut plastic pieces as shown in pattern. Finish edges.
- Drill holes in front panel, 1⅜" in diameter, for birds to go through. Drill holes ¼" in diameter, ⅝" below larger holes; insert wood or plastic dowels 3" long, to make perches for birds.
- Bevel the top edge of the back to line up with the slope of the sides.
- With solvent, cement sides to back; front to sides; and bottom to sides, front and back.
- Hinge top to top of back. Screw lower edge of back to house or window sill.

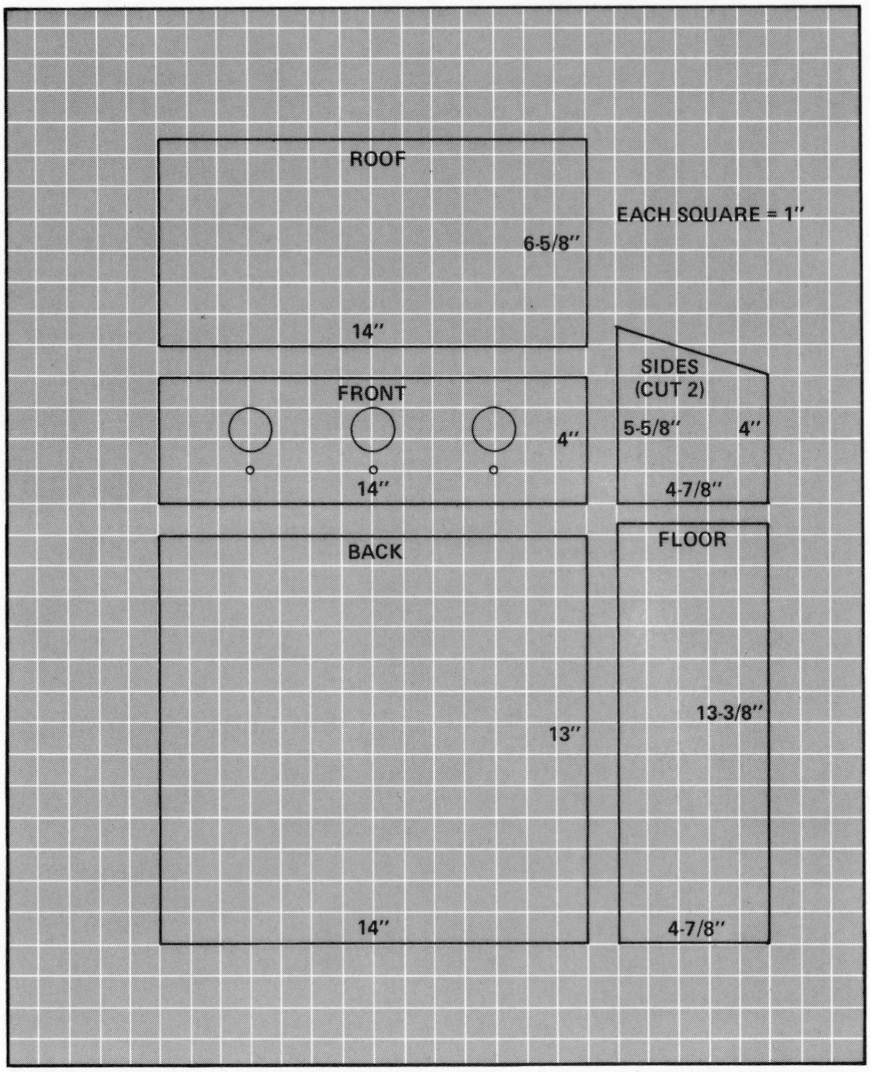

Clocks and desk accessories

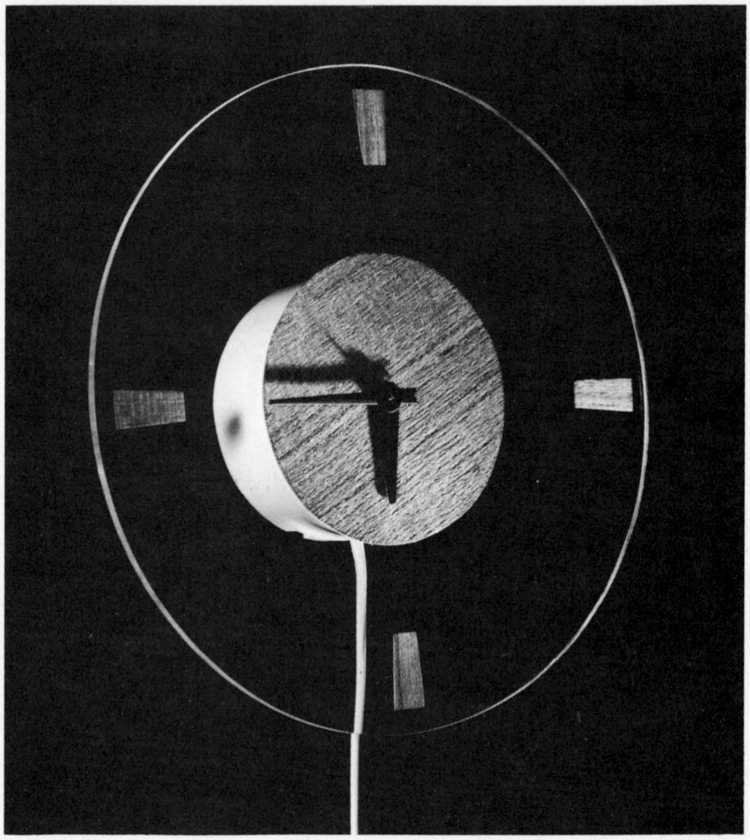

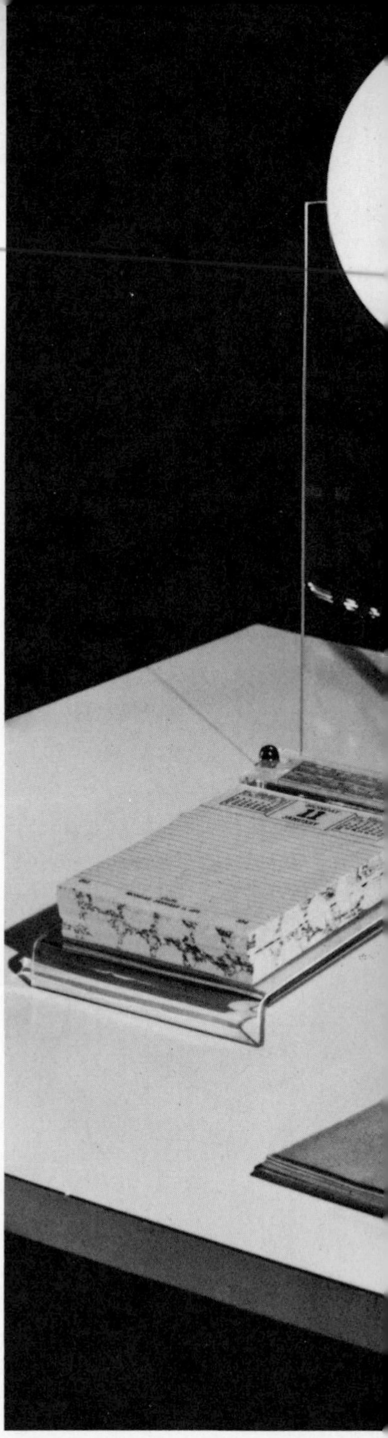

The desk top is covered with gift ideas for you to make in plexiglass—all easy to do. There's an elegant base for a globe light, a wood-and-plastic book rack and pencil caddy, a desk clock and calendar. Close-up pictures and directions are in the Appendix, where you'll also find information on working with plexiglass; directions for electric clocks follow:

Wall Clock

Materials: *Clear plexiglass 1/4" thick, 9" square; clock works (look for an inexpensive wall clock with a plastic case in back to house works); wood veneer; household cement.*

- Cut plastic to a 9" circle; polish edges carefully.
- Drill a hole in center of plastic to take stem for clock hands.
- Cut a circle of wood veneer large enough to hide clockworks; glue to face of plastic. Drill stem hole in it, too.
- Glue clock works to back of plastic, behind wood veneer, with household cement.
- Paint hands desired color and re-

place. Cut small pieces of wood veneer to mark numerals on clock face and glue them in place.

• Clock will look best if you can use a recessed wall outlet so cord is hidden, or use battery-operated works.

Desk Clock

Materials: *Black plastic ⅛" thick, cut 2 pieces 5½x6"; white plastic ⅛" thick, cut 1 piece 5x5" and 3 pieces 5x4¾"; black plastic tape; small alarm clock; solvent cement; household cement.*

• Polish edges of black plastic only.

• Remove case from clock. Drill hole in center of 5x5" white plastic to take stem for clock hands. Glue works to this piece which is face of clock.

• Drill one of the remaining white pieces with holes for clock setting and alarm buttons; cut a groove at the bottom for cord. Set aside.

• With solvent cement, attach remaining two white pieces to back of face flush with sides; this makes a 3-sided "box" around clock works.

• The black pieces are top and bottom of clock. Center one open side of works "box" on one black piece and solvent cement in place with solvent; then cement the other black piece on the other side.

• Push the back piece into the box as far as you can to cover clockworks, letting cord and buttons come through previously drilled holes. Cement in place with solvent.

• Cut very thin strips of black tape and apply to face at 3, 6, 9 and 12 positions.

• Spray paint hands black and alarm set indicator red. When dry, place on clock stem.

Plastic ornaments and jewelry

The possibilities in plastic intrigue artists and designers. You can paint on it, or appliqué pressure sensitive papers, tapes, cloth or plastics to make designs. You can scribe or texture it—on both sides, for dimensional effect. Try one of these easy beginner projects; also see Christmas Tree in Appendix. You'll be proud to give whatever you make in plastic.

Seascape

Three-panel plastic picture looks like an aquarium with waving seaweed.

Materials: *3 pieces ¼" plexiglass cut 5½x6½", 4¼x7¼" and 5½x8⅝"; tiny shells; colored glass; sand; fabric scraps; spray adhesive; wood 2¼x11x¾".*

- Polish edges of plastic.
- Enlarge pattern designs on white paper; peel masking paper off plastic and lay over designs; hold in place with masking tape. With a sharp-pointed instrument, trace on plastic the outlines of seaweed to be etched (outlined leaves in diagram). Cut masking tape to fit around leaves and etch them by rubbing with sandpaper or steel wool.
- Cut fabric leaves (solid black leaves in diagram) and glue in place.
- Spread glue along bottom and pour sand over; shake off excess.
- Glue shells in place, along with bits of colored glass arranged in fish shape.
- Sand wood base. Cut 3 grooves, ¼" with ¼" between each groove; first groove should be set back ⅝" from front edge.
- Insert plastic panels in grooves.

Mobile

Scraps of clear and colored plastic make a striking wind chime or mobile.

Materials: *Scraps of plexiglass; ¾" walnut, about 5x8" for hanger; clear nylon fishing line.*

- Polish edges of plastic scraps. Drill a hole at the top of each piece.
- Shape and sand a wood hanger (enlarge our pattern or design your own). Drill it with tiny holes here and there. Thread nylon fishing line through holes and tie on plastic pieces at varying levels.

Necklaces

Plastic makes a sparkling pendant.

Materials: *Scraps of colored plastic (black, red and white, or your choice); wire necklace, brass links, black ribbon.*

- Enlarge patterns. To make tiered pendant cut three pieces of black plastic. Finish edges, drill with tiny holes, attach to wire necklace with brass links.
- Cut other pendant pieces from red and white plastic. Finish edges, drill with tiny holes. Hang white center inside red piece with brass links. Make a wire link for top and put it on ribbon.

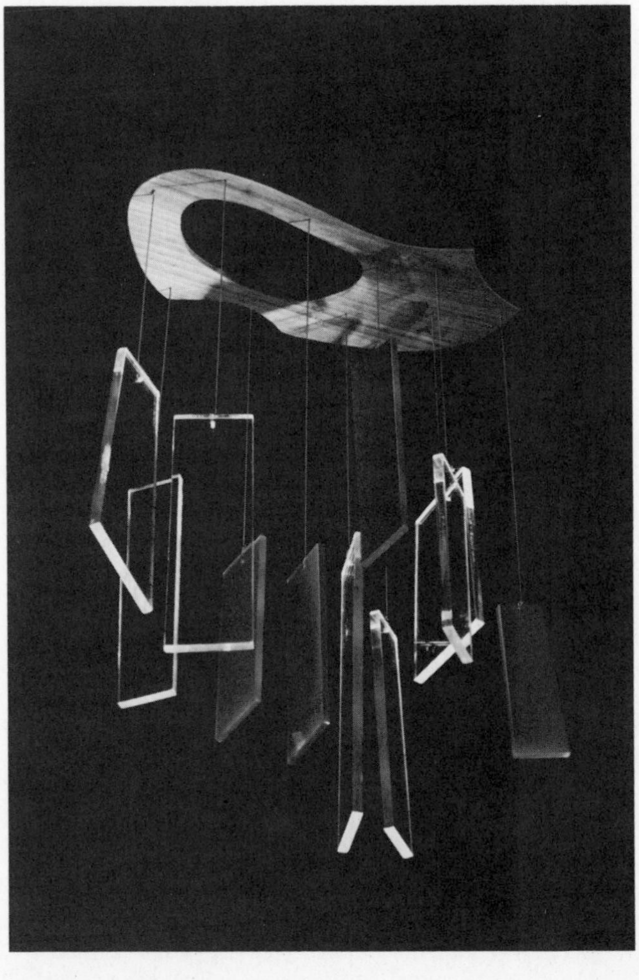

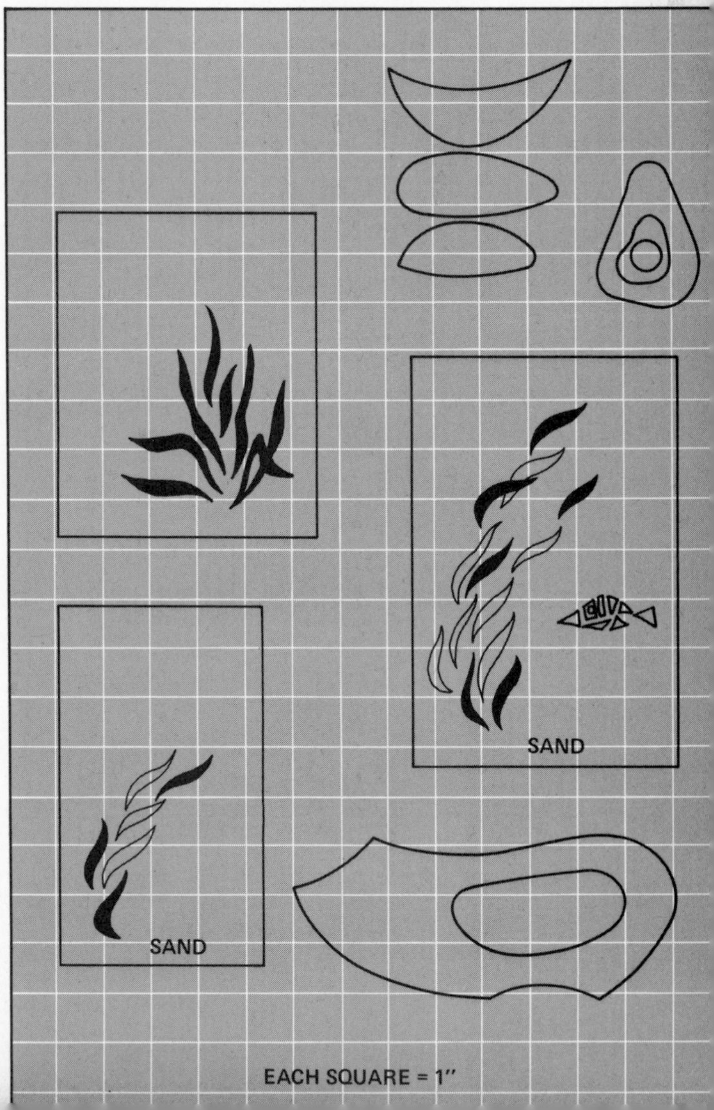

GIFTS TO DECORATE WITH
seeds and spices

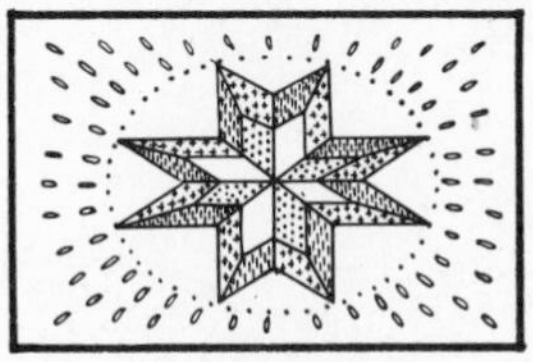

Your own garden and kitchen cabinets hold the materials for seed art.

• For large pictures and tray, use tempered masonite (it will not warp); use plywood for small pictures.

• Apply seeds with a white glue. To cover an area solidly with seeds, spread glue thickly within area; sprinkle seeds over glue and press firmly in place. To place seeds separately, use tweezers and dip seeds in glue.

• Spray with clear plastic.

Note: To kill any insects in grain, bake 10 minutes in preheated 140° oven.

Seashell Tray: Paint 20x15″ masonite a medium green. Glue on seeds: Large shell–solid poppy and chive in alternating bands, outlined with whole black peppercorns. Snail shell – solid white and brown rice outlined in turnip and radish seeds. Scallop shell–solid sesame seed outlined with barley. Starfish – solid mustard seed with arms of black peppercorns. Coral – solid barley and solid mustard seed. Dots–lentils.

Corn Shocks Picture: On 10½x12½″ masonite, paint sky coral; field, white; corn shocks, yellow; sun, white with red center.

Glue on seeds: Ring around sun–mustard seed. Sun–rice. Tassels–anise and caraway. Ties–poppy seed. Shocks –sesame. Field–rice and popcorn.

Flower Arrangement: Paint masonite medium blue with dark blue bowl.

Glue on seeds: Large leaves–split peas around black peppercorns, lentil stems. Medium leaves–Kentucky wonder beans on sesame seed stems, sunflower seed at tips. Ferns – caraway stems, leaves of cloves. Large flower–whole ginger with center of whole allspice. Medium flower–petals of baby lima beans dotted with turnip seed, centers of poppy seed. Tiny flower–rice petals, mustard seed center.

Recipe Box: Spray-paint metal recipe box yellow. Glue solid areas of turnip, celery and poppy seeds in star pattern; turnip seed and rice around star.

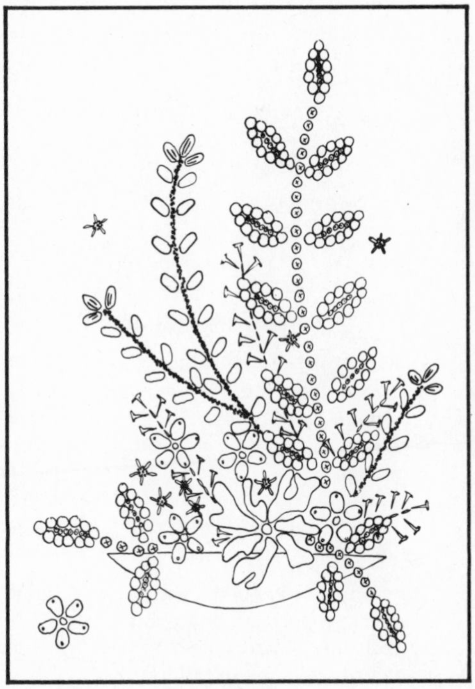

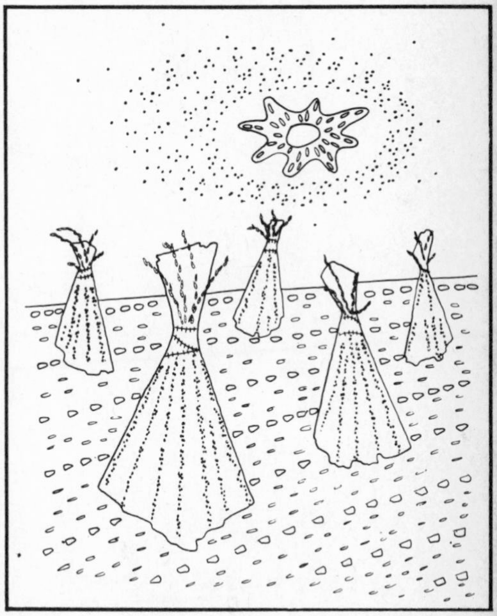

Patterns are ¼ actual size.

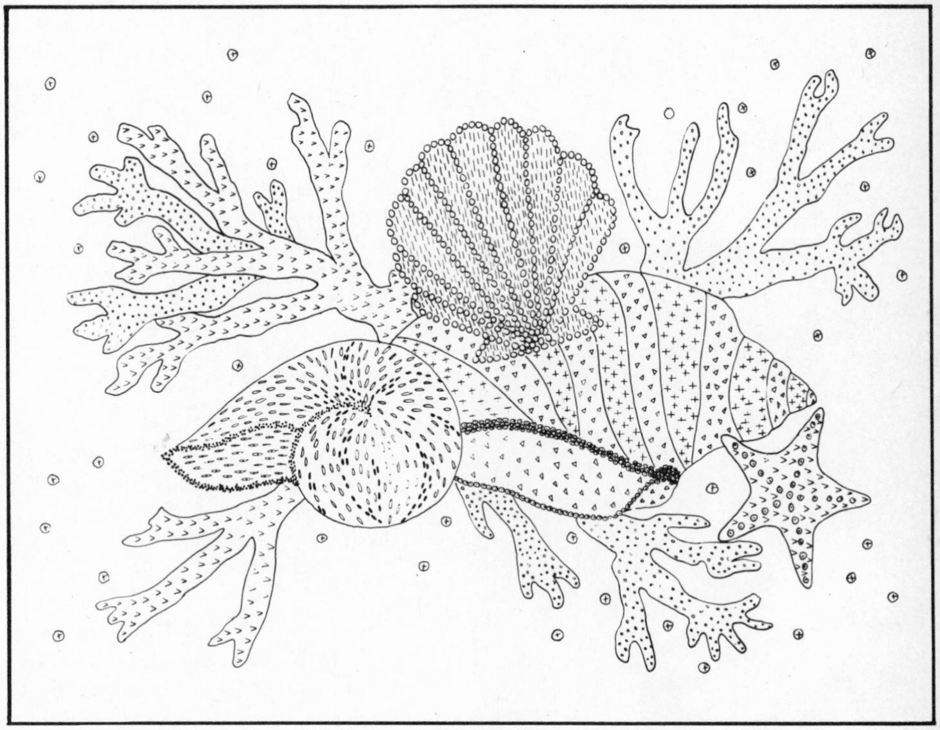

Jigsaw gifts

Gift-wrap paper designed by clever artists makes attractive toys, ornaments and bookends for you. Shop for papers decorated with storybook characters and glue them to plywood; then cut out the figures with a jig saw, paint the edges and backs and coat with a shiny protective finish. You'll be so pleased with the results, you'll start thinking of other things to make or decorate with your cutouts . . . toy chest, recipe file, tissue box, spice rack?

Before starting a project, test a small piece of the gift-wrap paper you've selected by gluing it to wood and brushing on two coats of the plastic finish. Some papers do not hold color well and it would be disappointing to spend time cutting out the wood and then lose your design.

A small brayer is handy for rolling the paper smooth when you glue it to the wood, but you'll find a drinking glass will also do the trick.

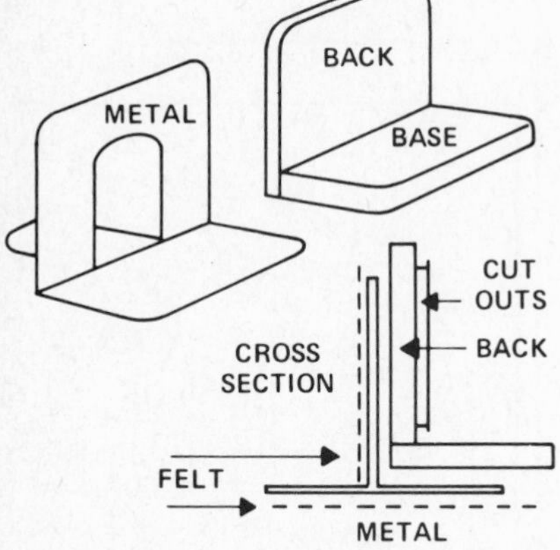

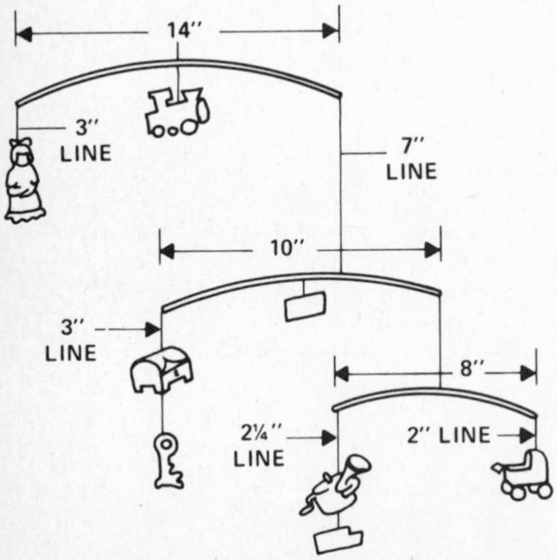

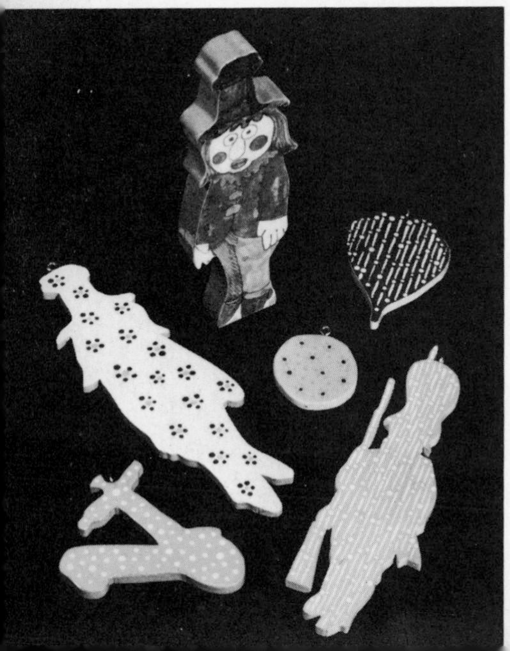

Ornaments and Mobile

Materials: *¼" plywood; gift wrap; white glue; sandpaper; wood putty; enamel undercoater; enamel paint in colors desired; clear plastic finish such as Patricia Nimocks' "Fun Finish" (a decoupage product available in hobby shops); tiny screw eyes; coat hanger wire and nylon fishline for mobile.*

• Brush plywood with white glue; press gift wrap designs to wood and roll out wrinkles with brayer (or with your fingers). Cut out figures.
• Fill any holes in plywood with wood putty and sand edges smooth. Coat edges and back of figure with enamel undercoat; let dry. Sand lightly, then paint edges and back with enamel in colors desired. Use two coats, sanding lightly between coats—a nylon scouring pad (Scotch-Brite) is good for this. Decorate the back of figures with dots, stripes or flowers, if you wish, using contrasting color enamel (see photo).
• When enamel is thoroughly dry, apply clear plastic finish to all surfaces. You do not have to sand between coats; three coats will give a smooth, shiny, very durable finish.
• Twist small screw eyes into tops of figures, for hanging.
• To make mobile: cut lengths of coat hanger wire, arc them slightly and string them together (see diagram). Tie on ornaments with nylon fishline, shifting their positions until mobile balances.

Toys

Follow directions for ornaments, except substitute ¾" gum plywood for ¼" plywood. The gum plywood is more expensive than fir plywood, but in this thickness, it is easier to cut.

Bookends

The little scene you'll compose to decorate bookends may be cut from two or three different gift wraps. You may even sketch a part of the design yourself—the cloud and tree on the "Little Girl" bookend are shapes we cut from plywood and painted.

Materials: *Same as for ornaments, plus metal bookends; ½" plywood to make base and back; epoxy glue; felt.*

• Measure the base and upright part of metal bookend and cut base and back from ½" plywood at least ¼" larger than metal so that wood will completely cover the metal. Or cut wood even larger if your design requires more background.
• Round the outside corners of back and base, fill holes with wood putty, sand smooth, paint with enamel undercoat and with 2 coats of enamel in colors desired, sanding between coats.
• Following directions for ornaments, glue gift wrap designs to ¼" plywood, cut out with jig saw; sand and paint edges.
• Apply 3 coats of clear plastic finish to all surfaces of base and back, and to cut-out figures.
• With epoxy glue, glue back to base and glue these pieces to the metal bookend (see diagram). Finally, glue the cut-out figures to the back in desired positions, also with epoxy glue.
• Cut felt to cover back and bottom of metal bookend and glue in place with white glue.

HAPPY
BIRTHDAY

FOR THE KNOTTING...

wood and yarn wall hangings

If you're looking for gifts that are almost ridiculously easy to make—but terrific-looking—try these wall hangings. You use only one knot, a plain overhand knot. The effectiveness of the pattern derives from selection of yarn colors and use of twigs or wood dowels and beads.

You'll find this an easy introduction to macramé, the knotting craft—especially if you've been discouraged by the more intricate patterns.

Twig Wall Hanging

Materials: *8 good-size twigs, about ½" in diameter and 20" long; rug yarn in colors desired (we used dark brown, ecru, black, medium brown, gold and avocado).*

- Cut rug yarn in 5-yard lengths, as follows: 9 lengths, dark brown; 4 lengths, ecru; 3 lengths, black; 7 lengths, medium brown; 5 lengths, gold; 8 lengths, avocado.
- Fold each 5-yard length in half and use as a double strand.
- Place the *center* of double strand over the first twig and tie the overhand knot, snugging it against the twig.
- Continue to tie strands around first twig in the color sequence given—that is, 9 dark brown, 4 ecru, etc.
- Now sandwich the second twig between the front double-strand and the back double-strand of each length of yarn and tie another overhand knot, again snugging it against twig. Continue across, knotting all yarn lengths.
- Work hanging in rows of knots, twigs and spaces as shown in diagram.
- Leave fringe in varying lengths.

Wood Dowel and Bead Wall Hanging

Materials: *21 wood dowels, 12" long, ⅜" in diameter; 42 wood beads, 14 mm. (available at most hobby shops); rug yarn in colors desired (we used black, ecru, dark brown and avocado); crochet hook.*

- Cut rug yarn in 8-yard lengths, as follows: 6 lengths, black; 7 lengths, ecru; 4 lengths, dark brown, avocado.
- Fold each 8-yard length in half and use as a double strand (do not clip loop end).
- Place the *center* of double strand over the first dowel and tie the overhand knot snugging it against the dowel.
- Continue to knot strands around the first dowel in this color sequence: black, ecru, dark brown, black, ecru, avocado, ecru, black, dark brown, avocado, ecru,

avocado, dark brown, black, ecru, avocado, ecru, black, dark brown, ecru, black.

• Next, weave in 3 dowels, sandwiching them between front double-strands and back double-strands. Tie overhand knot after third dowel.

• Leave a 1″ space, and tie a row of overhand knots, using *two* double-strands for each knot except the center ecru double-strand. Leave another 1″ space and tie a row of overhand knots, each double-strand tied separately (like the first knots).

• Continue to work hanging in rows of knots, dowels, beads and spaces as shown in diagram. When adding beads, use the crochet hook to pull the two loose ends of yarn through the bead, then pull through the loop end.

• Trim fringe to 4″.

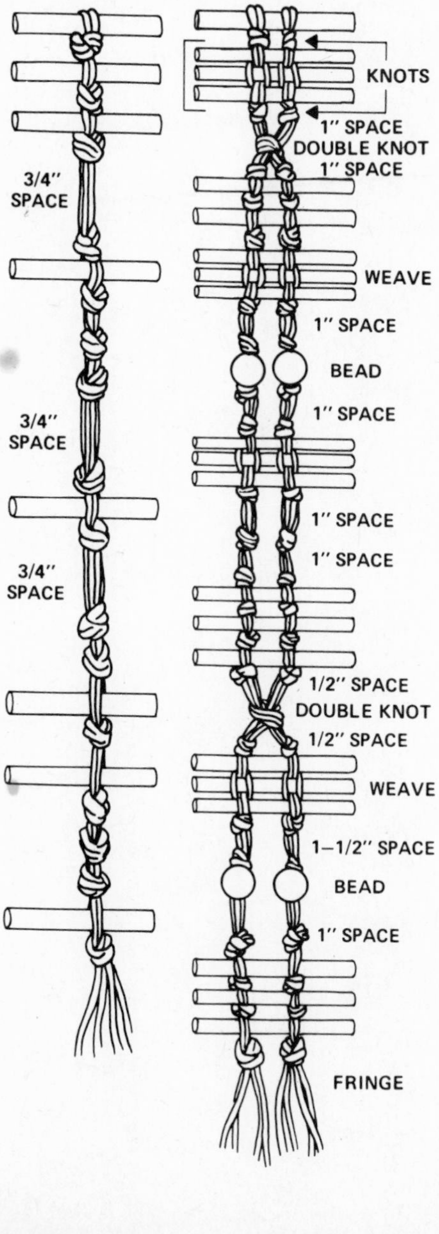

Cut-and-paste pictures

SOFA PILLOWS

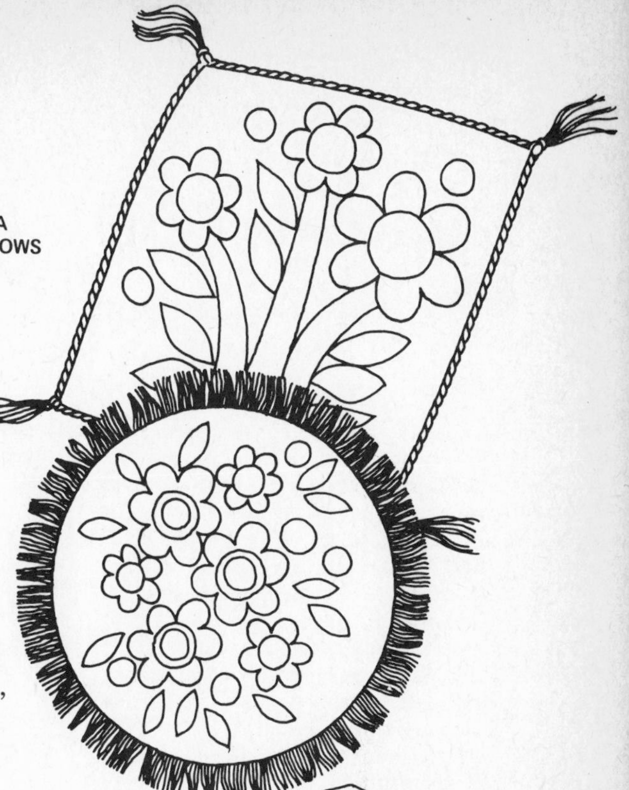

You can turn scraps of wood and felt into works of art you'll be proud to give, or sell at bazaars. Use the designs shown here, draw your own or look for outlines you can trace from Christmas cards, coloring books, gift wraps or magazine art.

PIN CUSHION

BOXED PILLOWS

TABLE MAT

WALL HANGING

Materials: *Pine wood, ½" thick, cut into rectangles of various sizes; white glue; several colors of latex paint; small paint brush; felt scraps in a good assortment of colors; picture hangers.*

• If you don't have scrap wood around the house, buy a pine board 4" wide and ask the lumber yard to cut it up in various short lengths.

• Paint the 4 edges of each board. Place board on waxed paper and paint the top. Let dry. You can use enamel instead of latex paint on the boards, but the wood must be primed or undercoated first. Tempera or poster paints also work well. If you are working on a lot of boards, or if several people are working together, it's a good idea to paint boards one day, and do felt work the next.

• Draw patterns and cut felt pieces.

• When paint is dry, place felt designs on wood, trying different colors and arangements. When you're pleased with your design, transfer it carefully to a piece of paper. Paint the entire surface of the wood generously with white glue thinned with a little water. Replace felt design, pressing it lightly into the glue. Do not be concerned if the glue coat is heavy; it will dry clear and give the wood a shiny look.

• When glue is dry, in about ½ hour, fasten a picture hanger to back of plaque.

Bonus suggestion: The same sparkling colors and design ideas can be adapted for other gifts and accessories–pillows, pin cushions, tablemats, wall hangings.

Felt, rope and rag rugs

Almost every home has a closet (or a drawer, or a box) which contains the essentials for making a rug–leftover yarns, faded blue jeans, used clothes or old curtains. Much of the joy and challenge in rug making comes from the use of these recycled materials – the whole idea of making something from almost nothing makes a game of it. We think you'll be especially intrigued by the Rag Bag Oval–it uses short narrow pieces of cotton fabric.

If you want to make a brilliant area rug and you want to accomplish it with great speed, then machine-appliqué felt is for you. Or, you can use the old-fashioned button rug technique to make the Crimson Bouquet rug, in which the flower petals are secured to the backing with French knots. For an unusually dramatic rug, try the Wrapped Rope design. Just imagine how it would please an indoor gardener!

Rag Bag Oval

Materials: *Cotton fabric (worn denim is ideal); scrap wood and nails to make loom; 2 large spools of string; cardboard; scissors; heavy-duty thread.*

To make loom: From lumber 1″ thick, cut a base 6x16″ and an upright 6x4″. Fasten upright to base from underneath, about 5″ from end, using long screws or nails. Pound 2 long nails into short section of loom, to hold spools of string; pound another long nail at other end of loom (see sketch). Pound 4 smaller nails into upright, in pairs, as shown in sketch. To warp loom, wrap string from each spool around its pair of nails on the upright in a figure 8, leaving enough string to extend to the single nail at the far end of loom. Tie the two strings together around this nail–your loom is ready.

To prepare fabric: For a 1″ thick rug, you will want strips of cotton about ½″

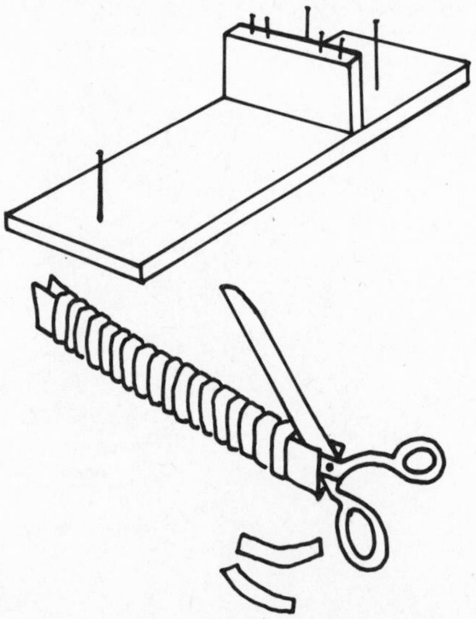

wide and 2½″ long. Here's the easy way to make all the strips the same length. First, tear fabric in long strips ½″ wide. Cut a cardboard gauge 2½x 8″ and fold it in half lengthwise. Wrap the cotton strips around the gauge, slip the blade of scissors into the open edge of fold and cut fabric (see sketch).

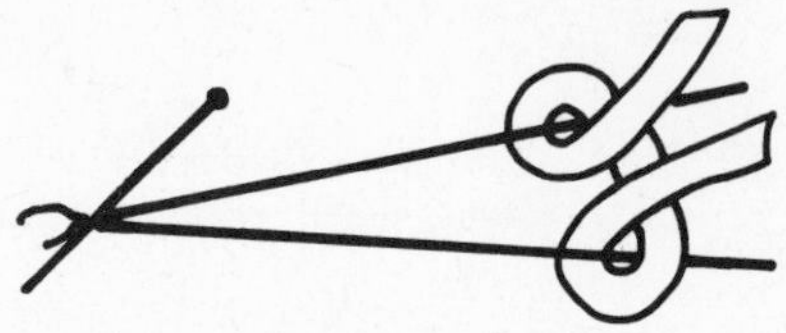

Knotting: Place a strip of fabric over the 2 warp threads (see photo), wrapping the ends around the warps and pulling them up between (see sketch). Slide the knotted fabric down the warp threads to the holding nail. Continue to knot pieces of fabric one by one, sliding them down tight until the warp threads are full. Then lift the string off the end nail and loosen the warp threads wrapped around nails in the upright. Draw a new length of string from each spool, slip the last knotted fabric over the end nail and tighten warp strings on the upright nails again. Continue knotting as before.

You will be making a continuous strip of knotted fringe which you can start sewing together when it is a few feet long. It is easy to work for a while making fringe, alternating that with coiling and sewing. Do not break the warp strings until you have the rug the size you want.

The proportion of an oval rug is determined right at the beginning, by the length of the center strip. Decide what you want the finished size to be and subtract the width from the length–the difference gives you the length of the initial center strip. For example, if you want an oval rug 20x36″, you subtract 20 from 36, make center strip 16″ long.

Coil the fringe clockwise around this center strip and whip together on the back with strong linen or cotton thread. Ease curves so that the rug will lie flat.

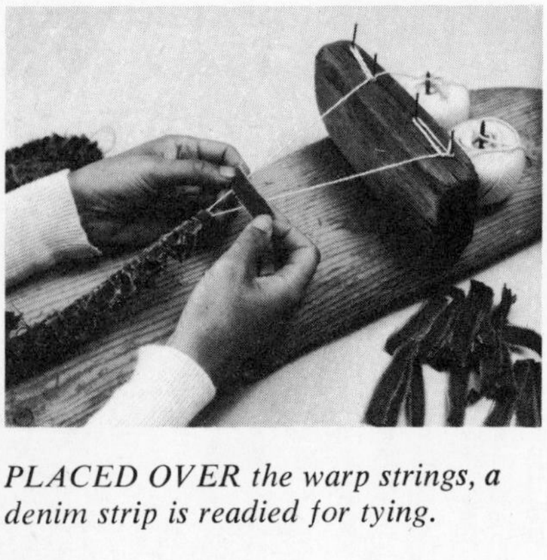

PLACED OVER the warp strings, a denim strip is readied for tying.

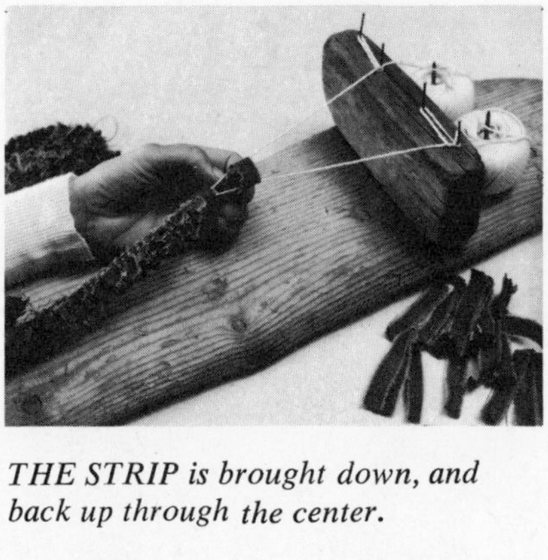

THE STRIP is brought down, and back up through the center.

Adapted from *Handmade Rugs from Practically Anything,* copyright © 1971, 1972 by Jean Ray Laury and Joyce Aiken, published by Farm Journal, Inc., Philadelphia, Pa., distributed by Doubleday & Co., Inc., Garden City, N.Y.

CRIMSON BOUQUET is a contemporary version of the old-fashioned button rug. The stacks of flower cutouts are attached to felt backing with French knots.

RAG BAG OVAL utilizes small bits of fabric not ordinarily used for rugs, knotted into a fringe on a simple string loom. The fringe is coiled and sewed together; rug has a soft surface texture.

PEDESTALS is machine-appliqué and quick to do. Bands of colored felt are folded and cut with decorative edges to make the design, then satin-stitched to felt backing.

Felt rugs

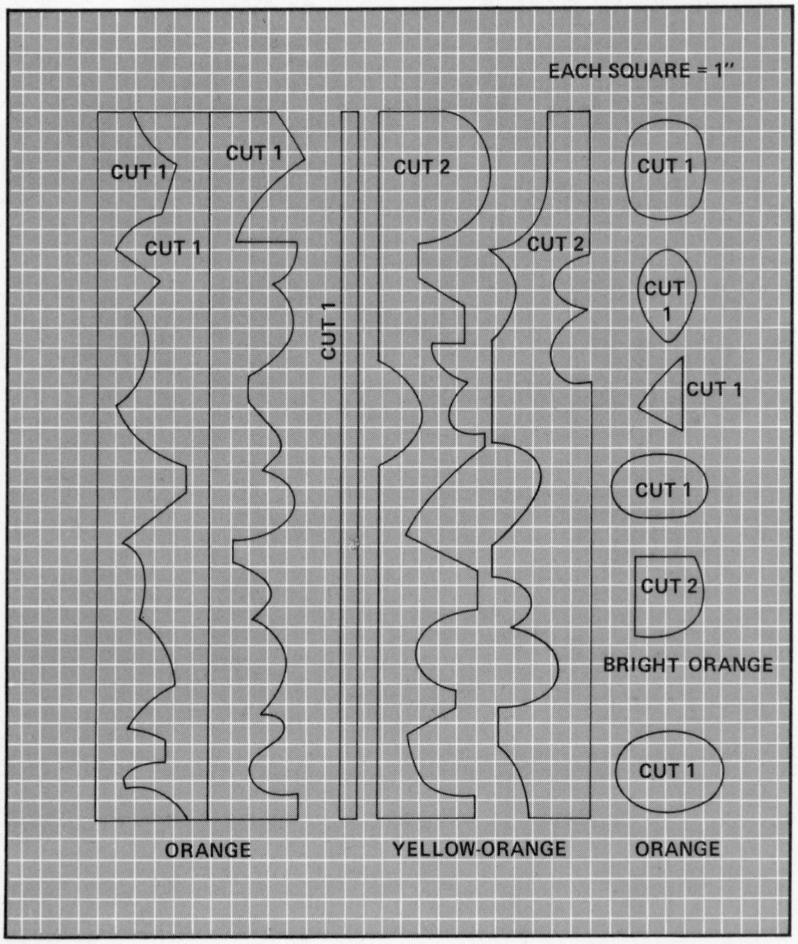

Felt is more durable than you might guess and, used in layers or overlapped, it becomes even stronger. Look for felts which are 50% wool (or more). Most are half wool, half rayon, but check—one that is 75% rayon will not wear as well.

Felts also come in different gauges or thicknesses. Hold the felt up to the light . . . if you can see through it, or if the fibers seem unevenly distributed, it may not wear well.

If you wish to use an *all*-wool felt, your best source for ordering it is through an interior decorator. Usual minimum cut of the 70" felt is one yard. If you use an all-wool background, it is then satisfactory to use a part-wool felt for the appliqué.

A finished felt rug lies flat and looks best when used as an area rug over carpeting. If you plan to use the rug on a smooth or polished surface, be sure to use a rubber rug pad under it to prevent skidding and slipping. Felts are not washable and must be dry-cleaned, though the wool fibers resist soiling to some extent. Polyester felts may soon be on the market and they would, of course, be washable.

Pedestals

Materials: *Deep orange felt for background 36x40"; felt for appliqué in yellow-orange, dull orange and bright orange; 13' of bright orange fringe; blending thread colors for machine appliqué.*

• Enlarge patterns (see Appendix) and cut pedestal bands in colors indicated—you'll have 3 dull orange, and 4 yellow orange plus 1 straight narrow band. Cut small shapes as indicated, 6 from bright orange, 1 from dull orange.

• Arrange bands on background felt (see photo for placement) and baste in position. Also baste small felt pieces in place.

• Appliqué bands to background on the sewing machine, using the satin stitch.
• Back your rug, if desired, with a second layer of felt or with rubber rug padding. Sew on fringe.

Crimson Bouquet

Materials: *Red felt for rug background 30x36" (plus a second piece for backing, if desired); 11 feet of matching red cotton fringe; wide assortment of felt in pink, orange, red, magenta and purple colorings; embroidery floss.*

• From the vari-colored felts, cut circles of all sizes from 1 to 6" freehand; then scallop or cut them into petal shapes (see sketches). Leave a few circles round.
• Stack the flower cutouts 4, 5 or 6 layers thick and attach them in a random arrangement all over the felt background. Use 3 strands of embroidery floss; secure flower in center with straight stitches making a cross or a star design; or with French knots. You may want to add French knots at petal points to help hold flowers in place (see sketches).
• Back the rug, if you wish, with the second layer of felt, or with rubber rug padding, and sew fringe around edges.

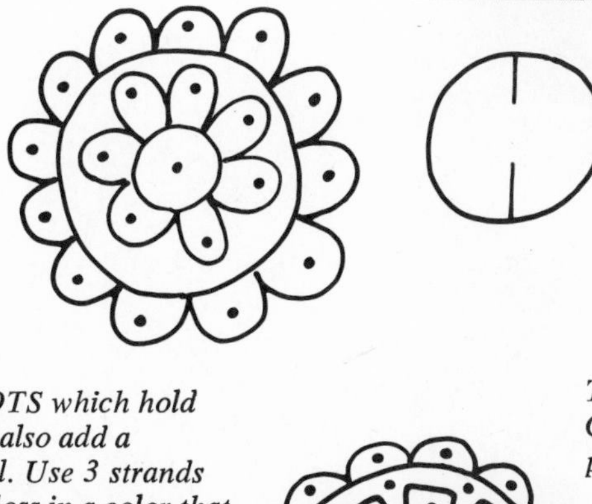

FRENCH KNOTS which hold flowers in place also add a decorative detail. Use 3 strands of embroidery floss in a color that blends with felt color without exactly matching—for example, pink on red felt.

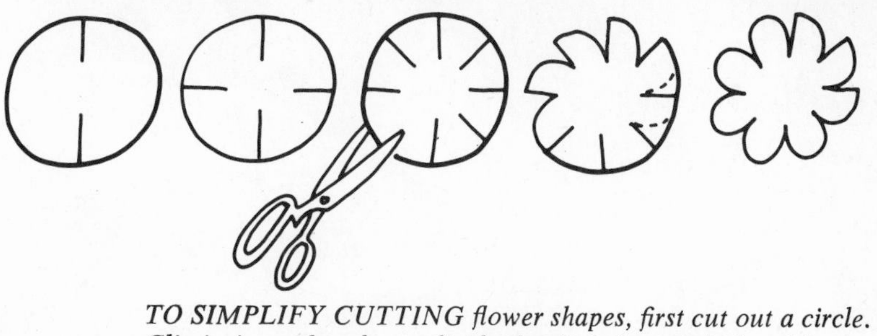

TO SIMPLIFY CUTTING flower shapes, first cut out a circle. Clip in from the edge to divide the circle into eight (or six) portions, then round off each portion.

CUT NOTCHED FLOWERS from circles, too. Clip as indicated, then notch the fabric at each clip.

Forest

Materials: *Dark green felt, 36x36" for background; white felt for tree appliqués; about 10' of white ball fringe.*

• From paper, cut a circle pattern 36" in diameter (see Appendix). Pin pattern to green felt and cut out rug.
• Use paper pattern to sketch tree designs: Divide the circle into wedges (see sketch) and fill the wedges with fanciful tree/leaf shapes.
• Cut the shapes in white felt and pin them to rug background. Machine-stitch ⅛" from edge, using a long stitch—8 to 10 setting on most machines (see close-up detail). Before machine stitching, you may want to hand-baste ½" from edge.
• Sew ball fringe under outer edge of rug. Back the rug with a second circle of felt, if you wish, or with rubber rug padding.

Note: This design would also make an attractive Christmas tree skirt. Slit it from edge to center and cut out a small circle in center to fit around tree trunk.

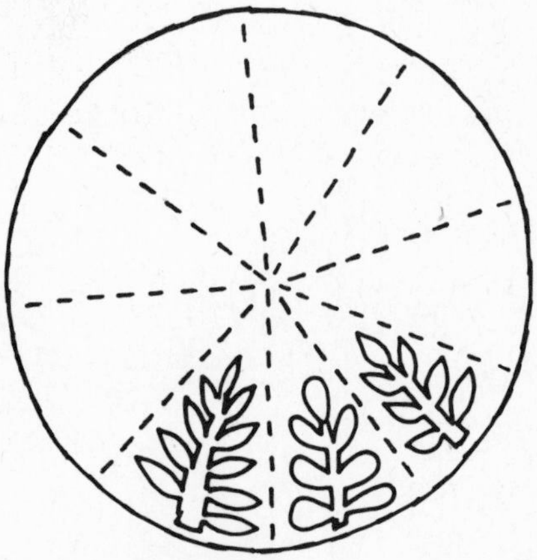

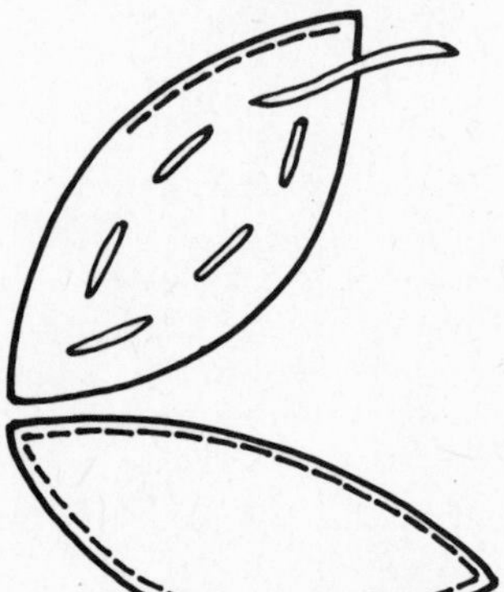

Green Grow the Flowers Oh

Materials: *White felt 36x72"; also dark green, light green, sharp pink, dark pink and coral pink felts; about 10′ of coral pink ball fringe.*

- From paper, cut a circle pattern 36" in diameter (see Appendix). Pin pattern to white felt and cut out rug and rug backing.
- Enlarge pattern (see Appendix) and cut stems and some leaves from dark green felt; cut other leaves from light green and flower petals from pink felts.
- Baste appliqué design to rug top, positioning stem appliqué first; then extra leaves and flowers. Stitch to background on sewing machine, using the satin stitch. Choose thread colors that blend with felt colors without exactly matching—for example, use coral pink thread on sharp pink felt (see close-up for stitch detail).
- Sew rug back to rug top, and stitch ball fringe around the edge on the top.

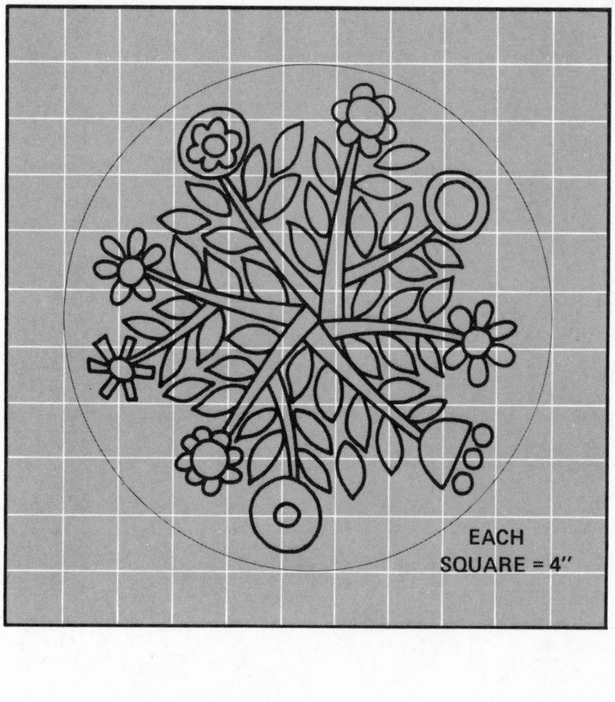

Wrapped rope rug

Materials: *About 45′ of sisal rope; 4-ply or rug yarn in colors desired; white glue; heavy, dark-colored upholstery fabric with latex backing about 15x18″; carpet thread.*

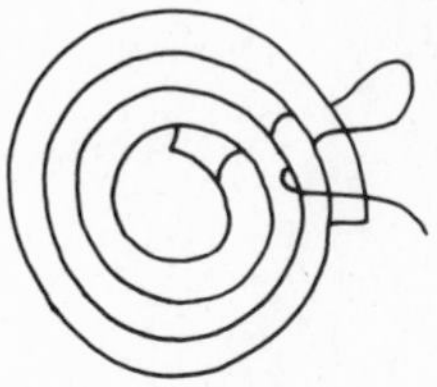

• Cut pieces of sisal approximately 3′ long. Wrap each with a single color of yarn (see photo), securing the ends with white glue.
• After all ropes are wrapped, coil some of them to lie flat and sew them together with matching yarn, using a weaving stitch (see sketch).
• Now arrange the coils, laying other wrapped ropes in place to connect one coil with another (see photo).
• When design pleases you, stitch the coils and connecting ropes to upholstery fabric with carpet thread.
• When all rope is sewed in place, cut the fabric away around outside edge of rug. Latex coating prevents fraying, so hemming is not necessary.

3 pillows in patchwork

END OF THE DAY

For a luxury-loving friend, patch flower-printed and plain velveteen to make a nappy-soft pillow. Note that you flip pattern #2 to cut the printed pieces. Follow velveteen rules for cutting "with nap."

This pattern makes a 14″ pillow. If you want "End of the Day" in a different size, the pattern block can easily be reduced to, say, 10″ in size. Draw a 10″ square, divide it into a checkerboard of 4 equal squares and rule in diagonal and triangle lines. This gives you the two pattern pieces in the smaller size. Enlarge pattern the same way.

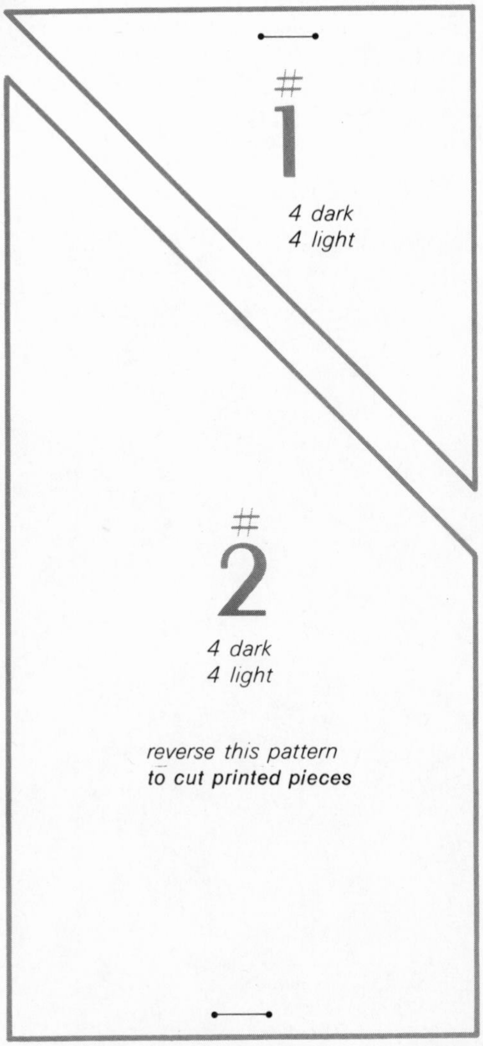

•——• grain of fabric
Cut fabric ¼″ from pattern line for seam allowance

MORNING STAR PILLOW

To make vinyl pillowtop pictured, cut four each of patterns 1, 2 and 3 from reptile-patterned vinyl. Cut 12 more diamonds (pattern 2) from black vinyl and 16 diamonds from brown vinyl. Allow ¼″ seam allowance around patterns.

See photo for arrangement of brown, black and reptile diamonds. Sew together each star point of 4 diamonds first; then sew the 8 points together and fill in with triangles and corner squares. In the center, where a lot of seams come together at one point, taper seams to about ⅛″ before you cross them with another seam.

Also see suggestions with Framed X tote, for sewing on vinyl.

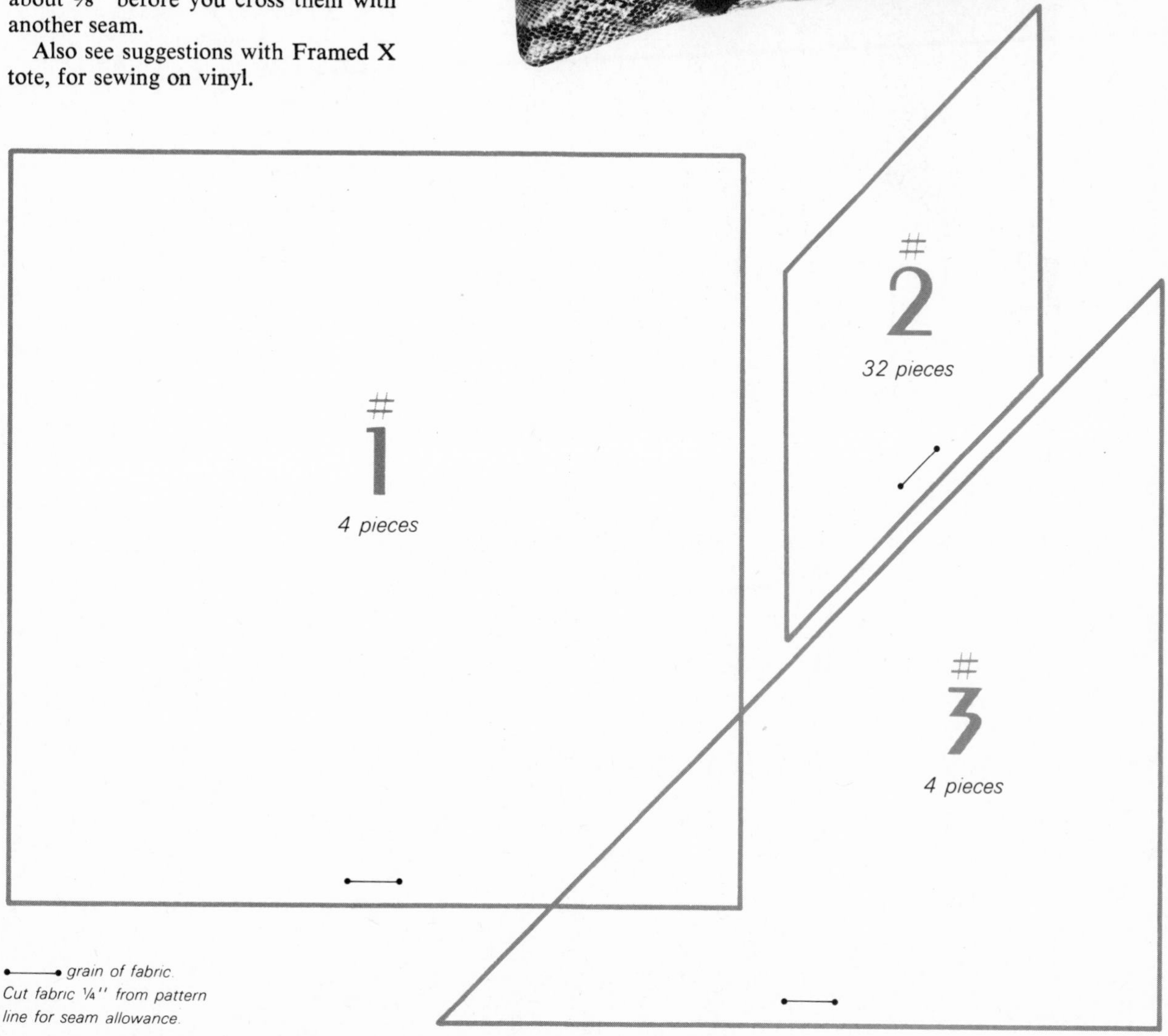

•——• *grain of fabric.*
Cut fabric ¼″ from pattern line for seam allowance.

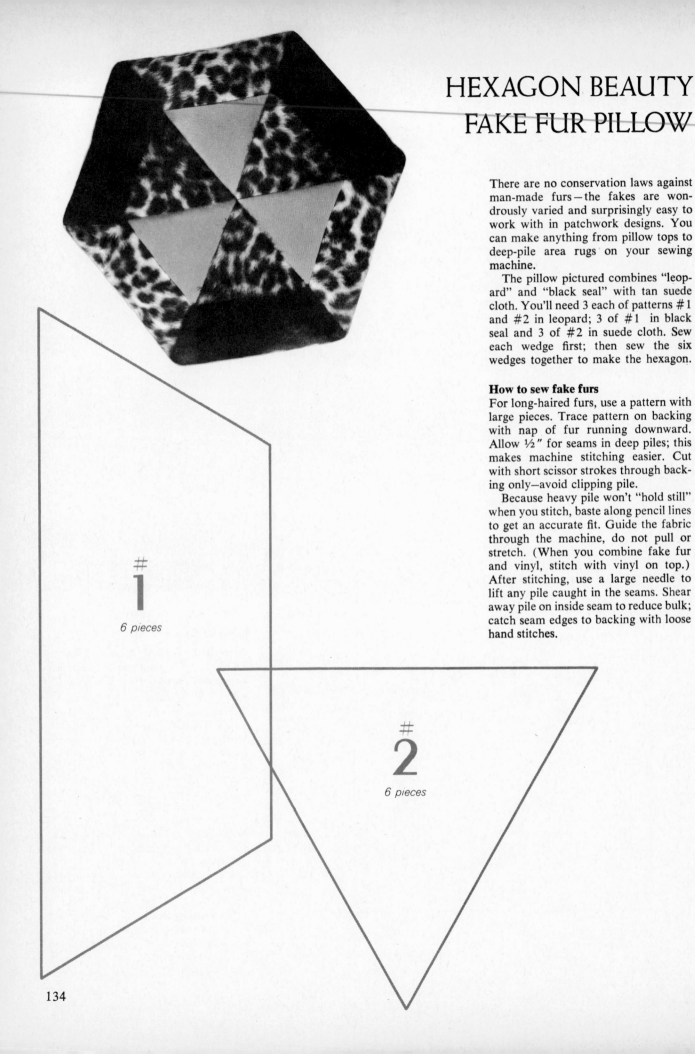

HEXAGON BEAUTY FAKE FUR PILLOW

There are no conservation laws against man-made furs – the fakes are wondrously varied and surprisingly easy to work with in patchwork designs. You can make anything from pillow tops to deep-pile area rugs on your sewing machine.

The pillow pictured combines "leopard" and "black seal" with tan suede cloth. You'll need 3 each of patterns #1 and #2 in leopard; 3 of #1 in black seal and 3 of #2 in suede cloth. Sew each wedge first; then sew the six wedges together to make the hexagon.

How to sew fake furs
For long-haired furs, use a pattern with large pieces. Trace pattern on backing with nap of fur running downward. Allow ½″ for seams in deep piles; this makes machine stitching easier. Cut with short scissor strokes through backing only–avoid clipping pile.

Because heavy pile won't "hold still" when you stitch, baste along pencil lines to get an accurate fit. Guide the fabric through the machine, do not pull or stretch. (When you combine fake fur and vinyl, stitch with vinyl on top.) After stitching, use a large needle to lift any pile caught in the seams. Shear away pile on inside seam to reduce bulk; catch seam edges to backing with loose hand stitches.

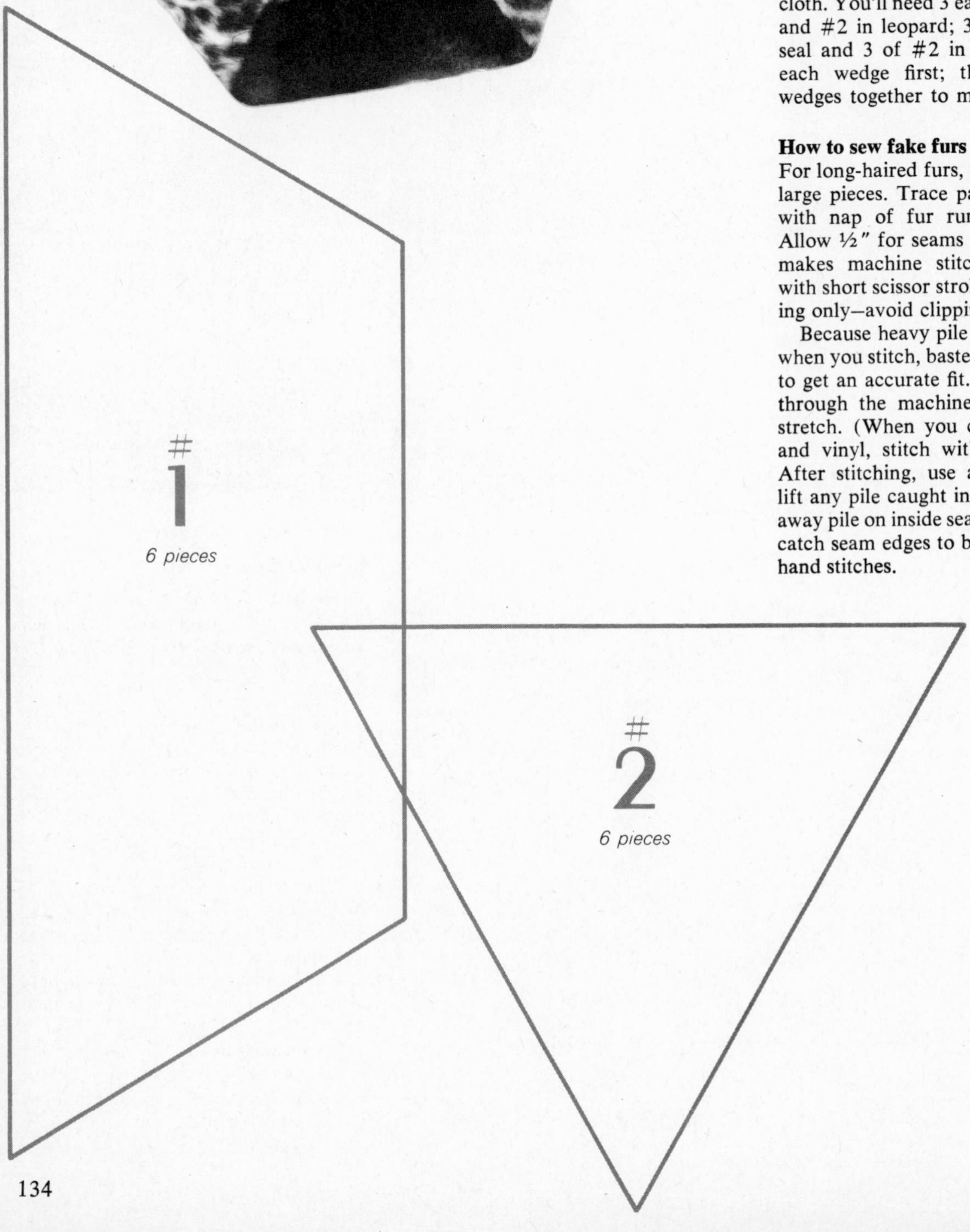

Gifts from scraps

Shoe Trees

Stuff fabric shoe trees with absorbent material (not foam rubber). Use old terry toweling cut in shreds, cotton batting, excelsior or kapok.

Materials: *Firm tightly woven fabric; stuffing; small brass rings; brass safety pins; fine gold-colored chain.*

• Enlarge pattern (see Appendix) and trace on fabric following "straight of goods" line. Cut 8 pieces for each pair of shoe trees. Stitch 4 pieces together for each tree, leaving end open; turn and stuff tightly; slipstitch opening. Sew on rings and pin the pair together with a 5" length of gold chain.

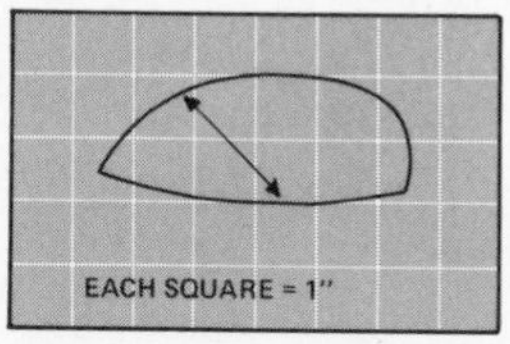

Pincushions

In Christmas colors and motifs, these pincushions will sell well at bazaars.

Christmas Tree: From bright green felt, cut 4 equilateral triangles, 4" each side. Decorate 3 with tiny snips of colored felt, sewed on or glued. Sew triangles together to make a pyramid, stuffing tightly before you close final seam.

Cube: Cut 6 (2½") squares of fabric—2 each of white, red and green. Trim one white square with green felt holly leaves and red French knot berries. Press ¼" seam allowance around all squares. Sew together using green embroidery floss and overcast stitch: red to white to red to white (forming a hollow square); sew green to top and bottom to complete cube. Stuff tightly before you close final seam.

Patchwork Tote Bag

The velvety texture of suede cloth contrasted with crocheted package twine makes a great looking tote.

Materials: *10 pieces of suede cloth (or leather) cut 4" square; plain white package twine; fabric for lining; No. 8 (H) crochet hook; eyelet punch.*

• To make crochet squares, chain 13 stitches plus 2 more for turning—or whatever you need to get 4" size. Single crochet in rows until piece measures 4". Crochet 8 squares.

• Crochet boxing and shoulder strap in one piece about 1½" wide (ch 5 st plus 2 for turning) and 5' long.

• Using eyelet punch (or ice pick), punch holes in suede cloth squares all around each square, 3/16" from edge and about ⅜" apart.

• Sew squares together with twine in a checkerboard pattern, making bag front and back, 12" square.

• Sew boxing to three sides of front and back; sew ends together to complete shoulder strap. Crochet through punched holes around top edge of bag. Line bag with fabric if you wish.

Hang-ups

Mr. and Mrs. Stockings

Trim a sharp turquoise boot with pink felt flowers for Her; cut His boot a little shorter, in light green, and decorate with green leaves and white beads for berries.

Materials: *Burlap for stockings — turquoise and light green; felt scraps—dark green, yellow-orange and 3 tones of pink/purple; embroidery floss; large white beads; cotton fabric for lining stockings.*

• Enlarge patterns (see Appendix) and cut 2 turquoise and 2 light green stockings. Seam and turn.

• Cut 6 pink flowers and pin around top of turquoise stocking, overlapping slightly. Place yellow-orange centers on each flower and embroider both center and flower to stocking with a circle of French knots.

• Cut 16 green leaves and pin them around top of green boot. Sew leaves to boot with light green embroidery floss, using the outline stitch to look like veining in the leaf. Sew on beads.

• Cut and stitch linings separately, slip into boots and slipstitch around boot tops.

Organdy Wreath Appliqué

Whether you hang it against the wall or in the window, an organdy panel looks ethereal. This design is a montage of tree-shaped triangles cut from green and blue printed fabrics. You can make the hanging any size; ours is big, 45″ square. You might want to hang up your paper pattern first, to check size before you cut into fabric.

Materials: *White organdy for panel; selection of green and blue-and-green printed fabrics (avoid fabrics with crease resistant finishes; untreated cottons are easier to appliqué); green and turquoise felt for letters; 2 (5/8″) wood dowels; paper and white paint.*

- On paper, draw a circle the size you want appliqué wreath to be; ours is 36″ in diameter on 45″ fabric.
- Cut paper triangles in four sizes and shapes. Ours are: 6″ base, 3¼″ high; 4¾″ base, 4¾″ high; 5½″ base, 6″ high; 3½″ base, 5½″ high. Cut 12 of each size.
- Lay paper triangles around the circle overlapping and varying the shapes until the arrangement pleases you. Tape in place.
- Decide on arrangement of colors and prints. If you've used 36 triangles in your wreath and you have 6 different fabrics, you could simply repeat the fabrics in sequence all around the wreath.
- Label the paper triangles according to fabric order and cut out appliqués this way: Lay patterns on wrong side of fabric with grain running from top to base of triangle. Trace around patterns with a pencil, directly on fabric. Leave space between each outline for hem allowance. Cut fabric pieces ⅛″ out from tracing line.
- Baste ⅛″ hems in all triangles, being especially careful at corners.
- Appliqué triangles to organdy following paper design. Use a small running stitch or blind stitch, as you prefer.
- Enlarge patterns for letters and cut from felt. Appliqué in place.
- Sew 1″ hems in organdy panel at top and bottom. Paint dowels white and insert in hems. Hang with yarn ties.

Frames

A gift sure to be appreciated is a picture frame (or mirror frame, or shadow box—see pages following). Custom-made frames are shockingly expensive, but the materials to make your own frames are immediately available at any building supply dealer. And our step-by-step directions are easy to follow.

Sportsman's Cork Frame

The frame for Audubon's "Canvasback Duck" print is a simple butt-joint frame covered with cork floor tiles. Butt joints are easier to make than mitered corners and they're just fine if you cover them up.

Materials: *Self-adhesive cork tiles (from floor covering dealer); ¾x2" white pine; Skotch cleats; white glue.*

• Measure the print (or the matted print) and subtract ½" from width and length. (This calculation gives you the necessary ¼" you need all around to mount print to back of finished frame.) Cut two pieces of white pine to the short measure. Add *twice the width* of the pine to the long measure (allowance for overlap) and cut two pieces. Cut straight across (sharp 90° angles) as neat and crisp as possible. (Photo 1)

• Apply glue to ends of short pieces and butt them against long pieces, face down on the table, to make a rectangle with tight square corners. Hammer Skotch cleats over joints, 2 cleats at each corner. (Photo 2)

• Measure strips of cork tile 2" wide to cover pine. Be sure you mark and cut cork with the grain. Cut enough to cover the frame, using your steel ruler and X-acto knife to make clean straight cuts (see Appendix). (Photo 3)

• Strip paper covering from back of cork and stick cork to frame. (Photo 4)

• To mount print, measure it and cut mounting board to fit. Fiberboard, plywood, Homasote and Upson board are all good mounting materials. Mix white glue with a little water and brush a thin layer evenly over mounting surface.

• Pick up the print, holding it by the corners, taut on one side; lay edge of print along edge of mounting surface and spread print smoothly across surface to other side. If it doesn't lie down evenly, *immediately* lift it by the corners on one side and peel it off. Try again. (Photo 5)

• Working from the center to edges, roll out air bubbles and excess glue with a brayer. Caution: Be sure the brayer doesn't pick up glue along the edges. For safety's sake, lay a piece of tissue over the print before you roll it out. (Photo 6)

• Cover the mounted print with another board the same size, laying them both on a flat surface. Lay a weight on top and let stand for several hours.

PHOTO 1

PHOTO 2

PHOTO 3

PHOTO 4

PHOTO 5

PHOTO 6

Shadow boxes

Build a shadow box from standard builder's molding for someone who has a collection to display. You can follow our design, using drip cap molding for the frame and red velvet for the lining—or choose other moldings and materials to best set off the collection.

Our directions tell how to make the box pictured which is 1" deep, 8x10" inside, fitted with two shelves. The tools you need to make the frame are: miter box and back saw, corner clamps, hammer, steel ruler and nail set.

Materials: *1/4" fir plywood, 8x10"; drip cap molding, 4'; 3/8x7/8" walnut, 3'; 1/4 x7/8" walnut, 18"; 1/4x3/16" basswood strip, 3'; 1/8" glass, 7 15/16x9 15/16"; nails (#17 brads—1", 3/4" and 1/2"); wood putty; gesso; sandpaper; red velvet; black latex paint; silver model airplane paint; 2 small cleats and screws.*

- To make frame: cut one end of the drip cap molding in the miter box set at 45° angle. Hold the drip cap upright with the slope facing out. (Photo 1)
- Measure drip cap against 8x10" plywood to mark where to make the second miter cut. (Hold the drip cap in position for framing plywood and measure precisely.) Measure, mark and cut drip cap for remaining 3 sides of frame in the same way. (Photo 2)
- Spread glue on the mitered end of one long piece and one short piece of drip cap. Put them in the corner clamps and draw them together tightly, making a corner. Hammer two 1/2" brads into one side of the joint; hammer one brad into other side. Remove from clamps (it is not necessary to wait for glue to dry—brads will hold the corner). Make another corner with the remaining two pieces of drip cap. (Photo 3)
- Spread glue on the remaining mitered ends of the two corners you've made and fit them together to make the frame. Place one of the new corners into the clamps and draw together tightly; hammer brads as before. Repeat with the fourth corner to complete frame. (Photo 4)
- Cut basswood strips which will be nailed to inside front edge of frame to retain glass: two pieces 7 5/8" long and two pieces 10" long. Cut wood straight across, 90° angle. (Photo 5)

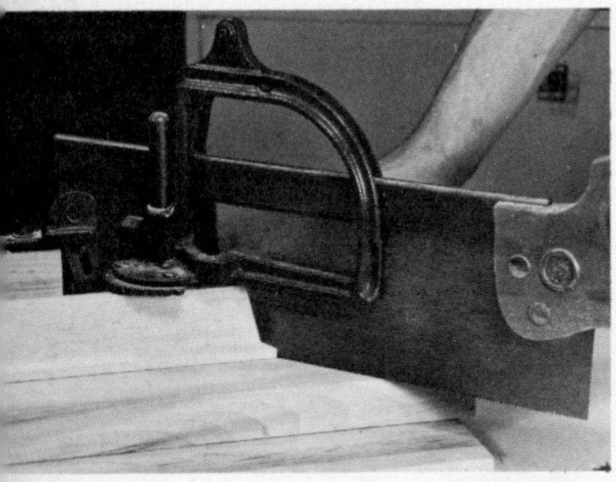

PHOTO 1

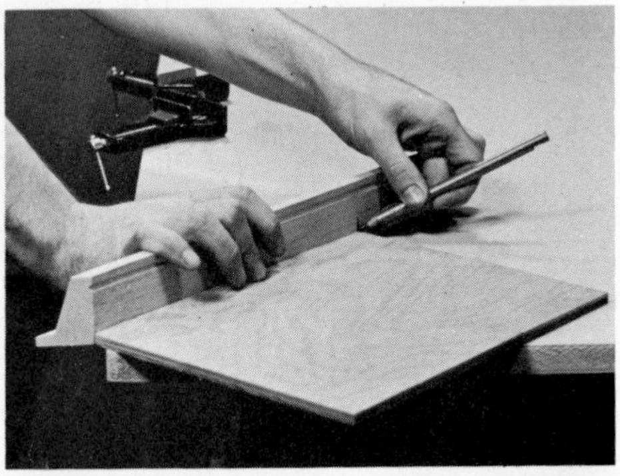

PHOTO 2

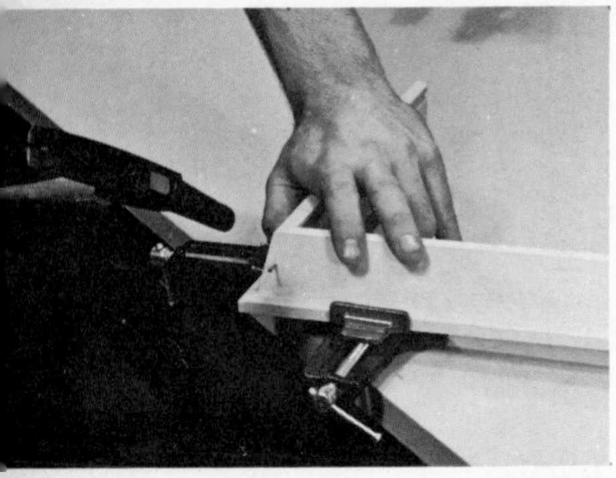

PHOTO 3

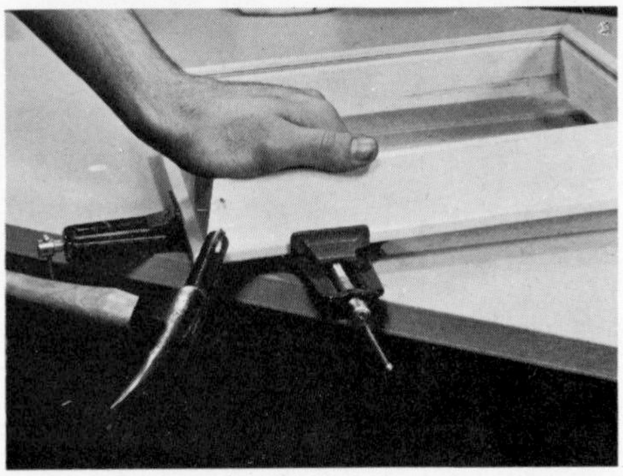

PHOTO 4

• Draw a line ⅛" from front edge on all four inside edges of drip cap frame. (Photo 6)
• Place the ¼" side of the basswood strips against the drip cap along the pencil lines; drive three ½" brads into each side. Counter sink all brads and fill holes with wood putty. (Photo 7)
• Glass will be sandwiched between basswood strips and inside walls of shadow box. To make inside walls: cut four pieces of ⅜x⅞" walnut with mitered ends (place wood on edge—the ⅞" side against miter box—see photo 8). Cut two pieces 8" long on the outside of miter; two pieces 10" long on outside of miter.
• If collection requires shelves to display it, cut two from ¼x⅞" walnut. To determine the length, fit the inside walls into drip cap frame and measure distance between them. Cut shelves straight across, 90° angles. (Photo 9)
• Remove inside walls from frame and nail shelves to walls with ¾" brads (see exploded drawing). Glue miniature figures to shelves.
• Sand entire construction with 200 or 400 grade sandpaper. Pay special attention to the inside edges of the bass strips—sand them to a slightly rounded edge.
• To finish: coat entire frame with gesso. Let dry; sand lightly. Apply a second coat of gesso. When dry, sand to a smooth finish. Paint frame with black latex paint—outside, face and the two visible sides of the basswood strip. Let dry. To add silver trim, cover outside half of face of drip cap with masking tape and paint exposed inner half of face plus basswood strip with silver model airplane paint. (Photo 10)
• Cut fabric 10x12" to cover plywood back of shadow box. Lay fabric face down on a clean surface and center plywood on fabric back. Cut away corners. Apply white glue along one edge of plywood and bring fabric over it. Press down and secure with masking tape. Glue opposite side of fabric, stretching it tightly across face so there will be no sagging. Repeat with other two sides.
• To assemble shadow box: Place drip cap frame face down. Clean glass and slide it in from back. Fit inside walls and shelves into frame. (See drawing.)
• Place fabric-covered plywood back in position. To secure permanently, hammer 1" brads through plywood into drip cap frame. If you want to change exhibit, use screw cleats instead of nails. Screw them into drip cap frame so they can be turned to hold plywood in place. (Photo 11)

PHOTO 5

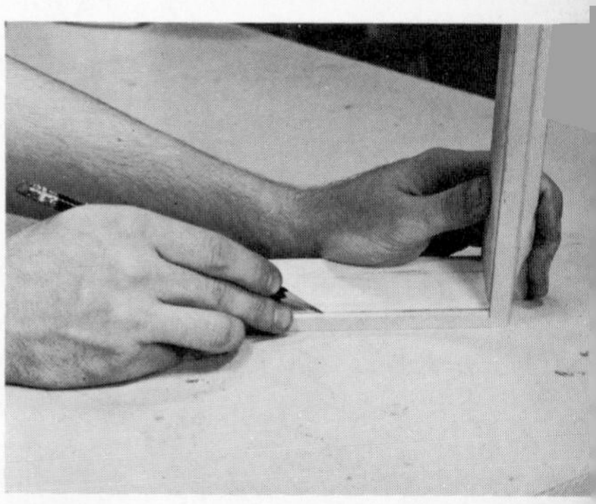
PHOTO 6

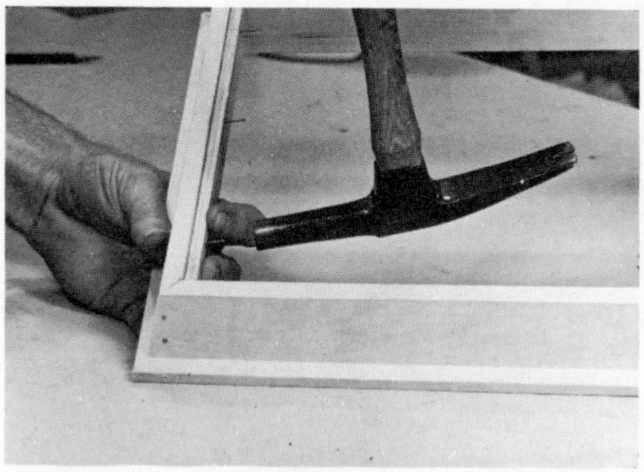
PHOTO 7

PHOTO 8

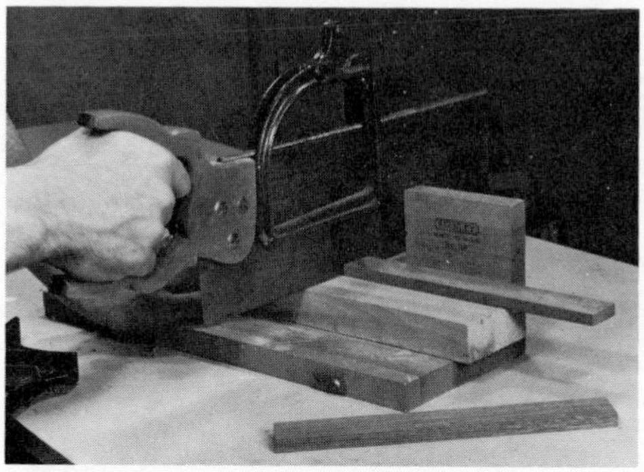
PHOTO 9

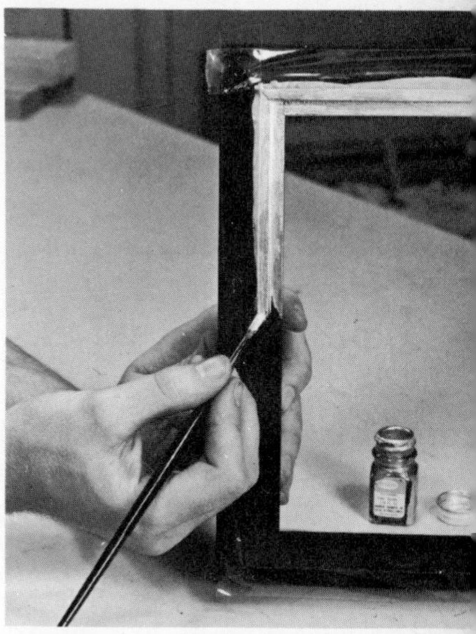
PHOTO 10

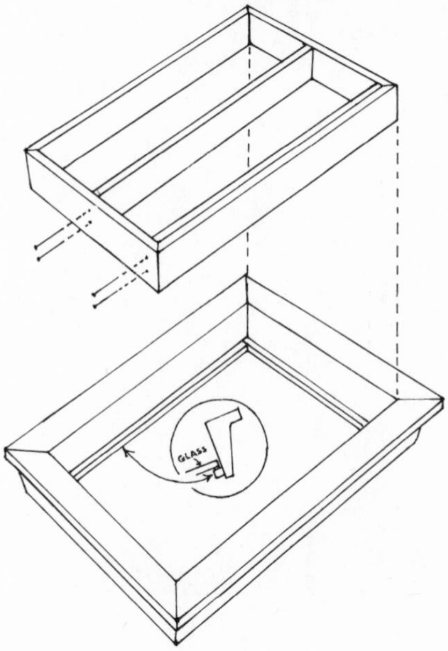

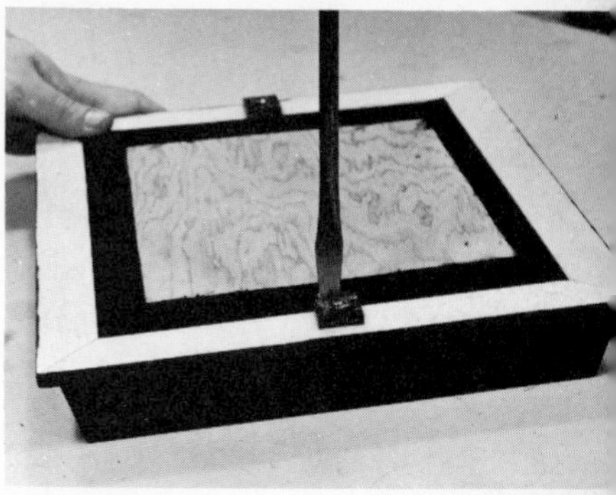
PHOTO 11

Spindle mirror

If your handcrafted gift will go into a Colonial home, consider making this early American spindle mirror. The bottom shelf gives it enough support to stand on a dresser—or it can be hung on the wall. It fits in almost anywhere, and it's easier to make than it looks.

First, you construct the inner frame for the mirror itself; then you assemble the top and bottom shelves with spindles and finials which you can buy at any large building supply store. Finally, you nail the two frames together and paint them—we suggest an antique green finish. Get your mirror cut and polished at the local glass and mirror shop and set it in the frame—your gift is ready to wrap.

Our directions tell how to make the frame pictured, which is 15½" wide and 21" from base to finial; the mirror itself is 10¼x15¼". The tools you need to make the frame are: miter box and back saw, corner clamps, hammer, steel ruler, nail set and drill.

Materials: *¾" capping stock, 4'; Colonial dado molding, 5'; ½x2⅛" window trim, 3'; 2 turned spindles 1 3/16" in diameter, 16⅞" long; 2 matching finials 3" long; ½" quarter round, 4'; white glue; nails (#17 brads, 1¼", ¾"); wood putty, gesso, latex paint (green or your choice of color); acrylic burnt*

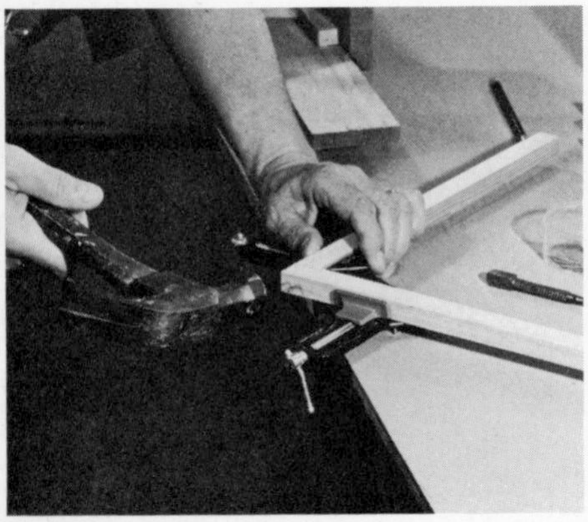

PHOTO 1

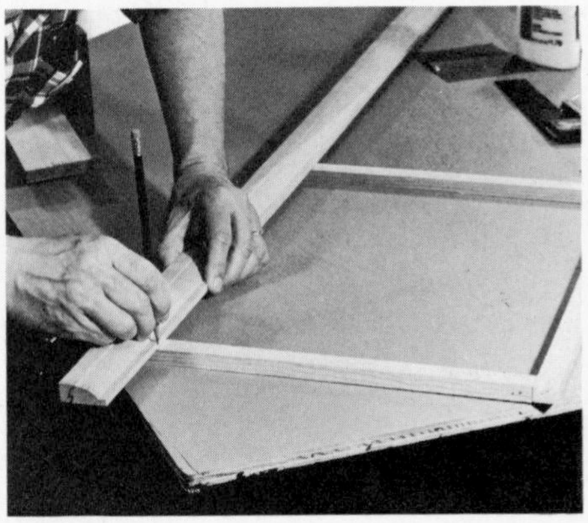

PHOTO 2

PHOTO 3

umber (for antiquing); mirror 15¼x 10¼".

• To make back of mirror frame: Cut 2 pieces of capping strip 16⅞" and 2 pieces 10⅜"—cut wood straight across, 90° angles. Spread glue on the cut end of short piece and press it to side of long piece; put them in the corner clamps and draw them together tightly, making a corner. Hammer two 1¼" nails into the joint. (Photo 1) Repeat with other corners, to complete butt-joint frame 16⅞x12".

• Use this frame to measure Colonial dado molding to make face of frame. Lay molding over frame along each of the four sides in turn, and mark molding at *outside* edges of frame. (Leave some cutting space between markings.) (Photo 2)

• Set the miter box to receive the back saw at a 45° angle. Cut the four lengths of molding you've marked off, so that the cuts slant toward each other—that is, from the outside edge of molding toward what will become the center of the frame. (Photo 3)

• Apply glue generously to cut end of one long piece and one short piece; press ends together in corner clamps and tighten clamps to make a snug corner. Wipe up any glue that oozes out. Nail the joint together with three 1¼" nails. Drive two nails into corner from one side; one nail from other side. (Photo 4)

• Repeat with the other two pieces of molding; then fit the corners together to make a rectangle—glueing, clamping and nailing each corner in turn. Countersink all nails; fill holes with wood putty and let dry. Sand smooth.

• To assemble frame, place the butt-joint frame over back of Colonial dado frame, lining up edges so they're square and flush on all sides. Use masking tape to hold them flush while you nail them together. Drive three ¾" nails into each side, through back frame into molding. (Photo 5)

• To make spindle frame, cut 2 pieces of window trim 15¼" long. Measure ⅞" from ends and back (straight edge) and mark for spindle holes. Check the dowel-like ends of spindles and finials to ascertain size of drill holes—ours were ½" for spindles, ¼" for finials. Cut off the dowel-like ends to a ¼" depth. Drill two ½" holes into the top of the bottom shelf, only ¼" deep. In the top shelf, drill two ½" holes from bottom for spindles, and two ¼" holes from top of shelf for finials (study top sketch).

• Photo 6 shows how the six pieces fit together. Coat holes and dowel ends of spindles and finials with white glue and push dowel ends into holes.

• Set mirror frame into opening in spindle frame and nail in place—hammer three ¾" brads through window trim into frame, both top and bottom. Countersink nails and fill holes with wood putty.

• Sand entire frame and coat with gesso; sand again to get a smooth finish. Coat with green latex paint. When dry, mix burnt umber with a little water and brush over entire frame. Let set for 2-5 minutes, then wipe off with a soft cloth.

• Cut two pieces of quarter round 9" long and two pieces 14" long. Set mirror in inner frame and secure it by nailing the quarter round to back of frame on all four sides; use ¾" brads (see sketch).

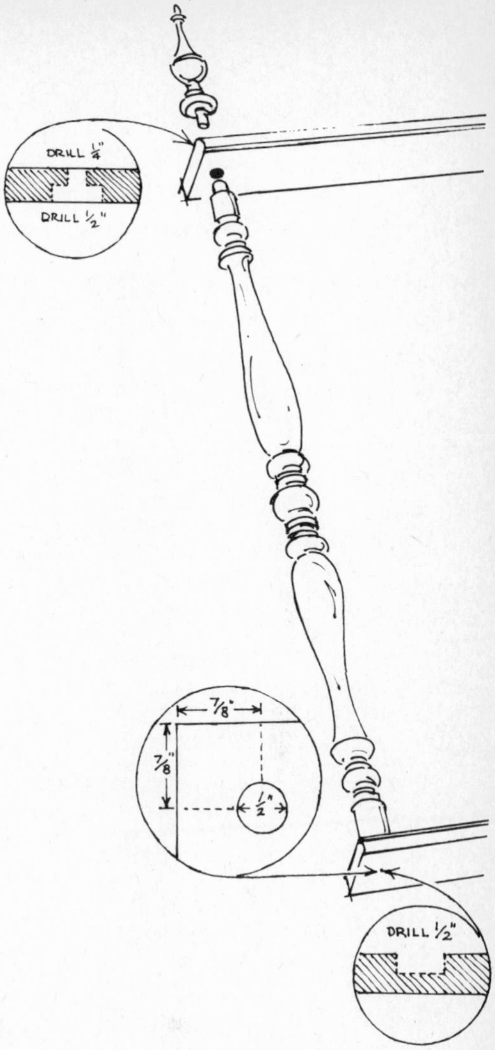

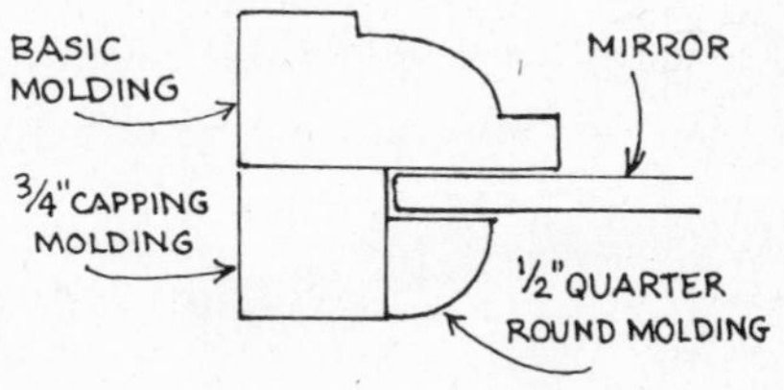

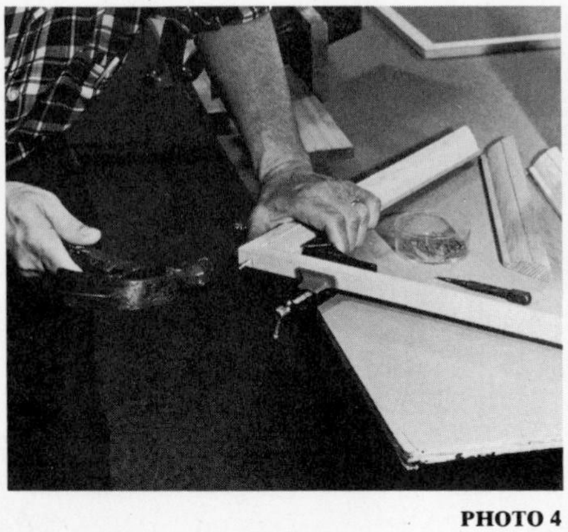

PHOTO 4

PHOTO 5

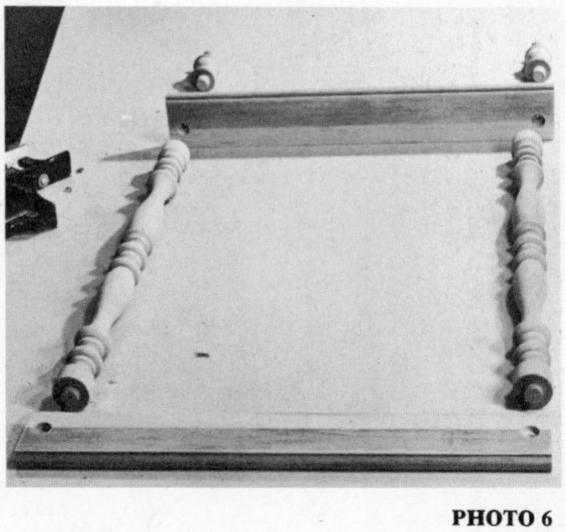

PHOTO 6

Bean and nut mosaics

Bean Mosaics

Dried beans come in enough colors and sizes for you to work out some attractive designs. Choose food motifs for kitchen plaques; animals for family room or playroom; or mix your motifs.

Materials: *Assorted dried beans: black, mung, kidney, navy, coffee, red; also split peas, lentils, whole pearl tapioca; black frame 7x9" for each picture, plus 2 pieces cardboard and 1 piece burlap, also 7x9"; white glue.*

• Glue burlap to one piece of carboard. Draw a line 1" from edge, all around. Glue black beans on line to form border.
• Sketch design on burlap (see photos for suggestions) and glue beans in place.
For *Frog,* use black and mung beans plus split peas.
For *Salamander,* use black, mung and kidney beans and split peas.
For *Turtle,* use black, mung, kidney and navy beans, lentils and split peas.
For *Cherries,* use black, mung, coffee and red beans and whole pearl tapioca.
For *Pear,* use black, mung and coffee beans and split peas.
For *Apple,* use black, mung, coffee and red beans, and split peas.
• Place finished picture in frame, securing it with second piece of cardboard and tiny brads.

Nut Mosaics

Fashion nutty flowers on a background of crushed shells.

Materials: *Black frames, 8x10"; heavy cardboard 8x10"; white glue; nuts and nut shells as follows:*
For Brazil Nut Flower, 29 Brazil nuts, 1 whole pecan, crushed pecan shells.
For Almond Flower, 13 almonds, 10 filberts (hazelnuts), crushed walnut shells.

• Place cardboard in frame. Spread white glue thickly on cardboard and cover well with crushed shells. Let dry; shake off loose bits of shell.
• Glue on whole (unshelled) nuts to form flowers (see photos for designs).

Bean Jewelry

Project for youngsters: making gift brooches and tie-tacks from dried beans, lentils and tapioca.

Materials: *Balsa wood (1/16"); assorted dried beans, lentils and pearl tapioca; white glue; brooch or tie-tack hardware (from hobby shops); model airplane glue.*

• Cut brooch circles and squares from balsa wood with scissors; also tiny circles for tie-tacks.
• With white glue, glue large beans in place first (see photo for design ideas); then fill in with lentils, split peas and small tapioca. Let dry. Attach hardware to back of balsa wood shapes with airplane glue. For a nice finish, paint edge of balsa wood to match outside row of beans.

Candle formations

If you've done all the ordinary things in candlemaking–like molding them in milk cartons and frosting them with whipped wax–it's time to graduate. You can, almost as easily, make unusual candles like these, richly colored and textured, exotically shaped.

Our directions (next page) explain how to mold the mushroom candles and the color-streaked hanging candle; and how to cast the other shapes, like free-form sculpture, in sand. Some of the sand candles are nested in driftwood; each one is unique.

Candles like these require professional know-how and materials. But professional doesn't mean difficult – it just means better techniques and better results. Try these recipes and see for yourself.

Read and follow directions carefully. Wax is flammable; when you work with it, you must be alert and know what you're doing.
Here is a description of the supplies and equipment you will need:

Candle Wax: You can buy candle wax at most hobby shops, at candle supply stores and some oil refineries. It is usually available in individual 10 lb. slabs or in cartons of 5 or 6 slabs. Candle wax is sold according to its melting point–the temperature at which it becomes liquid. A good melting point for general candlemaking is 140° or 145°F. Do not use supermarket paraffin for these candles; not only is it dangerous to work with, it is not desirable wax for candles because it burns very quickly.

Dyes: Do not use liquid dyes or crayons; they will not dissolve properly in wax. Instead, ask for chips or powdered dyes made especially for candles. Dyes may be added to wax at any time during melting. When the wax hardens, the color will appear lighter.

Wicks: There are two kinds of wicks–cotton and wire core. Cotton wick is used primarily for candles made from commercial molds. The wire core wick is a better choice for the sand candles, and for any mold which does not have a hole in the bottom.

Melting and Pouring Containers: Use a seamless bucket to heat wax over direct heat. Stainless steel is best, but a porcelain-coated bucket is an inexpensive substitute. You can melt wax for the mushroom ice candles in a double boiler or a coffee can placed over a pan of water–but the higher wax temperatures required for sand candles cannot be reached over water. Don't try to lift a heavy bucket of hot wax–instead, use a small pitcher or handled pan to dip out wax and fill mold.

Candy Thermometer: To pour successful candles, you should know the temperature of the wax. But the thermometer is even more important for safety reasons. If you don't watch temperature closely, it rises quickly to the flash point –the point at which wax will burn, 400°F.

Never Leave Wax Unattended: If it should catch fire, smother it with a pan lid or a piece of asbestos–keep it handy. Water will not put out a wax fire. If you spill hot wax on yourself, don't try to remove it immediately–instead, quickly flood the area, wax and all, with cold water. When wax cools, carefully peel it off and treat as for burn.

Molds: You can mold candles in any container which widens at the top, and which can withstand temperatures up to 210°F. Avoid glasses or cans which have lips or grooves in the side. You'll also find a variety of commercial molds where candle supplies are sold. Before you fill the mold with wax, give it a light coating of liquid soap, cooking oil or spray silicone, so the mold will release the candle more easily.

Hanging Wok Candle

This candle is molded in a Chinese wok —a round-bottomed iron or steel cooking pan 14″ in diameter.

Materials: *10 lbs. candle wax, dye chips in 2 or 3 colors; wire core wicks; leather thongs plus equipment listed.*

• Break the wax into chunks by hitting it with a hammer, and put it in bucket to melt. Insert candy thermometer and watch temperature carefully.
• Coat the inside of the wok with releasing agent. Also fill sink or tub near your work area with water at room temperature.
• When the wax reaches 210° remove it from heat. Dye it a light color.
• With dipping pan, pour wax into wok, filling just below the top.
• Wait a few minutes for the wax to heat the metal wok; then drop small bits of contrasting color dye along the sides of the wok. You'll see the dye slide down the sides to the bottom of the wok, leaving a streak of color in the wax. If the streak is light and seems to disappear, let it cool a little and try again.
• When you have a nice pattern of streaks, protect your hands with hot pads or oven mitts and carefully place the wok in the tub of water. Let it float. This will "freeze" the pattern and hasten the cooling of the candle.
• When a thin layer of wax sets on top of the candle, pour on more wax to bring it to original level (wax shrinks as it cools).
• Cut 3 leather thongs, 30″ long. Tie double knots at one end of each thong. When the wax in the wok cools enough to form a ¼″ layer on top, push the knotted ends of thongs into the wax about 1″ from sides of wok and at equal distances from each other.
• Push four wire core wicks into the wax. Place them in the center of the wok, about 2½″ from each other. Be sure their flames won't come close to leather straps when you hang the candle.
• Let the candle cool completely; this will take 3 to 4 hours; lift it from wok and tie leather thongs so that the candle hangs level, and place it where you can see the sunburst pattern on the bottom. When wicks burn into candle, you can drop votive candles into the depressions or refill them and wick them again.

Mushroom Ice Candles

Use any size bowl to mold the lacy mushroom cap and buy a cylindrical candle of appropriate diameter to be the stem.

Materials: *Candle wax (amount depends on size of candle); purchased cylinder candle; dye chips (same color as purchased candle); ice cubes; equipment as listed.*

• Break up candle wax and melt it over hot water.
• Coat the bowl with releasing agent (see Molds).
• Put ice cubes into a bag and break them into small chunks with a hammer, but do not crush too much.
• Place cylinder candle, wick down, into bowl and fill the bowl with the ice chunks (don't use tiny slivers). Keep the cylinder candle centered in the bowl of ice.
• Dye melted wax to match candle and pour it into bowl. (You can pour ice candles at almost any temperature under 210°).
• Let candle cool completely. (Patience is the first rule of candlemaking.) When cool, lift candle out of bowl and let the remaining ice melt out.

Note: When you burn a *large* mushroom candle almost to the depth of the cap, insert a votive candle in the depression. Otherwise, with continued burning, the cap will tilt to one side or slide down the stem.

Sand Candles

The hole you dig in packed wet sand becomes your "mold" when you cast sand candles. The surface of the candle will be covered with the sand which adheres to the wax when you dig the candle free; this gives it texture and color, too—you can buy sand in several colors at your building supply dealer. Avoid very fine sand, like beach sand; it caves in when you dig into it.

You will need a container for the sand; the best is a wooden box, but beginners can make do with a garbage can, bucket or heavy cardboard box. Cut a piece of plywood to fit in the bottom of any improvised container.

You will also need wicking rods—make them by cutting straight sections from wire coat hangers.

Casting candles in sand tends to be messy, so it's best to work in the garage or basement. Use a hot plate to melt the wax.

Materials: *Candlewax, dye chips, sand, wire core wicks, equipment as listed.*

• Moisten the sand just enough to make it pack well; mix it thoroughly and pack it into your box or container. Dig a hole in the sand the shape you want the candle to be. Spoons are useful for digging and for smoothing the sides of the hole. To make sure your candle will stand, dig to the bottom of the box so the base of the candle will be flat. You can press jars or cans into the sand if you want to make a more geometrical mold. You can give your candle legs simply by pushing your finger into the sand in 3 places (anything will stand on a tripod).
• Break up the wax and melt it. Dye it if you wish. Insert thermometer and watch it carefully. The temperature of the wax when poured is extremely important in making sand candles. You can pour at any temperature from 160° to 275° depending on how thick a sand coating you want on your candle. The hotter the wax, the thicker the sand coat will be. A candle poured at 215° or 220° will retain sand, but will glow through the walls when lighted.
• With your dipping pan, pour wax into the hole slowly. Let it cool until it skims over. Insert wire rods where you want wicks—a large candle may have several wicks. But be careful not to put them too close to the sides.
• Let the candle cool completely. Dig sand away from the sides and lift the candle out of the sand. Brush off loose sand.
• Pull out the wire wicking rods with pliers. Cut wire core wick(s) the depth of the candle; dip the wick in wax to make it stiff and easier to work with. Insert it into the hole left by the rod. Refill the candle with wax at 200° to seal the wick.
• If you wish, you can dip your candle in hot wax at this point—this gives the candle the look of glazed pottery and prevents the sand from falling off. Dipping is tricky because you must work with very hot wax—270°. The best way is to hold one side of the candle, dip it half way into the bucket and bring it out right away. Let it cool; then hold the dipped side and dip the other side into the wax. Pour a final topping of wax at 200° to finish and smooth top of candle.
• The triple candle pictured is made by digging tunnels between the three candle shapes in the sand.

Sand Candles on Wood

You can pour sand candles to look like they grew out of the side or top of a piece of driftwood, bark or any interesting piece of wood. First, decide the shape you want candle to be and where to place it on the wood. Bury the wood in sand, packing it tightly. Dig the candle hole against the wood, scrape wood free of sand in this area so that wax will adhere to wood. Pour wax at a temperature of 220° to 250°. Cool, wick and finish as for sand candles. Coat both wood and sand with wax if you wish.

Nursery art

Painted plaques of children's favorite stories are easy to make, even if you can't "draw a straight line." Find, in a story or coloring book, the subject you want to copy enlarging it if necessary (see Appendix for directions).

Your subject may suggest a design idea. For example, we used four separate plaques to illustrate the poem, "The Little Turtle" by Vachel Lindsay. The turtle himself is painted on a wood board 14" square. The three tiny creatures he snapped at–mosquito, flea and minnow–are on boards 4x5".

Materials: *Tracing tissue; boards in sizes desired; sandpaper; paint (any kind – enamel, latex, acrylic, poster paints); primer (needed for enamel); picture hangers.*

• Trace design on paper; cut boards and sand smooth. Paint boards desired background color. With a soft pencil, black the reverse side of traced design, and trace it onto painted boards (or use carbon paper.)

• Paint in design details. Paint edge of boards a contrasting color or black. Attach picture hangers.

How to give a plant

Florists, for some obscure and unlovely reason, wrap Christmas poinsettias and other gift plants in a big crinkle of colored foil. If you'd like to surprise your friends with more imaginative packaging, here are some ideas to start you thinking.

CUT A CIRCLE of leather and slash it to make a leather-mesh hanger. To figure size, measure base of pot and draw circle on paper pattern. Add concentric circles ½" apart, enough to equal half the depth of pot. Slash leather as indicated on diagram. Knot 4 leather thongs through outside edge of leather and tie together above plant.

MAKE A SIMPLE LEATHER sling for a hanging plant. One way is to cut three pieces of leather about ¾" wide—2 long pieces for the hanger and 1 short piece, enough to go around pot with a little overlap. Lay the 2 long pieces on the table to make a + and rivet. Set pot where they cross; bring strips against sides of pot and weave with the short piece, through 1" brass rings. Fasten short piece with rivet or glue to fit snugly around pot.

IF YOU GIVE A BIG houseplant, roll it in on a dolly. You can buy one at garden supply stores, fitted with a 1" deep pan. Or make your own from plywood and ball bearing casters. Give it a rim, or fit it with a large shallow pan.

USE GIFT-WRAP YARN in brightest colors to weave a cover for a plastic pot—it will make a green plant look as colorful as a centerpiece bouquet. First, tie rows of different colors of yarn around pot—these will be your "warp" threads. Thread a needle with more yarn and glue one end to bottom of pot; weave needle over and under warps from bottom, loop around top row and weave back to bottom; glue yarn end in place on bottom. Repeat with a different color; continue until pot is covered. Add small yarn bows for trim. Tie napkins with matching yarn.

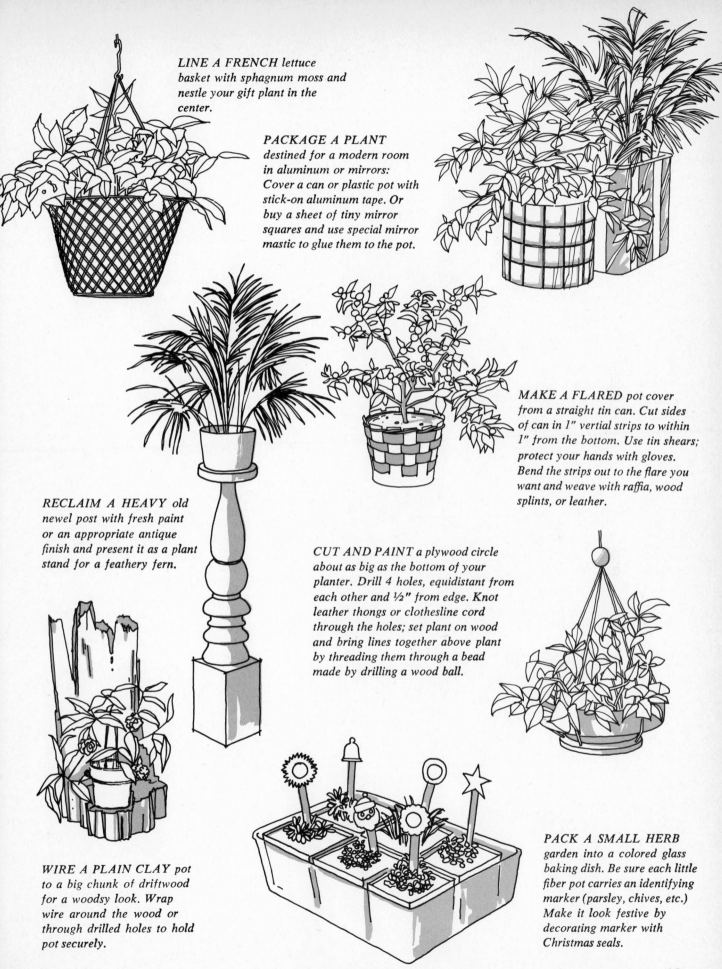

LINE A FRENCH lettuce basket with sphagnum moss and nestle your gift plant in the center.

PACKAGE A PLANT destined for a modern room in aluminum or mirrors: Cover a can or plastic pot with stick-on aluminum tape. Or buy a sheet of tiny mirror squares and use special mirror mastic to glue them to the pot.

MAKE A FLARED pot cover from a straight tin can. Cut sides of can in 1" vertial strips to within 1" from the bottom. Use tin shears; protect your hands with gloves. Bend the strips out to the flare you want and weave with raffia, wood splints, or leather.

RECLAIM A HEAVY old newel post with fresh paint or an appropriate antique finish and present it as a plant stand for a feathery fern.

CUT AND PAINT a plywood circle about as big as the bottom of your planter. Drill 4 holes, equidistant from each other and ½" from edge. Knot leather thongs or clothesline cord through the holes; set plant on wood and bring lines together above plant by threading them through a bead made by drilling a wood ball.

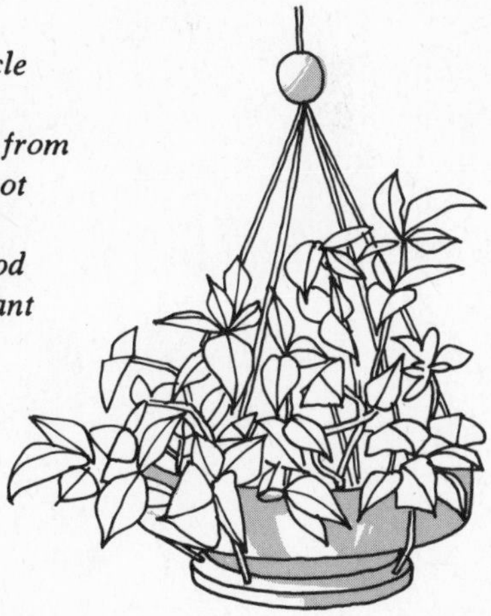

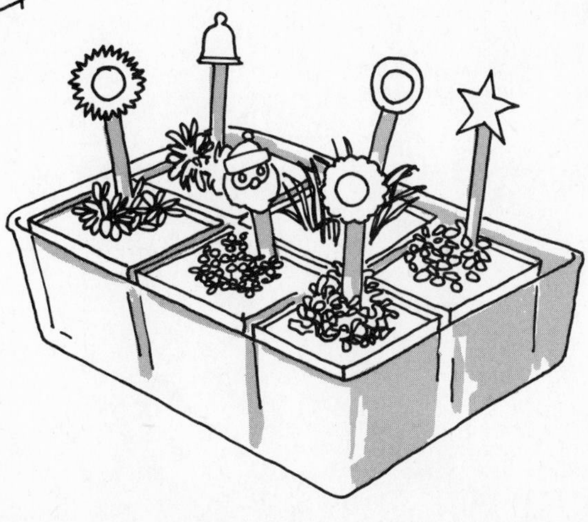

WIRE A PLAIN CLAY pot to a big chunk of driftwood for a woodsy look. Wrap wire around the wood or through drilled holes to hold pot securely.

PACK A SMALL HERB garden into a colored glass baking dish. Be sure each little fiber pot carries an identifying marker (parsley, chives, etc.) Make it look festive by decorating marker with Christmas seals.

Mirror

Bower of Flowers

A pretty way to frame a pretty face.

Materials: *Mirror 6x9", bright green felt 12x25" (or color you prefer) plus scraps in assorted colors; heavy cardboard; white glue; wood dowel; package sealing tape; cord for hanging.*

• Cut felt as shown with V-bottom and oval cutout 5x8½" for mirror. Cut flowers from felt scraps and sew to felt frame.
• Cut cardboard backing 1" shorter than felt at top; cut oval for mirror slightly larger than felt cutout.
• Brush cardboard with white glue and cover with felt; glue felt around dowel at top, and tape to back of cardboard.
• Tape mirror to back of cardboard with package sealing tape. If cardboard buckles, tape or staple wood strips to back of frame.

Paperweights

Every secretary needs one on her desk.

Materials: *Modeling clay that dries hard; small mirrors; acrylic or poster paint; polymer medium or shellac; special mirror mastic.*

• You can find small thin mirrors (1/16") in various shapes at many hobby shops. Or salvage mirrors from pressed powder compacts or handbags.
• Model clay designs just a bit bigger all around than mirrors. One way to decorate them is to press objects into the surface. Be sure they're flat and smooth on the bottom.
• When clay is thoroughy dry (up to 2 days), paint and coat with glossy polymer medium or shellac. Glue mirror to bottom with mirror mastic, and glue a gold cord around mirror to cover the sharp edge.

fancies

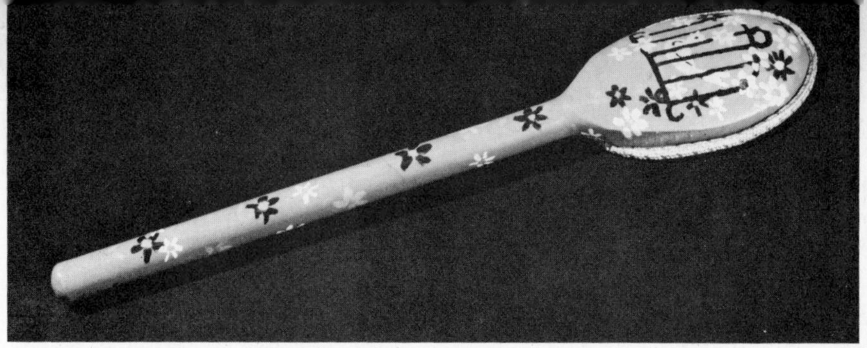

Paper Plate Mirror

The raised flower design is made from paper pulp egg cartons and string.

Materials: *2 (8") paper plates with wide rims; 6" round mirror; newspaper; white glue; egg carton; string; gesso; acrylic paint; package sealing tape; felt; small metal ring for hanging.*

• Cut out centers of paper plates and glue rims together. Cover rims with papier-mâché for added strength; dip 1x3" strips of torn newspaper in a mixture of white glue and water; apply to rims. When dry, glue on design of flowers cut from egg carton. Add swirls of string, dipped in glue mixture. Let dry.

• Coat frame with gesso. Paint flowers in bright colors. Tape mirror to back of frame. Sew ring to circle of felt near one edge, and glue felt to back of mirror.

Lipstick Mirror

Amusing whimsy for the powder room.

Materials: *Wooden spoon, primer and enamel paint; mirror; gold cord; glue.*

• Lay tracing tissue over bowl of spoon and trace edge line of spoon; take this pattern to glass company to get mirror cut.

• Sand spoon if necessary; coat with primer; then with enamel paint. Let dry; add flower design.

• Glue mirror to bowl of spoon and glue gold cord around edge.

Pie Pan Mirrors

For the kitchen, a tiny check-up mirror that looks like a flower.

Materials: *5" foil pans (saved from individual frozen pies); small round mirrors, enamel, spray enamel or acrylic paint; felt; mirror mastic.*

• Cut off rim of pie pan and cut sides into petal shapes. Paint or spray-paint entire pan. Cut felt petals to go behind pan, and glue mirror to center.

APPENDIX

How to work with plexiglass acrylic sheet

1. Scribing and Breaking (Up to ¼″ thickness)

Using a straight edge as a guide, place the point of the plexiglass acrylic sheet cutting tool at the edge of the material and, applying firm pressure, draw the cutting point the full width of the material (5 to 6 times for thicknesses from 0.100″ to 0.187″ and 7 to 10 times for 0.250″).

To break, the scribed line should be positioned face up over a ¾″ diameter wood dowel running the length of the intended break. Hold the sheet with one hand and apply downward pressure on the short side of the break with the other. The hands should be kept adjacent to each other and successively repositioned about 2″ in back of the

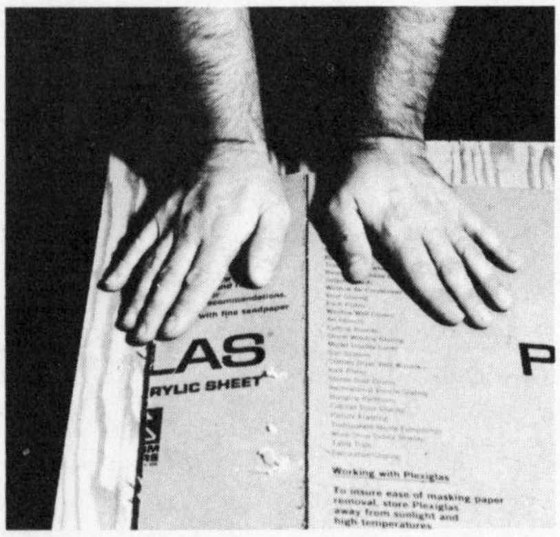

break as it progresses along the scribed line. The minimum cut-off width is about 1½″. Patterned plexiglass cannot be scored and broken.

2. Cutting with Saws

Do *not* remove protective masking paper before cutting. If cutting unmasked

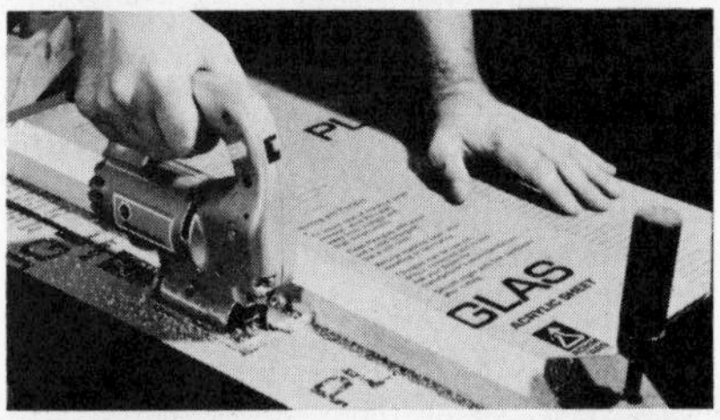

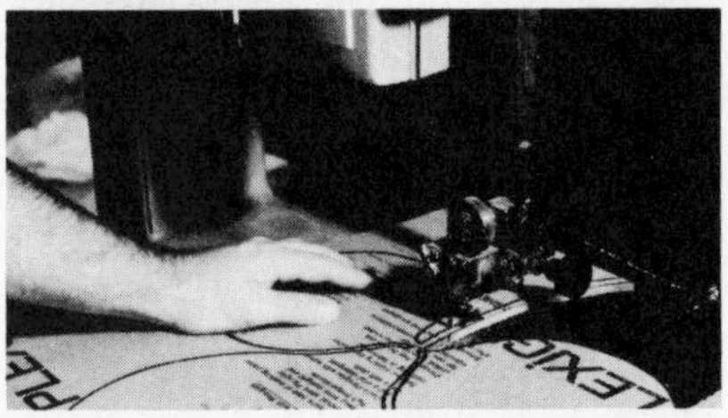

sheet is unavoidable, apply masking tape on both sides of intended cut to reduce friction and gumming behind blade.

Sabre, Band and Reciprocating Jigsaws

Curved shapes are easily cut with any one of these saws. Sabre and reciprocating jigsaw blades should have at least 14 teeth per inch. Straight cuts can be made with a sabre or hand jigsaw by

guiding the tool along a straight edge. Band saws should have at least 10 teeth per inch. Hold plexiglass down firmly when cutting—do not force feed.

Circular Saws

These are ideal for straight cutting. Use a steel crosscut blade which is recommended for finish cuts on plywood, veneers, laminates, etc. The blade should have at least 6 teeth per inch. All the teeth should be of the same shape, height, and point to point distance. Set the blade height just a little above the thickness of the sheet to prevent chipping. Hold plexiglass down firmly when cutting—do not force feed.

3. Drilling

By Hand with Standard Twist Drills

Standard twist drills commonly used for metals can be used to drill plexiglass if you take reasonable care. Back plexiglass with wood, clamp or hold firmly, use a sharp drill, very slow speed and minimum pressure. Caution: If you use too much speed, plexiglass will tend to

climb the drill; if too much pressure, chipping will occur on the back side of the hole.

With an Electric Drill

"Special Purpose High Speed Twist Drills for Plexiglass Acrylic Sheet" are required when using power equipment to drill plexiglass. Tighten drill securely in chuck. Back plexiglass with soft wood, clamp or hold firmly. Use highest speed available up to 3000 rpm. When drilling holes ⅜" or larger slower drill speed (1000-2000 rpm) will improve quality. Do not force feed. Slow feed as drill point penetrates second surface.

4. Edge Finishing

Sawed edges and other tool marks should be removed by scraping the edge with a sharp knife, filing with a fine tooth metal file and/or sanding with medium grit (60-80) paper. To further improve the appearance of the surface or edge, follow the initial finishing with "wet or dry" (150-220 grit) sand paper. For a transparent edge, follow this step with grits to 400 and buff with a clean muslin wheel dressed with a good grade of fine grit buffing compound. Finish up with a clean soft cotton-flannel wheel.

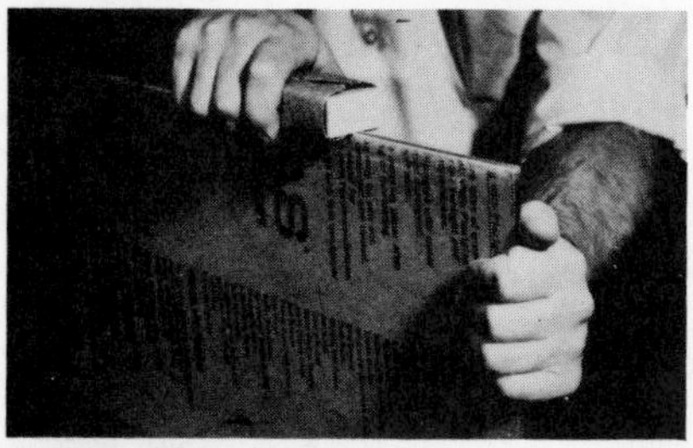

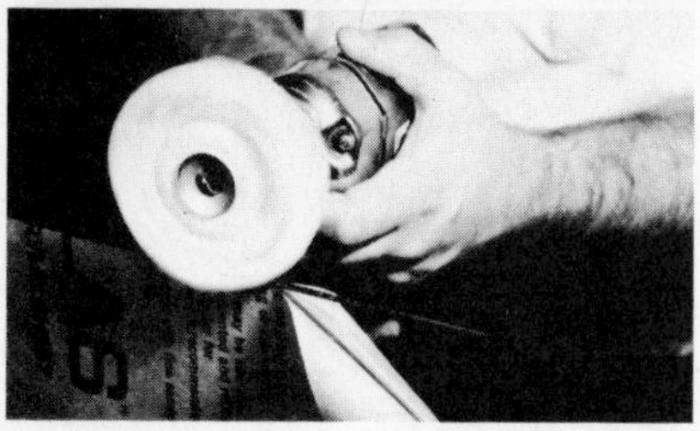

5. Cementing

Capillary cementing with a solvent (Methylene Chloride "MDC" or Ethylene Dichloride "EDC" or 1-1-2 Trichlorethane) is an easy method of joining two pieces of plexiglass. Sand surfaces to be cemented, do not polish. Remove protective masking paper. Hold pieces together with strips of masking tape as shown in photo below. Apply solvent to joint with the solvent applicator (available where plexiglass is sold) or with a syringe, oil can with a very fine spout, eye dropper or small paint brush. Let joint dry thoroughly. **Caution:** Solvents may be toxic if inhaled for extended periods of time or if swallowed; many are also flammable. Use in a well ventilated area; keep away from children.

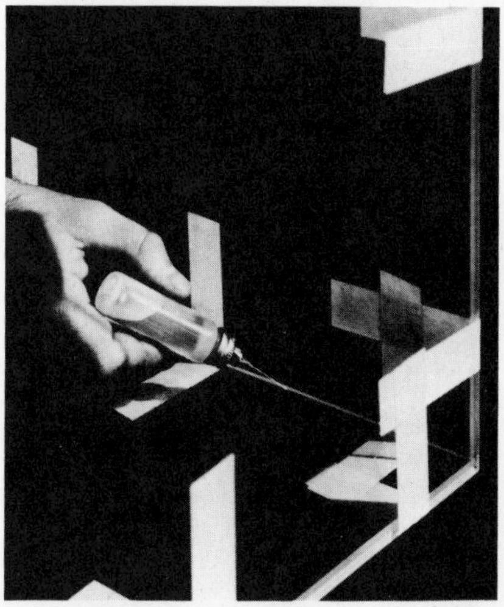

6. Strip Heat Forming

Information on constructing and using a strip heater is available where plexiglass and the heating element are sold.

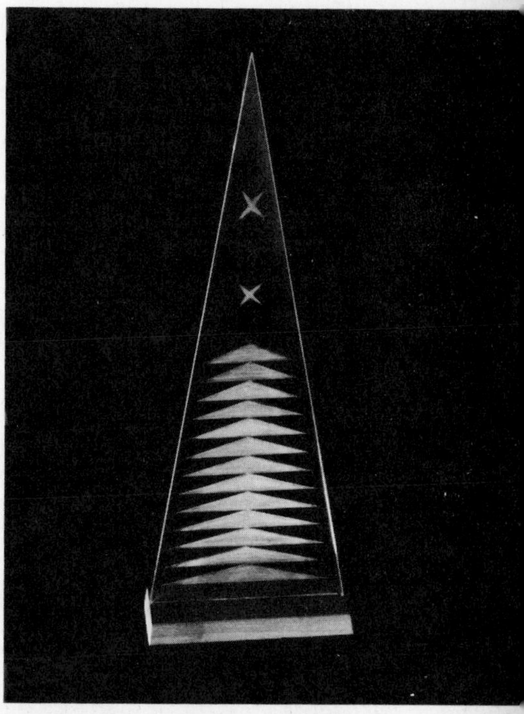

Christmas Tree

Stand this tree where it will catch the light, to show off the etched design.

Materials: *Clear plastic sheet ¼" thick, 4x11"; white paper; masking tape; sandpaper; wood for base, 2x4x½".*

- Cut a tree-shaped triangle from plastic 11" tall, 4" at base. Finish edges.
- On white paper, draw the same triangle and sketch in design. Remove masking tape from plastic and lay design on plastic. Hold it steady with masking tape. With a sharp pointed instrument, trace outline of design on plastic.
- Lay masking tape along edges of design to protect plastic and etch the design area by rubbing with fine sandpaper or steel wool.
- Sand wood base. Rout a ¼" groove down center and stand tree in groove. (Paint or stain wood base if you wish.)

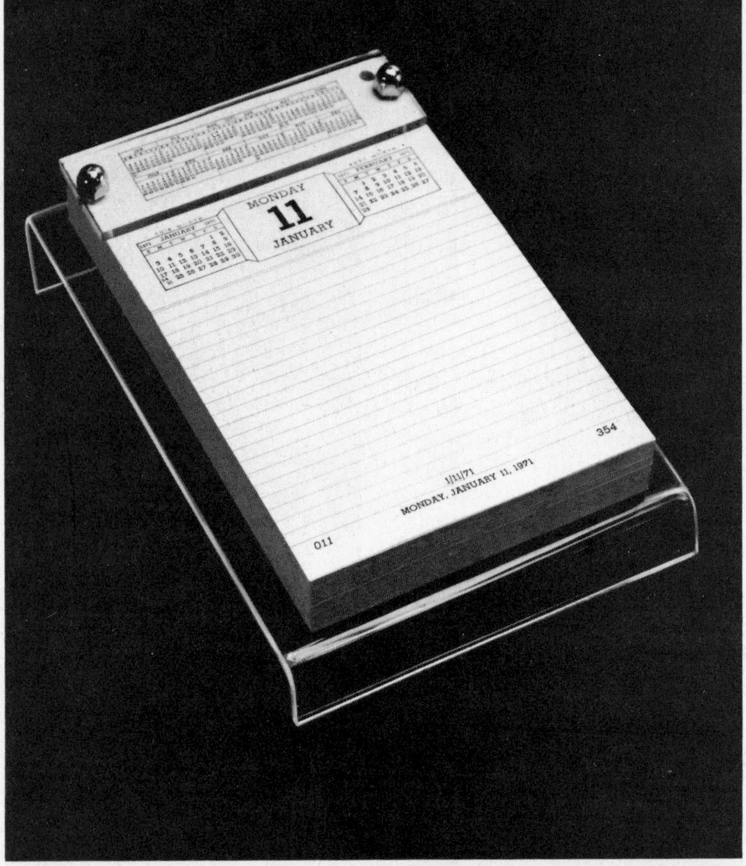

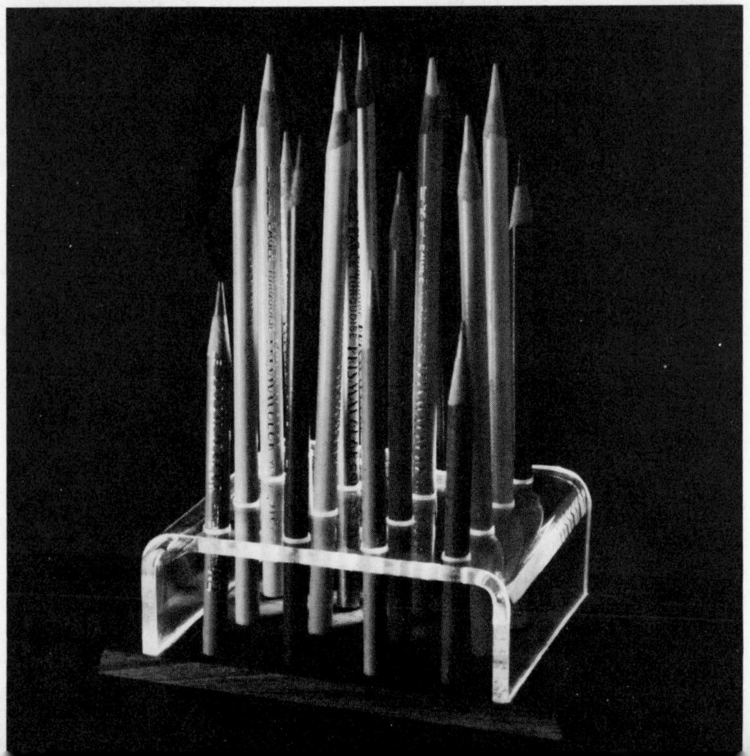

Plastic desk accessories

Not only can you saw plastic and cement the pieces together, but you can also bend it. For this, you need an electric strip heater made especially for forming plastic, and available where you buy plastic.

Desk Calendar

Materials: *2 pieces clear plexiglass, ¼" thick, cut 10¾x5" and 5x1½"; 2 3/16" bolts and nuts; calendar pad refill (from stationery store).*

• Polish edges of plastic. Using strip heater, make 90° bends in the large piece, ¾" from one end and 1½" from the other end.
• Drill holes in small piece to correspond to holes in calendar pad. Drill corresponding holes in base at tall end. Assemble with bolts.

Pencil Holder

Materials: *Clear plexiglass ¼" thick, 7x4"; wood for base, ¼" thick, 4x5¾"; household cement.*

• Polish edges of plastic. Drill ⅜" holes, 4 across and 4 down, beginning 1¾" from end and ⅜" in from edge.
• Using strip heater, make a 90° bend 1¼" from each end.
• Bevel short ends of wood base; sand and finish it; glue base to plastic with clear household cement.

Book Rack

Materials: *2 pieces of clear acrylic plastic sheet ¼" thick, cut 6x8"; 2 pieces of ½" hardwood (walnut, walnut plywood or your choice) cut 3¾" x 12"; 8 (⅝" oval chrome #8) wood screws; wood stain or boiled linseed oil to finish wood; black paint.*

• Round corners of plastic and polish edges.
• To find position for screw holes, enlarge pattern (see Appendix) and mark positions on the protective cover of the plastic. *Note:* Flip the pattern when you mark the hole positions on the second piece of plastic. Because you will countersink the holes, and they should be mirror opposites on your two plastic pieces.
• Make countersink in plastic first; then drill hole with ⅛" drill.
• Sand and finish wood. Paint ends of wood black. Drill holes for screws in ends of wood 1½" apart and equidistant from sides. To assemble book rack, screw plastic to wood (see photo).
Note: If you're mailing this gift to someone, you could mail it flat, with a tracing of this photo to show your friend how to assemble it.

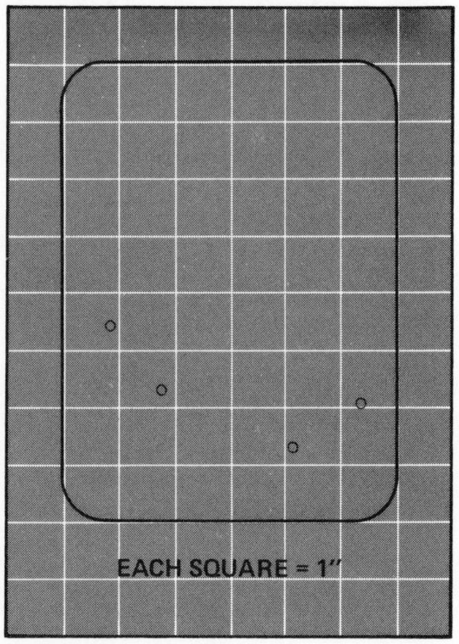

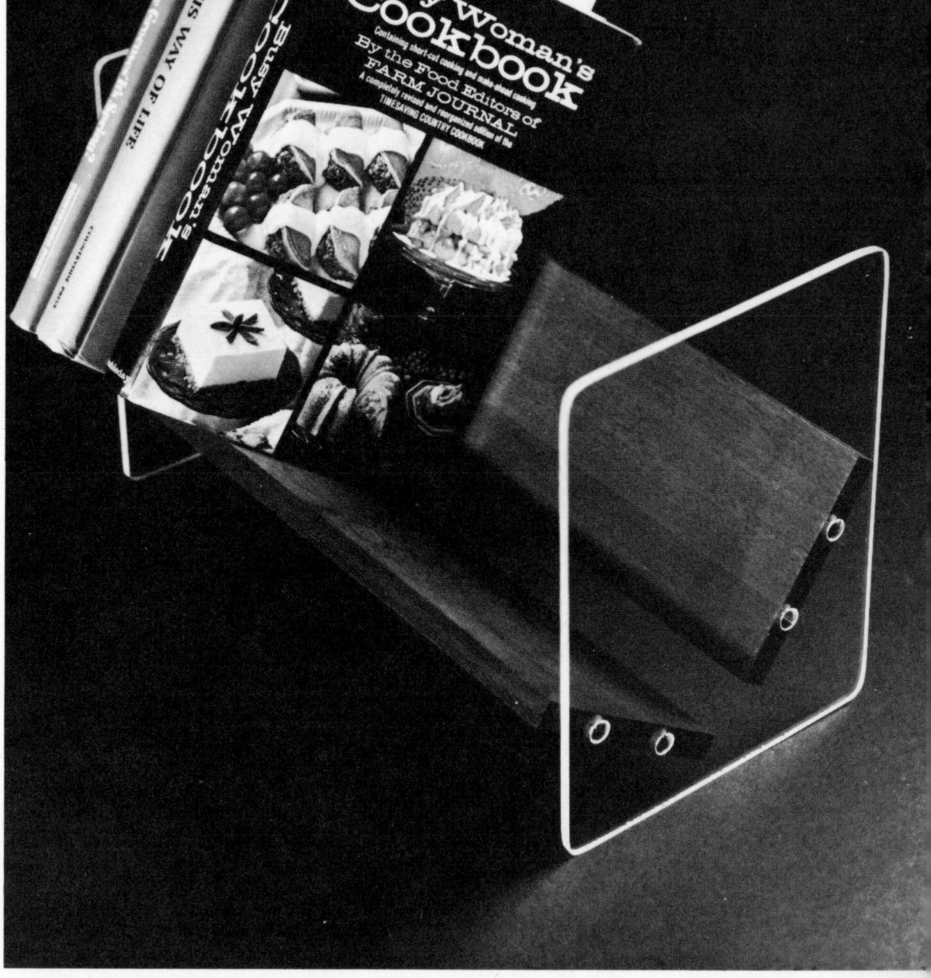

Plastic desk accessories

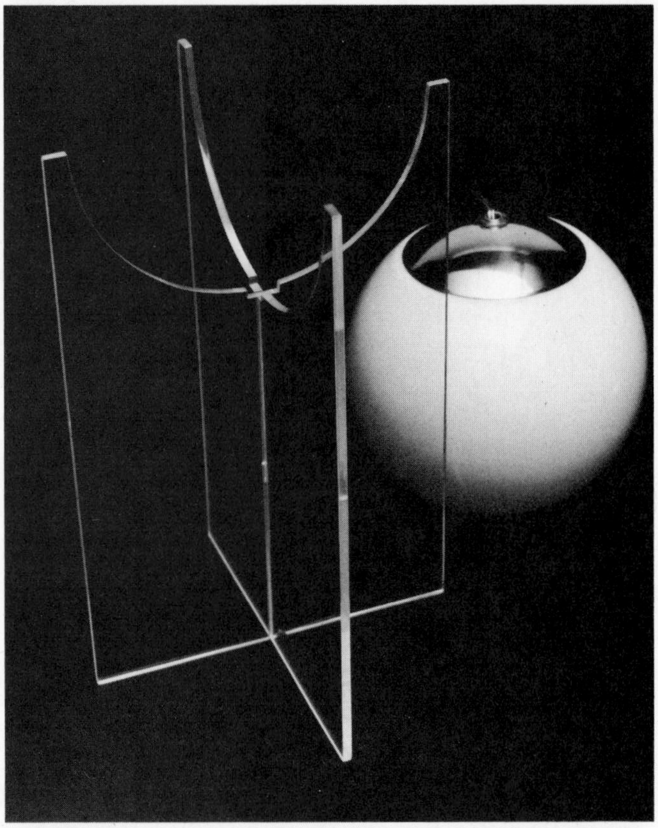

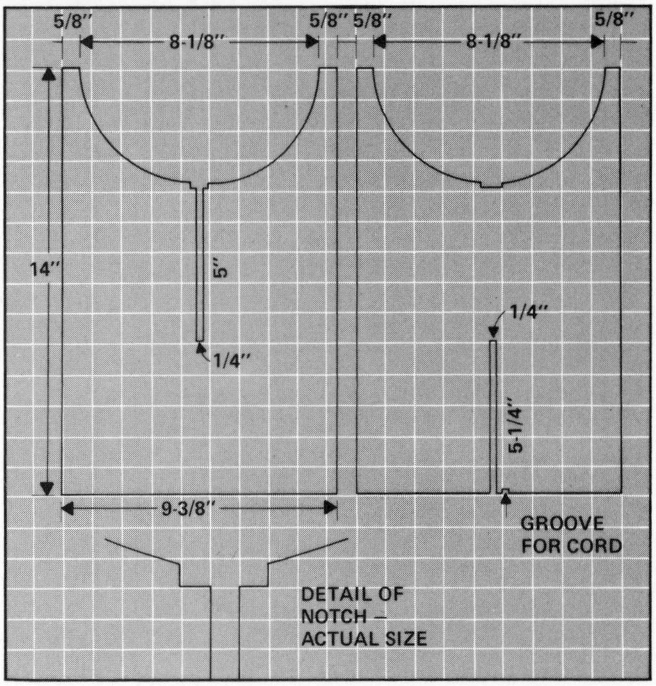

LAMP

Materials: *Clear plastic 1/4" thick, 14x 18½"; hanging light fixture with 8" diameter globe (available at Sears); 10 ft. clear plastic electrical wire.*

• Rewire lamp, to substitute clear plastic wire for white wire that comes with it.
• Enlarge pattern and cut two pieces of plastic with grooves as indicated. Polish edges.
• Fit pieces together and set globe in place. Bring electrical cord down center corner and under notch at bottom.

How to Draw Big Circles

You'll need a pencil, a tack or pin and a piece of string to make a compass. Lay a sheet of paper a little bigger than you want circle to be, on a surface that can be thumbtacked. Tie the string to the tack and stick it into the approximate center of the paper. Tie a pencil

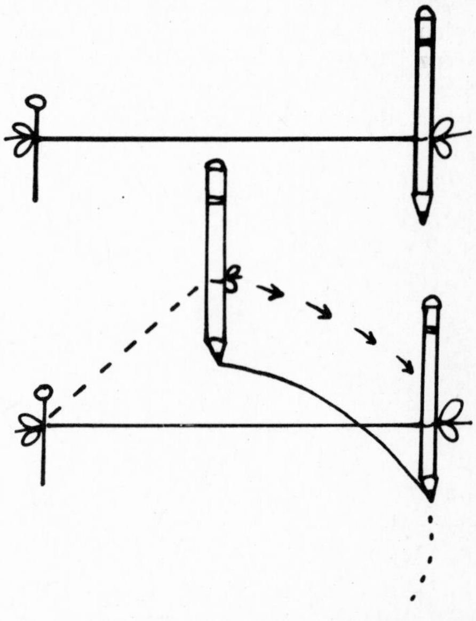

to the other end of the string; the distance from tack to pencil should be the radius of the circle you want, when the string is pulled taut. Keeping the string taut, trace the circle with your pencil.

How to Cut Paper and Cardboard

To make crisp, clean, straight cuts in paper or cardboard, learn to use an X-acto knife or mat knife and a steel ruler–the way the professionals do. The knife must be sharp, so keep a small whetstone handy for honing the knife edge. Always use a steel or metal-edged ruler–the knife will sliver a wood ruler.

The best surface to cut against is glass, but be sure it's clean; a smear of glue or speck of waste under your cutting line may cause the paper you're cutting to bunch up. If you don't have an old piece of glass handy, pad your work table with newspaper or cardboard. Replace them as needed – your knife will cut them to ribbons.

To help keep a steel ruler from slipping on the paper while you are cutting, cover the back of the ruler with a strip of masking tape. Lay the ruler along the cutting line and hold it there with firm pressure. Hold the knife tight against the ruler and try to make the cut with one firm stroke; you're apt to sliver or fuzz the edges if you take repeated strokes. If you're cutting cardboard and the edge is ragged, sand it lightly.

How to Enlarge Patterns

All patterns in this book are drawn on small squares and should be enlarged. Do this by marking off a sheet of paper with 1″ squares. Then copy the design outline from the small squares to corresponding large squares, using the squares as a drawing guide.

You can use this same method to enlarge or reduce size of designs in photographs or drawings anywhere. To enlarge item, make a tracing of photo or design. Mark off your tracing with small squares and proceed as above. Reverse the procedure to reduce size of design. You may want to invest in a clear plastic sheet ruled in ¼″ squares which you can lay over any photo or design. You'll find these sheets wherever artists' and draftsmen's supplies are sold.

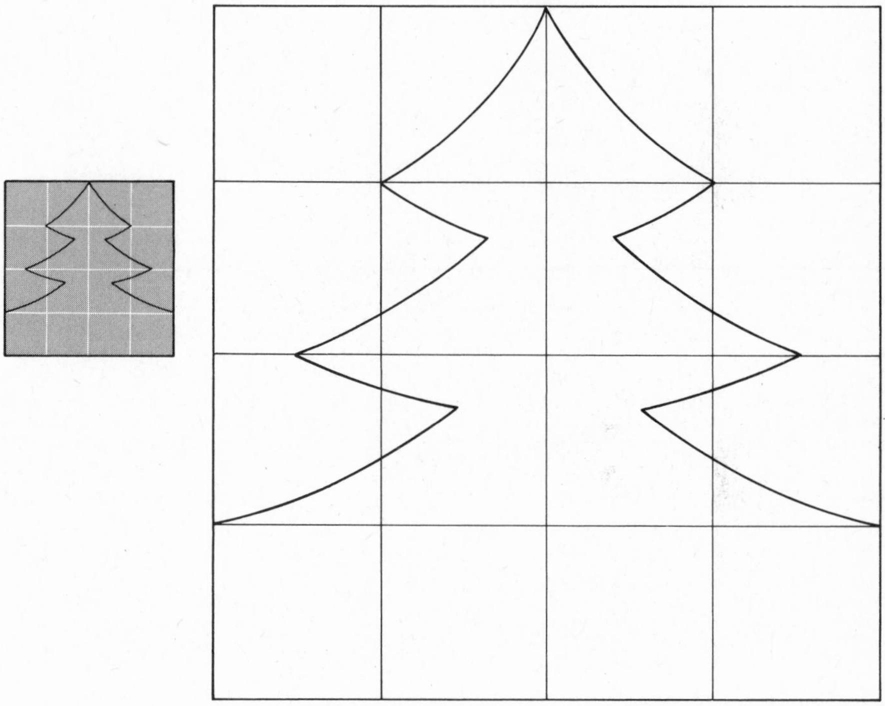

Credits

PHOTOS: Al J. Reagan except for page 42, Robert E. Coates; 90-93, Jo Dendel/Lee Payne; 139-143, Rich Erlich; 48, George Faraghan; 23, 47, Bruce Harlow; 4 10, 39, 52, 63, 71, 76, 79, 85, 138, 140, 142, 146, 147, William Hazzard; 111, Bill Miller; 7, 19, 50, 55, 58, 106, 116, Chas. P. Mills; 103, Gloria McNutt; 60, 61, Mike Nelson, Photography, Inc.; 13, 20, 25, 26, 29, 34, 66, Mel Richman, Inc.; 154, 155, Rohm & Haas; 71, 124-131, Gayle Smalley

DESIGNS: Page 71, 130, Joyce Aiken; 138-143, 157, Bauhof/Chapin; 69, Laurie Calkins; 90, Esther Dendel; 153, Dee Donovan; 116, 117, Patricia Grooms; 90, Pat Holtz; 68, 77, 85, 87-89, 99, 109, 135, 136, Kathryn Larson: 71, 79, 102, 122, 125-129, Jean Ray Laury; 90, Bici Linklater; 103, 119, Gloria McNutt; 110-115, 155, 156, 158, Ruth and Bill Miller; 93, Rosita Montgomery; 90, 93 Beverly Nemetz; 72, Nancy B. Peterson; 84, Ellie Simmons; 146, 147, Donna M. Sterman; 106, 137, 152, 153, Sally K. Stone; 125, Jenny Stukenborg; 90, Helen Trescott; 76, 100, 120, 121, 144, 145, 149, Jackie Vermeer/Louise Walker; 74, Grady Wright

DRAWINGS: Page 127, 128, Jean Ray Laury; 95, Bob Milnazik: 80, 81, 123, 150, 151, and how-to-illustrations, Mechanicals Unlimited; 96-99, 132-134, Don Wilder.

Recipe Index